D1426532

THE TYRANTS OF SYRACUSE: SYRACUSE: WAR IN ANCIENT SICILY

THE TYRANTS OF SYRACUSE: WAR IN ANCIENT SICILY

Volume I: 480–367 BC

by

Jeff Champion

Pen & Sword
MILITARY

First published in Great Britain in 2010 by
Pen & Sword Military
an imprint of
Pen & Sword Books Ltd
47 Church Street
Barnsley
South Yorkshire
S70 2AS

ISBN 978 1 84884 063 8

A CIP catalogue record for this book is
available from the British Library

Typeset in Sabon by
Phoenix Typesetting, Auldgirth, Dumfriesshire

Printed and bound in England by
CPI UK

Pen & Sword Books Ltd incorporates the Imprints of Pen & Sword Aviation, Pen &
Sword Maritime, Pen & Sword Military, Wharncliffe Local History, Pen & Sword
Select, Pen & Sword Military Classics and Leo Cooper.

For a complete list of Pen & Sword titles please contact
PEN & SWORD BOOKS LIMITED
47 Church Street, Barnsley, South Yorkshire, S70 2AS, England
E-mail: enquiries@pen-and-sword.co.uk
Website: www.pen-and-sword.co.uk

Contents

Preface

Throughout ancient and medieval times the island of Sicily was renowned for its wealth. This made it a tempting target for a whole series of conquerors: Greeks, Carthaginians, Romans, Vandals, Arabs and Normans. At the end of the eighth century BC the Greeks and Phoenicians had both sent colonists to the island. The Greeks were in search of new homes and farmlands. The Phoenicians were interested in trade. The two peoples would co-exist peacefully and trade profitably for nearly two centuries.

This was a period of great turmoil and change within the Greek world. The old, aristocratic governments would largely be overthrown and replaced by dictators, known as tyrants. The old form of warfare as described by Homer, where aristocratic heroes engaged in single combat, would also be swept away. A new class of wealthy farmers would arm themselves with armour, spear and shield. They were the first hoplites. They would form themselves into close-packed formations known as phalanxes, where co-operation was all important and individual heroics censured. These hoplite phalanxes would dominate the battlefields of the Greeks for three centuries.

Towards the end of the sixth century the peaceful relationship between the Greeks and Carthaginians would break down. The Greeks had continued to push further west, right throughout the Mediterranean, threatening Phoenician interests. This new expansionism worried the now dominant Phoenician city in the region, Carthage. In 480 BC, the same year that the Persians invaded Greece, they sent a large military expedition to Sicily to conquer the island and end the Greek threat. The campaign ended in disaster, as the Greeks, lead by Gelon, the first tyrant of Syracuse, decisively defeated them at the battle of Himera.

For the next seventy years the Carthaginians remained aloof from the affairs of Sicily while they concentrated on building an empire in Africa. Now that the Carthaginian threat had dissolved, the Greeks of Sicily no longer felt the need to be ruled by tyrants. In a widespread series of revolutions they would overthrow the tyrannies and set up democratic governments. The Greeks would then concentrate on which city among them would be supreme. Syracuse would emerge from these conflicts as the clear winner and leader of the Greeks of Sicily. This period of democratic rule, prosperity and relatively low levels of warfare was looked back upon by later Greeks as a golden age.

This serenity would be destroyed, not by the Carthaginians, but by their fellow Greeks, the Athenians, who would cast their covetous eyes over the wealth and particularly the wheat of Sicily. In 415 they would send their largest ever force to conquer Syracuse. The campaign would end in disaster, when in 413 the Syracusans and their allies would destroy the Athenian force.

Syracuse now appeared triumphant and unchallenged on the island. The Athenian invasion, and its openly discussed ambition of using Sicily as a base to attack Africa, had once again aroused Carthaginian anxieties. They feared that the Greeks of Sicily, united under a powerful Syracuse, might now be a threat to their cities in western Sicily and even to Carthage itself. In 410 they sent another invasion force to Sicily, beginning a long series of wars for control of the island that would not be settled until the Romans sacked Syracuse in 212, turning the island into their own private estate. These wars would be waged with extreme viciousness, even for ancient times, due to the ethnic and religious hatreds that the two peoples held for one another. Whole cities would be destroyed, populations massacred and temples defiled.

The initial successes of the Carthaginian invasion would lead to a political revolution in Syracuse. In 405 the population would panic and give emergency powers to a young soldier named Dionysius. He would use his new position to establish a thirty-eight year rule over the city. The tyrants of Syracuse had returned and the democracy was dead. For all but twenty of the next 195 years, Syracuse would be ruled by tyrants. For much of that time they would be at war with Carthage. This book and the following volume are an attempt to produce an easily accessible, narrative history of these events.

No attempt at writing such a narrative would be possible without the survival of the work of the ancient historian Diodorus, who described his work as one of 'the universal histories'. It covered events, in forty books, from the legendary times prior to the Trojan War until the beginning of Caesar's campaigns against the Celts. What information there is on Diodorus' life and work is, with one exception, contained within his own work. He was a citizen of the town of Agyrium in Sicily and probably wrote his history between the years 56–26 BC.

When assessing Diodorus' value as a historian it is essential to look at his methods of composition. Diodorus tells us that he deliberately set about writing a history that was both comprehensive and readable. As he said himself: 'for the benefit to the readers lies in understanding the greatest number and variety of events.' He claims that he sought to write an accessible account, surpassing all others in its usefulness, by reading the writings of other historians, visiting the sites to prevent errors and utilizing the public records in Rome.

Despite Diodorus' lofty ideals his value as a historian came under stinging attack by the German scholars of the nineteenth century, describing him as 'this most miserable of all writers'. Much of this severe criticism derived from the belief that Diodorus was simply an epitomizer, and long sections of his work were merely an abbreviation of an earlier author. In more recent times Diodorus' reputation as a historian has been largely transformed. He is generally seen as a competent historian who read widely and produced his own work. His major weaknesses are a tendency to moralize and, at times, overly abridge his narrative. Diodorus cites three earlier historians during his coverage of events in Sicily. These are Ephorus, Timaeus and Philistus.

Ephorus lived from *c.* 400–330 and was born in Cyme in Asia Minor. He was the first historian to write a 'universal history', named *Historiai*, in twenty-nine books, covering the period from the eleventh century until 356. Ephorus' work was highly praised and much read in antiquity, was freely drawn upon by other historians and the geographer Strabo.

Timaeus, *c.* 345–250 was born in Tauromenium in Sicily. He was exiled by the later tyrant Agathocles and sort refuge in Athens, where he lived for fifty years. Later he returned to Syracuse during the rule of Hiero II. While in Athens he completed his work, *The Histories*, probably in forty books, covering the history of Greece from its earliest days till the first Punic War. This included a section on the history of Sicily. Few fragments of his work remain. Unlike other writers of his time he repeated myths, gaining the nickname 'Old Ragwoman', in modern terms a collector of old wives' tales. He was often accused by ancient writers of bias, especially against the tyrants Dionysius I and Agathocles, while favouring Timoleon.

Perhaps the most important of Diodorus sources was Philistus, *c.* 432 – 356, who was a native of Syracuse and an important supporter of Dionysius during his early years in power. As such he would have been an eye-witness to many of the events he recorded. While in exile in Italy he wrote two works on the history of Sicily, in total twelve books, from earliest times until five years after the death of Dionysius. The main charge against Philistus as an historian is that he used his work to justify the rule of Dionysius in an attempt to be recalled to Sicily. It is known that both Timaeus and Ephorus used Philistus as a source for their works:

The coverage of events in this volume will be uneven. This is a result of the patchy nature of the surviving ancient sources. Much of the narrative therefore depends on how much interest Diodorus had in the events of Sicily, which largely seem to be centred on the Carthaginian invasion of 406 and the rise of Dionysius. For the Athenian invasions we do have additional accounts by Thucydides and Plutarch.[1] These two topics, although important will therefore, by necessity, occupy a disproportionate part of this volume.

I have generally used the Latin forms of names as I consider that these are better known. There are some exceptions, the most notable being the city of Akragas, where I have retained the Greek name as I believe the Latin version, Agrigentum, is too different. Where known, modern place names will appear in brackets after the first instance of the ancient name. During the work I will use the terms Sicilian and Italian to refer exclusively to the Greek populations of those regions. All dates, unless otherwise noted, are BC.

I would like to dedicate this work to my father, John Champion, who gave me my love of history. He was a proud man when my first book, *Pyrrhus of Epirus* was published. Unfortunately he did not survive to see the publication of this work.

List of Plates

Maps

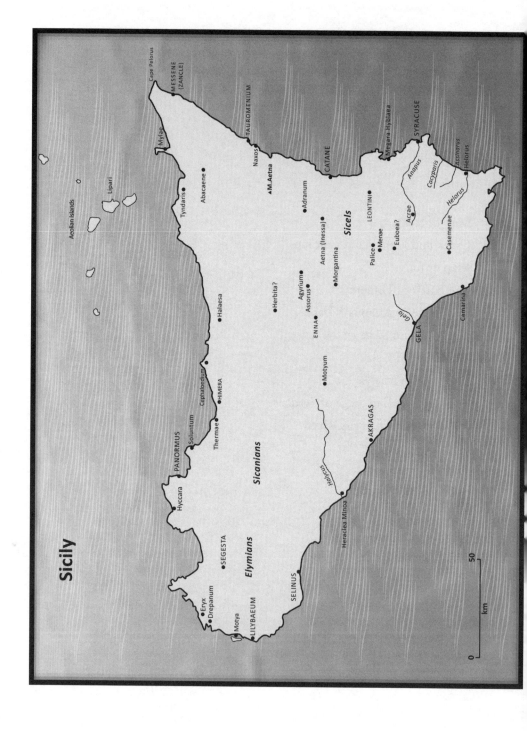

Sicily

Aeolian Islands

Lipari

Cape Pelorus

MESSENE
(ZANCLE)

Mylae

Tyndaris

Abacaene

TAUROMENIUM

Naxos

▲M.Aetna

CATANE

Adranum

Megara Hyblaea

SYRACUSE

Assinorus

Anapus

Cacyparis

Helorus

Aetna (Inessa)

Palice

LEONTINI

Acrae

Euboea?

Helorus

Sicels

Menae

Casemenae

Morgantina

Herbita?

Agyrium

Assorus

Halaesa

ENNA

Sicanians

Camarina

Gelo

Motyum

GELA

Cephaloedium

HIMERA

PANORMUS

Soluntum

Thermae

AKRAGAS

Halycus

Hyccara

Heraclea Minoa

Elymians

SEGESTA

Eryx

Drepanum

Motya

LILYBAEUM

SELINUS

0   50

km

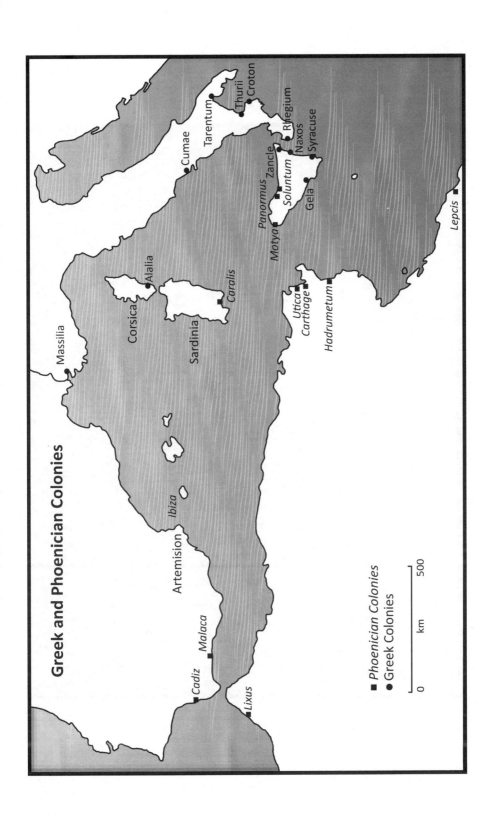

Greek and Phoenician Colonies

Lixus
Cadiz
Malaca
Artemision
Ibiza
Massilia
Corsica
Alalia
Sardinia
Caralis
Utica
Carthage
Hadrumetum
Cumae
Tarentum
Thurii
Croton
Panormus
Zancle
Rhegium
Naxos
Syracuse
Soluntum
Gela
Motya
Lepcis

■ *Phoenician Colonies*
● Greek Colonies

0   km   500

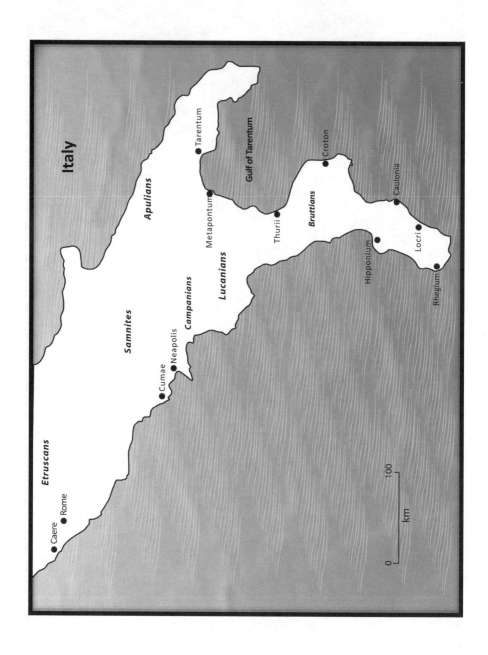

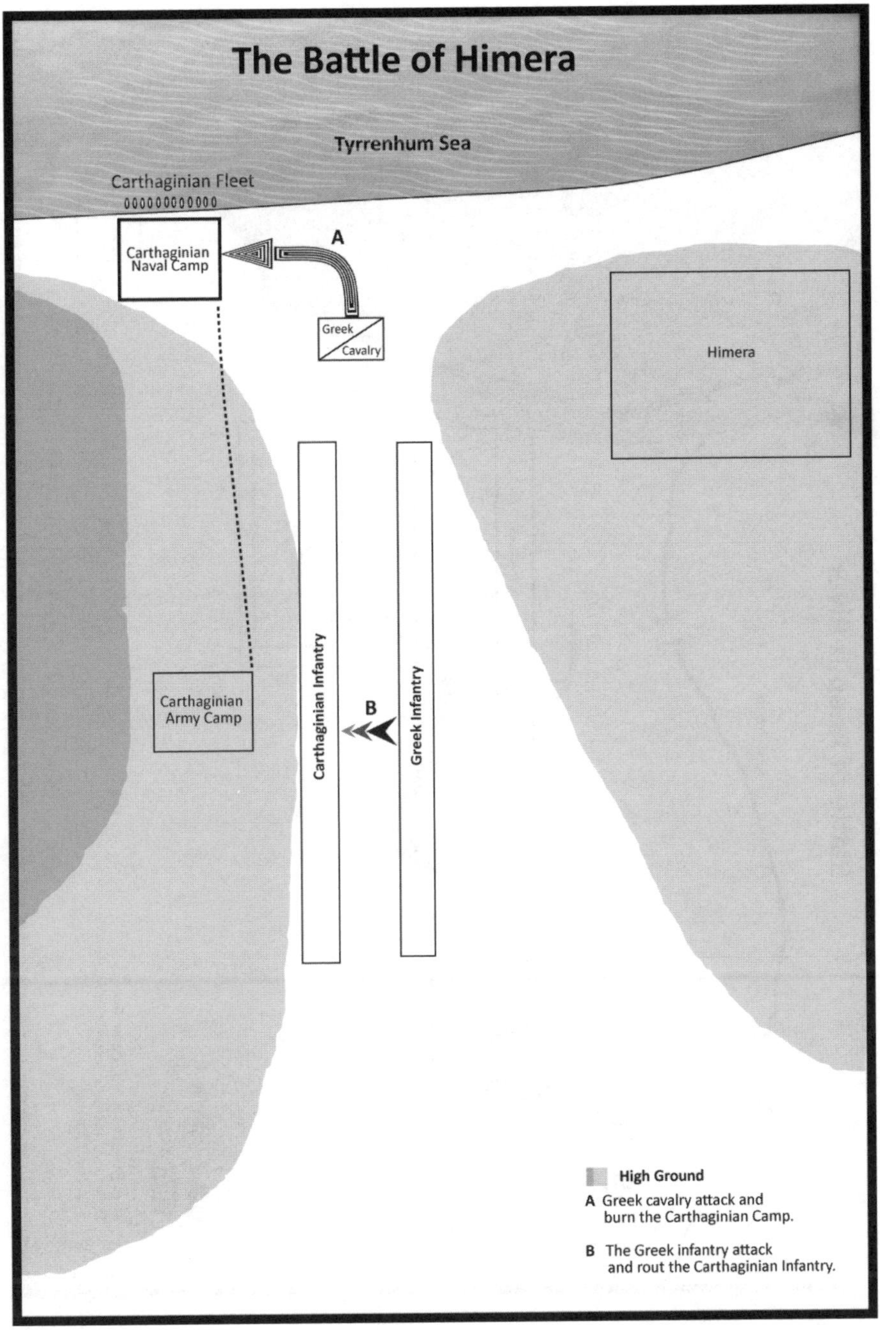

The Battle of Himera

Tyrrenhum Sea

Carthaginian Fleet
00000000000

Carthaginian
Naval Camp

A

Greek
Cavalry

Himera

Carthaginian Infantry

Greek Infantry

Carthaginian
Army Camp

B

High Ground

A Greek cavalry attack and
burn the Carthaginian Camp.

B The Greek infantry attack
and rout the Carthaginian Infantry.

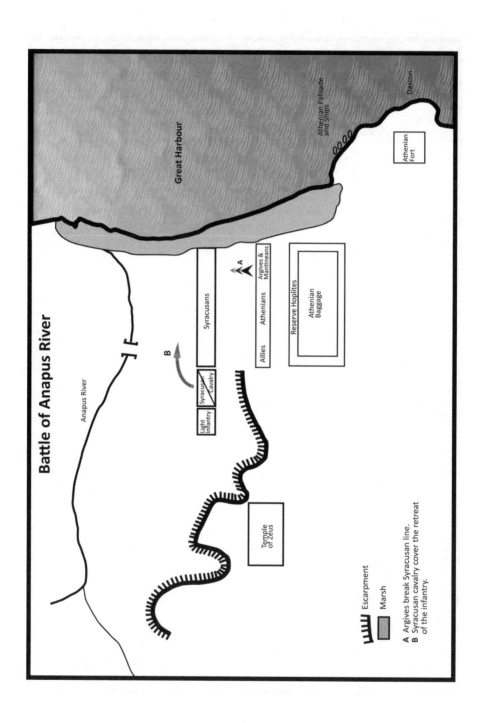

Battle of Anapus River

Anapus River

Great Harbour

Athenian Palisade and Ships

Dascon

Athenian Fort

Syracusans

Light Infantry

Syracusan Cavalry

B

A

Argives & Manitneans

Athenians

Allies

Reserve Hoplites

Athenian Baggage

Temple of Zeus

|||| Escarpment

Marsh

A Argives break Syracusan line.
B Syracusan cavalry cover the retreat of the infantry.

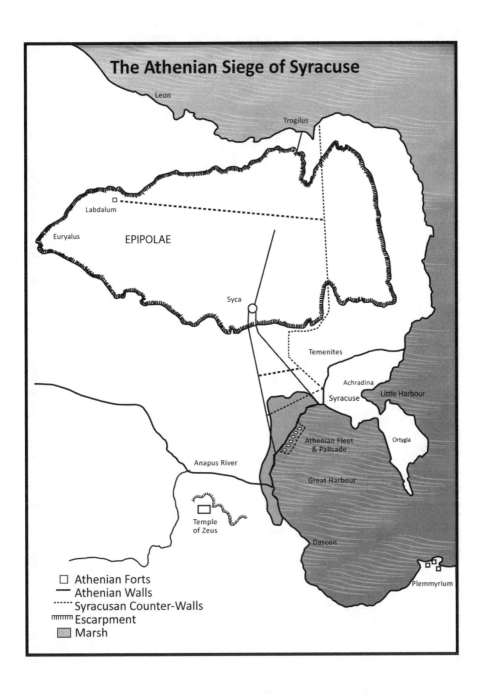

The Athenian Siege of Syracuse

Leon

Trogilus

Labdalum

Euryalus

EPIPOLAE

Syca

Temenites

Achradina

Little Harbour

Syracuse

Ortygia

Anapus River

Athenian Fleet
& Palisade

Great Harbour

Temple
of Zeus

Dascon

Plemmyrium

□ Athenian Forts
— Athenian Walls
······ Syracusan Counter-Walls
ⅿⅿⅿ Escarpment
▒ Marsh

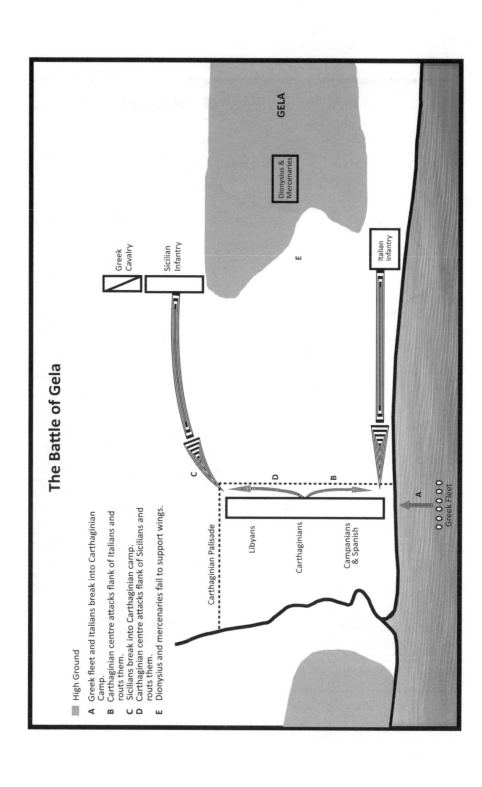

The Battle of Gela

High Ground

A Greek fleet and Italians break into Carthaginian Camp.
B Carthaginian centre attacks flank of Italians and routs them.
C Sicilians break into Carthaginian camp.
D Carthaginian centre attacks flank of Sicilians and routs them.
E Dionysius and mercenaries fail to support wings.

Carthaginian Palisade

Libyans

Carthaginians

Campanians & Spanish

Greek Fleet

Greek Cavalry

Sicilian Infantry

Italian Infantry

Dionysius & Mercenaries

GELA

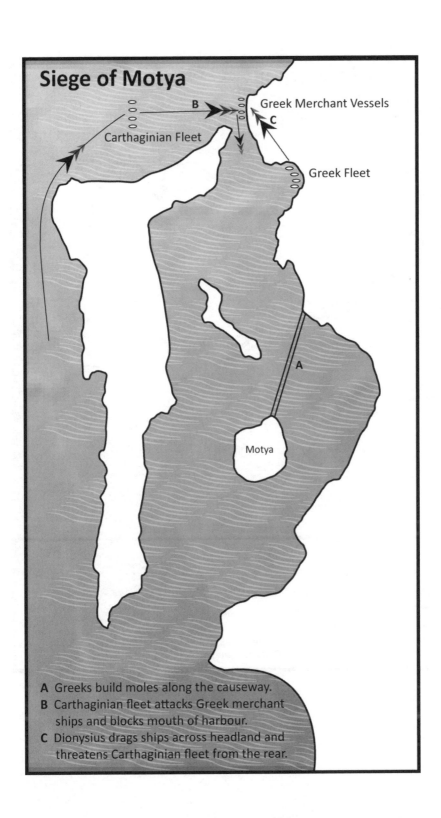

Siege of Motya

Carthaginian Fleet

B

Greek Merchant Vessels

C

Greek Fleet

A

Motya

A Greeks build moles along the causeway.
B Carthaginian fleet attacks Greek merchant
  ships and blocks mouth of harbour.
C Dionysius drags ships across headland and
  threatens Carthaginian fleet from the rear.

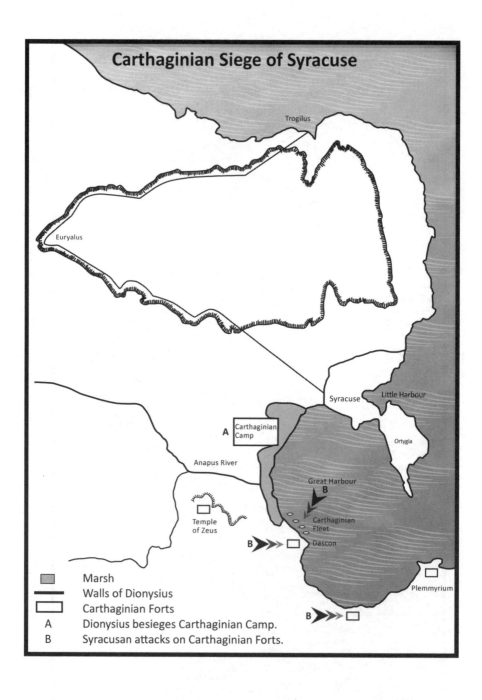

Carthaginian Siege of Syracuse

Trogilus

Euryalus

Syracuse

Little Harbour

A | Carthaginian Camp

Ortygia

Anapus River

Great Harbour

B

Temple of Zeus

Carthaginian Fleet

B ▶▶▶ Dascon

Plemmyrium

B ▶▶▶

Marsh
Walls of Dionysius
Carthaginian Forts
A Dionysius besieges Carthaginian Camp.
B Syracusan attacks on Carthaginian Forts.

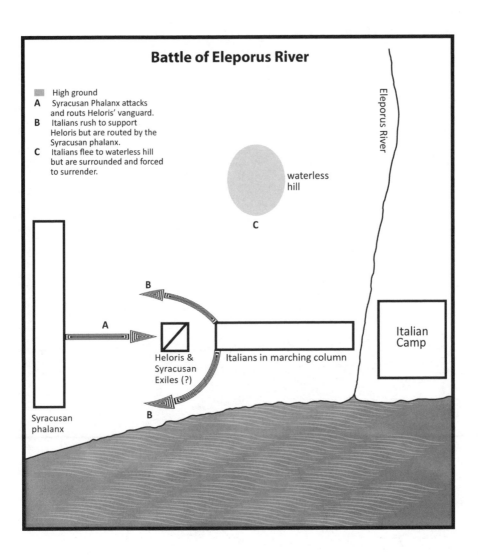

Battle of Eleporus River

High ground
A   Syracusan Phalanx attacks
    and routs Heloris' vanguard.
B   Italians rush to support
    Heloris but are routed by the
    Syracusan phalanx.
C   Italians flee to waterless hill
    but are surrounded and forced
    to surrender.

Eleporus River

waterless
hill

C

B

A

Heloris &
Syracusan
Exiles (?)

Italians in marching column

Italian
Camp

B

Syracusan
phalanx

Chapter 1

Colonies and Conflict

The fatness of the soil was such, that corn first grew here of itself,
which the most eminent of all the poets confirms in these words –
Within this island all things grow.
Without the help of seed or plough,
As wheat and barley, with the fine,
From whence proceeds both grapes and wine,
Which with sweet showers from above
Are brought to ripeness by great Jove.

Diodorus 5.2

In the year 734 an expedition of Ionian Greeks led by Theocles from the city of Chalcis in Euboea, and accompanied by another group from the island of Naxos, landed on the eastern most promontory of Sicily.[1] This point was created by an ancient lava flow from the nearby volcano of Mount Aetna. Here they founded the first Greek city of Sicily and named it Naxos after the homeland of part of the expedition. In many ways Naxos was an unusual site for the first Greek settlement on Sicily as there was only a limited area of cultivable land around the site. Nor was it the closest point to Italy, along whose coast the settlers must have sailed. It did, however, lie on a sheltered bay. Naxos is also the first point of Sicily on which the current from Capo d'Armi, the most southwestern point of Italy, strikes the island. The new city would thrive, but the limited area of its agricultural land would ensure that it would never be a power among the Greek cities of Sicily. Its position as the founding city would continue to be honoured by the Greeks. Ambassadors departing for missions to Greece, or returning to Sicily, would always offer sacrifice at the temple of Apollo in Naxos.

Within five years of their arrival in Sicily the Naxians had founded two more cities. The first was Leontini (Lentini), founded the following year, again by an expedition of colonists led by Theocles. Leontini was situated on the western side of the fertile Laistrygonian Plain. Five years later, another body of settlers founded the city of Catane (Catania), on the northern edge of the plain. With the creation of these two cities the Greeks had ensured that they had secured the richest wheat growing area of the island. These cities were founded by Greeks who spoke the Ionian dialect of their language.

A year after Naxos was founded another group of Greeks from the city of Corinth, who spoke the Dorian dialect, founded the city of Syracuse on the island of Ortygia further south along Sicily's eastern coast. The expedition was led by Archias, a member of the ruling aristocratic clan of the city. Archias had apparently agreed to lead the expedition in order to escape retribution for a murder he had been a party to back in Corinth. Syracuse was a much more promising site for a settlement, as it had two of the best harbours in Sicily and a large agricultural hinterland. Syracuse would continue to prosper and would eventually become the dominant Greek city on the island. According to the ancient geographer Strabo:

> The city grew, both on account of the fertility of the soil and on account of the natural excellence of its harbours. Furthermore, the men of Syracuse proved to have the gift of leadership, with the result that when the Syracusans were ruled by tyrants they lorded it over the rest, and when set free themselves they set free those who were oppressed by the barbarians.[2]

In 729 another group of Dorian settlers from the city of Megara founded the city of Megara Hyblaea, nineteen kilometres to the north of Syracuse. Two other colonies were also founded about this time by colonists from Chalcis, Zancle (Messina) in Sicily and Rhegium (Reggio) in southern Italy. Zancle was named after the native Sicilian word for the crescent shape of its harbour. Syracuse and Zancle were the only Greek cities of Sicily to have substantial harbours. The exact foundation dates of these settlements are unknown, but they were certainly before 720. The two cities dominated the important Straits of Messina, situated between the Italian mainland and Sicily. The original colonists of Zancle also included some who came from Cumae in Italy, having been expelled after gaining a reputation for piracy.

In 688 Antiphemus of Rhodes and Entimus of Crete came with their followers and founded a city on the southern coast of Sicily. It was built alongside the River Gela from which it took its name. With the foundation of Gela the first wave of Greek colonization of Sicily from overseas was complete.

The colonization of Sicily was a part of a much wider outflow of emigrants from the Greek mainland to such far-flung regions as Asia Minor, Italy and Sicily during the eighth century. It is sometimes argued that these initial colonies were established primarily as trading posts, and the strategic positioning of some and their occupation of good harbours gives some credibility to this proposition. There is, however, a much simpler reason: that of population pressure. The population of ancient Greece had collapsed after the fall of the Mycenaean civilization at the end of the twelfth century. It remained low for the following four centuries. Archaeological evidence shows that there was a rapid increase in the number of inhabitants during the eighth century. Good agricultural land had always been in limited supply in mountainous Greece and the increasing population would have placed what did exist under further pressure.

Modern commentators often overestimate the importance of trade and commerce to the ancient Greek cities. Agricultural production was by far the overwhelming method of producing wealth in the ancient world. Trade and industry played a role in that they encouraged the production of an agricultural surplus, giving the farmer a market for his extra produce and goods to purchase with the profits. Despite this, commerce accounted for an insignificant part of the economy during the Archaic period of Greek history (750–480), the period of colonization. As Snodgrass points out, 'that in the Greek scale of values, commercial and industrial activity were rated so low as to be thought unworthy of the expenditure of any intellectual effort.' He further claims that 'few economic decisions were taken by Greek states.'[3] The overwhelming cause for outflow of migrants from Greece would have been the search for new agricultural land. Thucydides, writing of Athens, gives the ancient view for the sending out of colonists. He claims that an increase in the number of inhabitants 'swelled the already large population of the city to such a height that Attica became at last too small to hold them, and they had to send out colonies to Ionia.'[4]

This pressing need for land is demonstrated by the rapid annexation and securing of agricultural land by the colonists of Naxos. The Syracusans also quickly set up their own colonies in the fortified outposts of Helorus forty kilometres to the south, Acrae (Palazzolo Acreide) forty three kilometres inland and further to the west at Casmenae, in order to defend their farmlands. Strabo explicitly states that the Greeks were attracted to Sicily because they 'clearly perceived both the weakness of the peoples and the excellence of the soil'.[5] The seizure of good agricultural land from the territory around the city was one of the first priorities of most Greek colonies. This surrounding territory was known as the city's *chora*.

The peoples that Strabo mentioned were the original inhabitants of the island. According to the Greek historians, when the Greeks first arrived in Sicily it was already inhabited by three distinct ethnic groups. Archaeological evidence from the sites of these inhabitants shows that they already had trade connections with the Greeks going right back to the Mycenaean period. The first Greek colonists were not therefore embarking blindly into an unknown region.

The three existing cultures were, from east to west: the Sicels, the Sicanians and the Elymians. After giving a fanciful description of the earliest inhabitants being mythical beings such as the Cyclopes and giant cannibals, Thucydides then goes on to give the traditional Greek view of the origins of these people:

The Sicanians appear to have been the next settlers, although they pretend to have been the first of all the aborigines; but the facts show that they were Iberians, driven away by the Ligurians from the River Sicanus in Iberia. It is from them that the island, before called Trinacria, took its name of Sicania, and to the present they inhabitant the west of Sicily. On the fall of Ilium, some of the Trojans escaped from the Achaeans, came in ships to Sicily, and settled next to the Sicanians under the name of Elymi; their cities being called Eryx and Segesta. With them settled some of the Phocians carried on their way from Troy by a storm, first to Libya, and afterwards from there to Sicily. The Sicels crossed over to Sicily from their home in Italy, fleeing from the Opicans . . . Even to the present day there are still Sicels in Italy . . . They went with a great host to Sicily, defeated the Sicanians in battle and forced them to withdraw to the south and west of the island, which thus came to be called Sicily instead of Sicania.[6]

Despite its proximity to the Italian mainland, Sicily has always been an island in modern human times. The best evidence suggests that the first human populations arrived on the island about 18,000 years ago. Thucydides appears to be correct in claiming that the Sicanian culture was the first of the indigenous cultures to develop, probably about 1600. The next group to be identified is the Elymians. They had succeeded in driving out the Sicanians from western Sicily by 1100. The Elymians appear to be the most urbanized of the native Sicilians, founding settlements that the Greeks recognized as cities at Eryx (Erice), Segesta (Segesta) and Entella. The Sicel culture is the last to be identified, developing sometime between 1200 and 1000. They too drove back the Sicanians into central Sicily.

There is some linguistic evidence to support Thucydides' claims that the three distinct cultures were the result of three separate, later, waves of migration to the island. Modern opinion, however, generally favours the theory that all three were indigenous peoples who were influenced by a cultural layer imported from overseas, rather than the product of later, large scale migrations. The limited amount of DNA evidence available tends to support the latter view. It must also be remembered that the only written sources that we have for the three separate cultures come from the descriptions of the Greeks. How great the cultural differences between these three peoples were, and what their origins were, is much debated.

Whatever the origins of the native peoples of Sicily, the reality was that the first Greek colonists were forced to confront the existing Sicel population. The sites of both Naxos and Ortygia show evidence of earlier occupation by the Sicels. Whether the Greeks integrated these populations into their own or drove them out by force cannot be determined. There is a traditional view that the Ionian settlers tended to have good relations with the Sicels and often lived side-by-side with Sicel communities.

The Dorians, by contrast, are accused of either driving out the Sicels or conquering them and reducing them to serfdom. The Dorians were the last of the Hellenic groups to arrive in Greece and tended to set up conquest-states where the existing populations were subjugated to the status of a bonded agricultural labour force. Examples are the *helots* of Sparta and the *penestai* of Thessaly. Their societies tended to be aristocratic and militaristic in nature. Whether this difference in dealing with the native population is real or imagined cannot be certain. Strabo does not differentiate between the different groups of Greeks when he states that:

> As for these barbarians, some were native inhabitants, whereas others came over from the mainland. The Greeks would permit none of them to lay hold of the seaboard, but were not strong enough to keep them altogether away from the interior.[7]

Polyaenus also relates a tale that tends to deny this simple generalization. According to him the Ionian Theocles founded Leontini with the assistance of the Sicels and was under 'an oath not to disturb the Sicilians [Sicels].' In order to get around his oath he allowed a group of Dorian colonists from Megara to enter the city in order to drive out the Sicels.

> 'They attacked the Sicilians, who, being unarmed and unprepared, were unable to resist the enemy. The Sicilians abandoned the city, and fled, but the Megarians undertook to take the place of the Sicilians, and became allies of the Chalcidians. They immediately attacked the Sicilians and drove them out.'[8]

Six months later the wily Theocles used a stratagem to disarm and to drive out the Dorians during a festival. Afterwards, they wandered for two years before one of the Sicel kings gave them the site for their city of Megara Hyblaea.

The archaeological evidence does, however, tend to show that Sicel communities continued to live alongside those of the Chalcidians and interact peacefully with them over the next century. The result of this activity meant that by about 500 the Sicel communities appear, at least at the material level, to have become largely Hellenized.

The Dorians of Syracuse do, however, appear to have immediately set out to either enslave, or drive out, the neighbouring Sicels. By 660 they had set up strong-points to defend the agricultural lands they had annexed and reduced the remaining Sicel population to the status of *kyllyrioi*, who were classified as slaves. Rather than chattel slaves they were more likely to have been in a position similar to the *helots* of Sparta: lacking freedom of movement, tied to their own plots of land and paying a substantial percentage of their produce to their Syracusan landlords. Those Sicels who refused to be subjugated were driven further inland or south to the mountainous region around modern Ragusa.

At about the same time that the Greeks were settling eastern Sicily, another people, the Phoenicians, were founding settlements on the western end of the island. The history of Phoenician settlement is, however, even more difficult to trace than that of the Greeks. It began further west, in southern Spain and northern Africa. The Roman historian Velleius Paterculus gives the traditional earliest date for these settlements. He claims that in 1104:

> The fleet of Tyre, which controlled the sea, founded in the farthest district of Spain, on the remotest confines of our world, the city of Cadiz, on an island in the ocean separated from the mainland by a very narrow strait. The Tyrians a few years later also founded Utica in Africa.[9]

This date is generally considered far too early as no archaeological finds for any Phoenician settlements can be dated to before the ninth century. Unlike those of the Greeks, the earliest Phoenician settlements do appear to have been established exclusively for purposes of trade or mining. The Phoenicians established what would later become their most important colony, the city of Carthage on the northern coast of what is now Tunisia. It was settled by Phoenician colonists in 813: 'the founding of Carthage, that is, in the thirty-eighth year before the first Olympiad.'[10] This date was previously considered to be too early by archaeologists. More recent radiocarbon dating has confirmed it, however, as a reasonable estimate.

Carthage's foundation is shrouded in legend. Whatever records it maintained were destroyed by the Romans when they sacked the city in 146. What evidence we have comes from the writers of its enemies, the Greeks and Romans. The city was originally sited on a limestone peninsula that stretched out into the open sea and provided a well-protected natural harbour. This has since silted up. The promontory was well supplied with water. To the north it was protected by steep cliffs and to the south by a long isthmus. Although not the first of the Phoenician colonies in Africa, it would eventually become the most powerful Phoenician city in the western Mediterranean.

Over the next two centuries the Phoenicians established numerous trading posts, and opened mines, in Africa, Sicily, Spain and Sardinia. Their trade routes extended out into the Atlantic Ocean and reached as far as Britain and Morocco.

Although the original Phoenician settlements may have begun as trading or mining centres, many later developed into large cities. In the last decades of the eighth century, at the same time that Greek colonization began on a large scale, the Phoenicians of Lebanon and Cyprus began to send out large numbers of settlers to these outposts. The reasons for this apparent shift to mass migration can only be guessed. One theory is that the first wave of migration was caused by the expansion of Assyria under Tiglathpileser III (745–727). It is more certain that a second wave of migration was the result of a large-scale exodus of refugees who fled Phoenicia after the Assyrian king Esarhaddon (680–669) ravaged the region. Nor can the mother cities of the Phoenician colonies be attributed accurately, except that it is certain that Carthage was colonized by Tyre.

The Italian historian Giovanni Garbini has observed that the Phoenician colonies were established to the west of those of the Greeks, separated by 'an invisible line that ran from the northeast of Sardinia down to the *Arae Philaenorum* [Ajdabiya] on the Libyan coast' and is 'too precise to be a question of chance.' This has led him to conclude that 'it is reasonable to infer that an understanding was reached between the Greeks and the Phoenicians, enabling the latter to keep their seaways through the Mediterranean free.'[11]

It would appear, however, that any agreement between such scattered and disparate peoples would be impossible to negotiate, let alone enforce. It is more likely that the differing goals of the earlier colonists kept them apart largely by accident. The later movements of large numbers of Phoenician settlers into the western Mediterranean during the seventh century would ensure that this convenient situation did not survive.

According to Thucydides the Phoenician settlements in Sicily were originally only trading posts:

> There were also Phoenicians who occupied promontories upon the sea coasts and nearby islands for the purpose of trading with the Sicels. But when the Hellenes began to arrive in considerable numbers the Phoenicians abandoned most of their stations, and drawing together took up their abode in Motya, Solontum, and Panormus, near the Elymi, partly because they trusted their alliance with them, and also because these are the nearest points for the voyage between Carthage to Sicily.[12]

Like much of the pre-history of Sicily this statement is much disputed as there is no archaeological evidence for such settlements. Some scholars argue that because the settlements were only temporary in nature they would leave no permanent record. Others claim that even trading stations would require some buildings and the population would have to leave some remains, even if only burial sites. Whatever the truth of the matter, it is clear that after the coming of the Greeks to the east of Sicily the Phoenicians confined themselves to the western end of the island. Settlements were founded at Motya, Panormus (Palermo) and Soluntum.

Thucydides' claim that the founding of the Phoenician cities came after the migrations of the Greeks is supported by the archaeological evidence, which can find no physical evidence of Phoenician settlements at these sites prior to 700. Motya was probably the first to be settled and would grow to be the most important. It occupied an island less than two kilometres in diameter in a lagoon to the north of modern Marsala. It is protected to the west by a larger island and to the north by the mainland, giving a safe anchorage to vessels.

Panormus was also founded on a bay, one of the few along the northern coast of Sicily. Its name translates from the Greek as 'all weather', meaning that the port was safe for ships all year round. Soluntum was located eighteen kilometres to the east of Panormus near the promontory called Capo Zafferano. It occupied a naturally strong situation with a commanding view of the sea. These locations support the premise that the Phoenician colonies were sited primarily as trading posts. The cities also occupy that part of Sicily that is closest to Africa, leading some historians to posit that the colonists came from the newly colonized Phoenician cities of North Africa rather than those of the eastern Mediterranean.

The outflow of Phoenician refugees at the beginning of the seventh century appears to have had an impact on the cities in Sicily. Motya continued to grow during this century from a small trading post occupying only a small area to a large city covering the whole of its island site. Another source of settlers for Motya was the Greeks, most likely tradesman involved in the manufacturing or building industries.

The Phoenicians also appear to have enjoyed good relations with the nearby indigenous people, the Elymians. Thucydides speaks of an alliance between the two peoples. This collaboration is most likely a result of the apparent lack of interest by the colonists in annexing the inland farming areas to any large extent. Both peoples would have benefited from the trade that these cities brought. At the same time that the Phoenicians were colonizing Sicily they were also establishing similar outposts on Sardinia.

The foundation and subsequent growth of these Phoenician cities did not go un-noticed by the Greeks of Sicily. In the middle of the sixth century two new colonies were founded, this time mostly by the Greeks of Sicily them-selves rather than from outside. The first was most likely to have been Himera, on the northern coast, by colonists from Zancle and political exiles from Syracuse, probably about 648. The other was Selinus, on the southern coast, founded by migrants from Megara Hyblaea, settled either at the same time or twenty years later.

Neither is an immediately obvious location for a new colony. Himera did not have much suitable grain-growing land nearby and the colonists had bypassed much more promising farming country further east. It did have the advantage of having a beach by a river mouth and occupied a defensible hilltop. The countryside around Selinus had a large amount of arable land, but it was in a poor defensive position and needed strong fortifications. There was possibly a small harbour, although even this is disputed. The basin of what may have been the port is now silted up and may have already been so in ancient times. The surrounding marshes made the location very unhealthy. Malaria would continue to be a problem in Sicily until modern times. The colonists of Selinus had also bypassed much more promising sites further east.

The impulse for the settlement of these two colonies was most likely driven by the need for more agricultural land for the expanding populations of the eastern cities. This is especially so for Selinus, as Megara Hyblaea was hemmed in by Syracuse to the south and Leontini to the west. It is, however, difficult not to conclude that other considerations caused the choices of location. Both cities were sited as far west as was possible without encroaching into the lands of the Phoenicians and Elymians. In effect the Greeks were laying claim to everything to the east of these two cities; the seventh century equivalent of planting a national flag.

After the foundation of Selinus the Greeks of Sicily then back-filled the fertile southern coast of Sicily with new colonies. Syracuse founded Camarina in about 599, Gela established Akragas in 580, and Selinus settled Heraclea Minoa probably in the 570s.

In ancient times Sicily was renowned for the richness of its agricultural lands. This fertility allowed the Greek cities to become grain exporters, unlike their founding cities in Greece who were mainly grain importers by the fifth century. The export of grain was a major factor in the rapid economic expansion of the Sicilian Greek cities. Eventually they would become famous for their prosperity. Syracuse in particular was renowned for its wealth and extravagance. The 'tithe of the Syracusans' was a common simile for describing extreme affluence.

At first the founding of Himera and Selinus do not appear to have troubled either the Phoenicians or the Elymians. There is evidence of extensive trade between the Greek and Phoenician cities. The Elymian city of Segesta seems to have had, at least initially, a friendly relationship with Selinus. It adopted the Greek alphabet and developed the architecture and layout of a Greek city. The other major Elymian city, Eryx, being closer to the coast, adopted a Phoenician appearance and alphabet.

Despite their shared border, the first clashes between the Greeks and Phoenicians in the western Mediterranean did not occur in Sicily but as a result of the expansion of another group of Greek colonists. In about 600 a group of colonists from the Ionian city of Phocaea (Foca, in Turkey) founded a colony at Massalia, modern Marseilles. The Phocaeans were originally colonists of Athens. According to Herodotus they were the first Greeks to sail long distances 'and it was they who showed their countrymen the way to the Adriatic, Tyrrhenia [Italy] and the Spanish peninsular,' where they supposedly developed a friendship with one of the Spanish kings.[13] The Phocaeans were great traders and Massalia is one possible example of a Greek colony set up, at least initially, as a trading post. The site was on a well protected bay.

There is a legend recorded by Justin that one of the local Ligurian chiefs gave the site to settlers. Following the death of this chief, however, one of his advisors told his son that 'Marseilles would one day be the ruin of the neighbouring people, and that he ought to suppress it in its rise, lest, when it grew stronger, it should overpower him', and that 'the people of Marseilles, who are now regarded as your tenants, will one day become masters of your territory.'

The new king formed a plan to overthrow Massalia by a surprise attack during a festival, while the city was 'overcome with sleep and the fumes of wine.' The plan was betrayed by a Ligurian woman to her Greek lover. The Greek fell upon their would-be attackers and killed 7,000 of them including the king. After that, the Massalians during festivals always 'shut their gates, to keep watch, to place sentinels on the walls, to examine strangers, to take all kinds of precaution, and to guard the city as carefully in time of peace as if they were at war.'[14]

The Massalians then went to make war against both their Ligurian and Gaulish neighbours and 'their valour enabled them to take in some of the surrounding plains'. They set up a number of 'strong-hold cities' to defend their newly won lands against the native peoples, as had the Syracusans.[15] Although Massalia had possibly been founded as a trading city, it had, in a manner similar to that of other Greek colonies, quickly conquered its own *chora*.

The Massalians were not content with this and they soon founded a number of other colonies along the coast of southern France. This expansion brought them into conflict with the Phoenicians. The cause of the war was probably the establishment of a fortified settlement at the mouth of the River Rhone, 'a stronghold against the barbarians who live round about the River Rhodanus.'[16] This directly threatened the Carthaginians land passage, across southern France from the Atlantic to the Mediterranean, which avoided the dangerous passage through the Straits of Gibraltar. Burn claims that this gave the Carthaginians 'something important at stake; probably the hither end of the short land-passage to the Atlantic, important for the tin-trade.'[17] Details of the fighting are sketchy but Thucydides records that 'while they were founding Marseilles, they defeated the Carthaginians in a sea fight.'[18]

This victory only increased the Massalians' ambitions and they went on to establish a string of other colonies along the coast of Spain. This expansion most likely involved further aggression against the Phoenicians as according to 'archaeological inquiry: between 600 BC and 550 BC all the Phoenician colonies east of Gibraltar met their end.'[19] It is probably this period that Justin is referring to when he claims that the war with the Phoenicians was ongoing and that the Massalians 'often routed, and granted them peace under defeat; with the Spaniards they made an alliance.'[20]

The Phocaeans were not the only Greeks from the east to shatter the peace. In about 580 an expedition from Cnidus and Rhodes, led by Pentathlos, tried to set up a colony on the headland of Lilybaeum (Marsala), just south of Motya. This was at about the same time that the Rhodian colony of Gela founded Akragas. War had already broken out between Segesta and Selinus. These three events may very well have been linked in a new policy of Greek aggression. An alliance of the Elymians and Phoenicians defeated the combined forces of the Selinuntians and Pentathlos in battle. The allies then went on to capture and destroy the new Greek settlement at Lilybaeum. As a result of this campaign, Motya began to build the first walls of what would later become impressive fortifications.

The surviving Greek refugees escaped to set up a new colony on the Aeolian Islands off the northern coast of Sicily. Here they conducted a successful campaign of piracy against the Etruscans of Italy for the next century. They also attempted to solve the constant conflict over land ownership within Greek cities by making all land the property of the state. It would be leased out and redistributed at regular intervals.

The defeat does appear, at least for most of the next century, to have cooled the ambition of the Greeks of Sicily to conquer the western end of the island. Instead the new city of Akragas embarked on a successful campaign of conquest against the native Sicanians. These conquests were carried out under the rule of Phalaris, one of the first of the tyrants of Sicily.

Chapter 2

Cities, Hoplites and Tyrants.

In aristocracies revolutions are stirred up when a few only share in the honours of the state; a cause which has been already shown to affect oligarchies; for an aristocracy is a sort of oligarchy, and, like an oligarchy, is the government of a few, although few not for the same reason; hence the two are often confounded. And revolutions will be most likely to happen, and must happen, when the mass of the people are of the high-spirited kind, and have a notion that they are as good as their rulers.

Aristotle, Politics 5.7

The Greek city, or *polis*, was not just a city; it was an independent, sovereign state. Not only did it rule over the city itself but also over a surrounding area of countryside. The *chora* would contain outlying villages but the political and military centre of the state was the city. If the *polis* was lucky, or well-situated, this countryside might contain metal deposits, the mining of which would be a valuable source of revenue for the city. Nonetheless, the main purpose of the *chora* was to provide agricultural land. Aristotle lists six methods, in order of importance, by which a state, or governor of a region, could raise regular revenue. In order of importance they were: by a tithe on produce; special products, for example gold or silver; levies on markets or merchandise; taxes on land and its sale; taxes on cattle or other livestock; poll-taxes and taxes on industry or trade.[1]

From this list it can be seen that tithes on agricultural produce and land taxes were the most numerous and important. The control and exploitation of agricultural land was still the major source of wealth throughout the ancient Greek world. The conquest of new agricultural land was the most reliable method of increasing a state's wealth and revenue base. Although referring to the later Hellenistic dynasties, Austin's view of the relationship between the control of territory and power is just as applicable to the Greek *polis*:

Increase of territory meant increase of revenues hence of power, while decrease of territory had the opposite effect and might send the dynasty into decline.[2]

This simple, albeit brutal, logic explains the origins of the conflicts between the Greek colonists and the native peoples of Sicily.

By the end of the Archaic period, the Greek city would have evolved into the familiar form that it would continue to follow over the coming centuries. The city would be a walled settlement around a fortified strongpoint, usually the highest point of the city, the *acropolis*. The heart of the *polis* was, however, the *agora*, an open space in the centre of the city. The usual purpose of the *agora* was as a market-place, but this was not its most important function. The *agora* also served as the political centre of the city. In earlier times the citizens would assemble to hear proclamations from the city's rulers or to gather for war. As time went on the *agora* would develop into a much larger and important centre. It would eventually come to be surrounded by public buildings, statues and temples, and trials would often be held there. Perhaps most importantly it would become the place where the citizens of the city would gather to discuss political issues.

This classical version of the Greek city had not, however, developed at the time of the original colonization of Sicily. During the eighth, and well into the seventh century, the Greek city was still little more than a village, or collection of villages, usually settled around an *acropolis*. Corinth, the founding city of Syracuse, was a collection of such villages, each with its own market, and one of which may have had its own private fortifications.

The development of the classical model of the *polis* began during the population increase of the eighth century but would not be completed until the end of the sixth. Not only was there a rise in the number of people during this period, but also a rapid growth in wealth and technological advancement, particularly in military technology.

The period between the fall of the Mycenaean kingdoms and the archaic period is usually referred to as the 'dark ages'. During this period the kings of the old Mycenaean realms had largely been removed by the aristocracy. Only the most conservative of the Greek states, such as Sparta, would continue to have kings. The Greek cities were now ruled by a narrow clique of nobles, usually referred to as the *aristoi* (the best men) or the *hippeis* (horsemen or knights). For example, in Corinth under the rule of the Bacchiads, citizenship was confined to this clan alone, consisting of perhaps as few as two hundred families. Society at the beginning of the archaic period was largely divided between two classes: the aristocracy and the rest, the *demos* (people).

The power of these nobles within their small communities was absolute. In the memorable words of Forrest, the local aristocrat was 'mayor, police-chief, magistrate, lawyer, draft-officer, commander, minister of religion, and a dozen other things rolled into one.'[3] In a world where there were no written laws, for the Greeks had lost the art of writing, the lower classes were completely at the mercy of his whim. The gulf between the two classes was vast.

The power of the aristocracy rested on the two pillars of their wealth and their military prowess. Only the wealthy had the resources to adequately train and equip themselves and their retainers for war. With the collapse of the Mycenaean kingdoms the means to conduct large-scale warfare, and to field the large numbers of chariots that these kingdoms had, vanished. Thucydides describes this period as one in which:

> Wars by land there was none, none at least by which power was acquired; we have the usual border contests but of distant expeditions with conquest the object we hear nothing . . . what fighting there was consisted merely of local warfare between rival neighbours.[4]

In such a society warfare would have largely consisted of raids on livestock, wife-stealing, punitive raids and revenge attacks. The horse-borne warrior would have excelled in this type of warfare, being able to either get in and out of hostile territory quickly or respond to raids on one's own land. The local militia was probably only called up in response to large-scale raids on their own villages. These levies would have largely been ill-armed and poorly trained. They probably acted as little more than a cheer squad for their local aristocrats and their retainers. It is unlikely that during this period the *hippeis* were genuine cavalry. More likely, they rode a horse, or chariot, to the battle-field then dismounted to engage in heroic single-combats, throwing javelins and closing to fight with swords against the opposing noblemen, in a manner similar to that described in Homer's *Illiad*. Although the poem was set in the earlier Mycenaean era, it was composed during the early archaic period and is generally believed to reflect the warfare and politics of its own time.

Along with the population increase in Greece during the eighth century, the opening up of new lands and trade through colonization led to a significant increase in the wealth of the society. Enough of this wealth appears to have trickled down to the people that a significant proportion of them rose above their neighbours to form a new class of wealthy non-aristocrats. This led to a corresponding increase in the numbers of men who could now afford to arm themselves properly. The archaeological record shows that during this time there was significant change in the use of bronze to produce armour, rather than luxury items or goods produced to be donations to the temples.

The wealthiest of these men armed themselves in the latest fashion of military equipment, ideally a bronze breastplate, greaves and helmet. The earliest preserved example comes from a tomb in Argos dated to the late eighth century. This defensive equipment was augmented with a round, nearly one metre-wide shield. The evidence suggests, however, that breastplates and greaves were relatively rare. The ownership of a spear and a shield was the minimum necessary requirement to serve in the line of battle. The men so armed came to be called 'hoplites' (armed men). Even a hoplite shield was, however, a considerable expense, beyond the means of the poorer citizens. When a state wished to increase the size of its number of hoplites it would do so by providing the poor with state-funded shields.

At some point the nature of Greek tactics also changed. The old 'heroic' manner of fighting was replaced by a new formation, the hoplite phalanx. Here the heavily-armoured spearmen would form up almost shoulder to shoulder, usually around eight ranks deep, with their shields touching and their javelins replaced by a heavier stabbing spear. They would maintain a solid line as they advanced, rather than run out from the ranks to seek individual foes. In fact such actions came to be frowned upon. This view is demonstrated by the refusal of the Spartans at the Battle of Plataea (479) to give a prize for valour to a certain Aristodemus, despite the fact that he 'had indeed fought magnificently, but that he had done so merely to retrieve his lost honour, rushing forward with the fury of a madman'.[5] This attitude spelled the end of the combat of heroes and helped break the military power of the aristocrats.

The traditional view of such fighting is that the strength of the new close formation was in shock combat. When two armies so armed fought, the two phalanxes would smash into each other in the hope of breaking the enemy's force through their impetus. If that failed, the battle would degenerate into a pushing match, with the braver individuals trying to force open a hole in the enemy line. This maneuver was known as the *othismos*.

An alternateive view is that the earlier, more heroic form of fighting lasted much longer. Herodotus' accounts of fighting at the start of the fifth century do contain some descriptions of battle that resemble the earlier style. This, along with the continuing representation of heroic combat in art, has led some modern commentators to argue that true phalanx warfare may not have come to dominate the battlefield until the middle of the fifth century.[6] Such Homeric descriptions and artistic representations of battle are, however, common long after this period, and still influenced historians as late as the sixth century *AD*.

In a recent study of hoplite warfare, involving much physical re-creation, Chris Matthew has argued that neither view is totally correct and that 'the word *othismos* cannot be subject to only one exclusive definition; nor, more importantly, can it be subject to only one school of thought.' Matthew argues that hoplites fought in two distinct orders. One very close, that was adopted for defence or for a deliberate advance, with overlapping shields and two ranks of spears projecting forward of the line. The other was in a slightly more open order, allowing the hoplites to charge at speed. In order for a clash of lines and the traditional shield-to-shield push to occur, both sides would have to adopt this formation and be willing to charge into contact. This did occur on a number of occasions. At other times, if one, or both sides, adopted the more closely packed formation the number of spears protruding from the lines made it 'not physically possible for the two formations to close to that proximity and the initial fighting would have been conducted at 'spear length' as Xenophon and others describe it.' The strength of the closer formation was such that, 'in every account of a battle where a close-order formation engaged with one in a more open order (or even against cavalry) the hoplites deployed in close order were always victorious.' He concludes that 'hoplite warfare was much more varied and dynamic in its nature than either of these totally opposing views can readily concede.'[7]

The exhausting nature of hoplite fighting meant that the clash of the battle lines rarely lasted more than an hour. The advantage of the hoplite phalanx was that in an open battle on level plain it would simply overwhelm infantry fighting in the traditional, open style of fighting.

The preferred method of fighting for the Greek states during this period was to solve disputes quickly in a single set-piece battle. This both limited the destruction of the countryside and allowed everyone to go home quickly. The Persian general Mardonius exclaimed that the Greeks 'when they declare war on each other, they go off together to the smoothest and most level bit of ground they can find and have their battle on it.'[8] This stylized form of warfare was possible because these early disputes were generally over the control of agricultural land, mostly plains. Once one state had adopted the phalanx, all the Greek cities capable of fielding enough hoplites were forced to follow suit.

A number of the enemies of the Greeks, such as the Etruscans of Italy and later the Carthaginians, probably adopted the same tactics for much the same reasons. Other peoples who lived in wooded or mountainous regions, such as the Thracians or the Lucanians of southern Italy, tended to remain with skirmishing tactics. In their native terrain they could outmanoeuvre the Greek phalanx. In such regions the Greeks were often forced to remain clinging to their coastal cities as they could not expand inland beyond the coastal plains.

Just when the new form of warfare developed is open to considerable debate. Victor Davis Hanson, writing on the mechanics of hoplite warfare, claims that close order fighting already existed during the dark ages and pre-dated the development of the equipment as 'military technology of itself rarely invents tactics; more often new designs are responses to existing needs.'[9] The more common view is that at first these newly armed men probably emulated their betters, throwing javelins and fighting in an individual manner. This form of fighting is still being described by the poets until the middle of the seventh century. At some stage, as the numbers of heavily armed troops increased, the phalanx evolved and came to dominate the battlefield.

The traditional view is that 'hoplite warfare' developed sometime in the middle of the seventh century in the Peloponnesus. This argument is based on circumstantial evidence. The naming of the equipment, the 'Argive' shield and the 'Corinthian' helmet gives the location. The famous Chigi Vase, dated to the mid-seventh century, shows men armed in the hoplite manner apparently marching in step to the sounds of a flute player. Artistic representations of hoplites with spears rather than javelins dominate from the middle of the seventh century. The Spartan poet Tyrtaeus, writing in the same period describes men as fighting 'side by side, and serried close'.[10] Some posit that the victory by the Argives over the Spartans at Hysiae in 669 was the first victory by the new phalanx over the older style of fighting. This defeat, the argument goes, forced the Spartans to adopt the new formation. As we have no description of the battle this can only be pure speculation. Certainly both the Argives and Spartans were willing to settle one battle by a fight of 300 champions as late as the middle of the sixth century.

Given the fragmentary nature of sources, all that can be said for certain is that hoplite equipment was common by the end of the seventh century and that true 'hoplite warfare' had probably developed by the beginning of the fifth century. These are the troops that would be the backbone of the armies of the Sicilian Greeks in their long struggle against the Carthaginians, and each other. For the purposes of this work it will be accepted that the phalanx was used by the Sicilian Greeks in their great victory over the Carthaginians at Himera in 480.

Although the hoplite phalanx would dominate the battlefields of the Greeks for three centuries, they did raise other types of troops. Both cavalry and missile-armed light infantry were used. In a large-scale battle neither could stand against the closely-packed phalanx. Their role was to serve as scouts, protect the flanks of the phalanx, and, if possible, to harass the flanks and rear of the enemy phalanx. Cavalry were also important after the battle; if one side had a marked superiority they could protect the flight of their own hoplites or ride down the fleeing enemy.

As the Greek states became larger and wealthier, campaigns were not always decided quickly in a single battle. A weaker state might remain behind its walls and refuse to fight. The usual manner of forcing them to come out was for the invading army to ravage their countryside. In order to do this the hoplites would have to disperse across the countryside in small units. Now they could be attacked with some chance of success by both cavalry and light infantry if surprised while out of formation or isolated in small numbers. Xenophon describes how an isolated unit of Spartan hoplites, while on the march, was successfully attacked by a unit of Athenian light infantry, peltasts, armed with javelins and shields.

If they marched along the road they would be shot at by javelins on their unprotected side and mown down; and if they tried to pursue their attackers it would be perfectly easy for peltasts, light and fast on their feet, to keep out of the way of hoplites.[11]

Despite such successes, and the increasing usefulness of such troops, it was still the case that pitched battles were almost always won by the clash of the hoplite phalanxes.

The rise in wealth led not only to a military revolution but also to a political one. If, as the Marxist philosopher Frederick Engels claimed, the state is a body of armed men, the politics of the archaic Greek state were about to undergo a fundamental change. We know from the poet Hesiod that many in archaic Greece resented the arbitrary nature of the power of the nobility. He complains that 'there is a noise when Justice is being dragged in the way where those who devour bribes and give sentence with crooked judgments, take her.' For Hesiod, writing some time at the end of the eighth century, such injustice seems natural given the monopoly on power of the *aristoi*, for 'he is a fool who tries to withstand the stronger, for he does not get the mastery and suffers pain besides his shame.'[12] Hesiod was one of the new rich and his ideal man was one who, like himself, owned his own land, two oxen and slaves, and hired the poor as labour. He was not complaining on behalf of the landless poor, but advocating on behalf of the newly wealthy.

The Greek nobles, like most aristocracies, believed that they ruled by divine right; most even believed that they were descended from gods. Naturally they despised the new rich. For them there were only two groups of people, themselves, the good (*agathoi*), and everybody else, the bad (*kakoi*). This contempt is displayed by the poetry of an exiled aristocrat, Theognis of Megara who sneers that 'money the *daimon* [spirit] gives even to the most utterly *kakos*, Cyrnus, but a portion of *arete* [virtue] attends few men.' He further goes on to whine that after the breaking of the power of the aristocracy 'those who before were *agathoi* now are *kakoi*, while the former *kakoi* now are *agathoi*. Who could endure seeing these things, the *agathoi* without honour or position, while the *kakoi* fall upon both?'[13]

Unlike the farmer of Hesiod's time, the newly emerged hoplite was able to challenge the monopoly held on political power by the nobles. Even if, as Forrest states, 'they did not want a share of political power' and were motivated simply by resentment for something as trivial as having been fined 'a sheep for an offence which had only brought their neighbour a caution', their resentment did lead to rebellion.[14] Over the next century and a half, beginning in Corinth in 657, the non-aristocratic *demoi* were able to break forever the monopoly of power of the nobility in the majority of Greek states. As Andrews puts it, the result of this period 'was to take power from the narrow aristocracies to leave it in the hands of a much wider class.'[15]

The very fragmentary evidence from the period does make it impossible to prove beyond doubt the claim that the newly rich hoplites were the driving force for the changes. The coincidence of their growing numbers and the widespread revolt against the aristocracy does, nonetheless, make it an attractive theory. There are many instances from later dates, however, that demonstrate how experience in war did allow the people to challenge the aristocracy. One from Aristotle describes how the people of Thurii challenged their nobles who:

> Had previously acquired the whole of the land contrary to law; for the government tended to oligarchy, and they were able to encroach . . . But the people, who had been trained by war, soon got the better of the guards kept by the oligarchs, until those who had too much gave up their land.[16]

Initially, the non-nobles appear to have lacked the confidence to carry out the early rebellions themselves. Instead they turned to powerful leaders, invariably disgruntled noblemen, who promised to remedy their grievances. These were the first tyrants. The Greek word *tyrannos* means sole or absolute ruler. The word was originally neutral in meaning, the oldest known use of the word is by the poet Archilochos describing King Gyges of Lydia (680–644). Only later would it come to have the same pejorative meaning that it does in English.

The first known Greek tyrant, Cypselus, seized power in Corinth, the mother city of Syracuse, in 657. The Corinthians had been ruled by the Bacchiads, one of the most exclusive of Greek aristocratic clans, generally not even marrying outside the family. According to Diodorus they were descendents of Hercules:

> two hundred in number when they seized the rule, and they all maintained control over the state as a body; out of their own number they annually chose one man to be chief magistrate, who held the position of the king, this form of government continuing for ninety years until it was destroyed by the tyranny which Cypselus established.[17]

Cypselus was, reputedly, the son of a Bacchiad mother and a non-Bacchiad father, the marriage only being allowed because of his mother being lame. Despite this he managed to obtain a post in the government, that of *polemarch*, usually a military post but often involving some civilian functions. He increased his popularity by being kind to debtors and managed to build a large following. Cypselus seized power by assassinating the ruling chief magistrate. When in power he exiled the Bacchiads and confiscated their property. Cypselus introduced a council and minor magistracies, allowing those citizens who previously had no experience of government to hold offices. He is reputed to have ruled Corinth mildly and to have been so popular that, unlike most tyrants, he had no need of a bodyguard.

His son Periander was a much less popular and more brutal ruler. Following his death, his successor Psammetichos was murdered by the aristocrats, with the help of Spartans, only three years later. Corinth then reverted to rule by a narrow oligarchy, a council of eighty members. This was eventually overthrown by a democratic revolution at the start of the fourth century.

Unfortunately, we have little evidence of the political platforms of the early tyrants of the seventh century. Other than that of Cypselus, the only other hints come from Aristotle who claims that 'Theagenes at Megara slaughtered the cattle of the wealthy, which he found by the river side, where they had put them to graze in land not their own.' Cypselus' rise to power does, nonetheless, appear to be fairly typical of that of the earlier tyrants, Aristotle further goes on to state that:

> Most of the ancient tyrants were originally demagogues . . . moreover, in those days, when cities were not large, the people dwelt in the fields, busy at their work; and their chiefs, if they possessed any military talent, seized the opportunity, and winning the confidence of the masses by professing their hatred of the wealthy, they succeeded in obtaining the tyranny.[18]

Some cities attempted to solve their social problems without resorting to tyrannies, usually by granting one of the aristocracy extraordinary powers to carry out political reform. In Sparta, one of the few cities to still have a king, in this case two of them, these changes are attributed to the person of Lycurgus. Little can be determined for certain about Lycurgus, some historians believing that he was probably a mythical figure. Even the period of his reforms is not certain. Most of the ancient authors dated him to the eighth century, whereas modern opinion varies from the eighth to the seventh. The reign of the king Polydorus, 700–665, is the most likely time as he had a reputation as being a reformer and friend of the people. Sparta does appear to have suffered from the same civil strife as other states, with Plutarch describing how:

> The people grew bold, and succeeding kings were some of them hated for trying to force their way with the multitude, and some were brought low by their desire for favour or through weakness, so that lawlessness and confusion prevailed at Sparta for a long time.[19]

The Spartan kings and aristocracy solved this problem by creating a new constitution that entrenched the rule of the nobility but gave the *demos* an outlet through which they could voice their opinions. Real power was centered in the *gerousia*, a council of twenty-eight aristocrats aged over sixty and elected for life, plus the two kings. They would put proposals to an assembly consisting of the hoplites who had the right to accept or reject them.

The assembly did not, however, have the power to propose their own legis-
lation. Even these minor reforms were too much for some; Polydorus was
assassinated by a disgruntled aristocrat, a certain Polemarchos. This appears
to have been a popular action, at least among a part of the population, as
eight centuries later we are told by Pausanias: 'there also exists at Sparta the
grave and memorial of Polemarchos.'[20]

Athens, in addition to the conflicts common to the other Greek cities, also
had the problem that its citizens resented the threat of being sold into slavery
for the inability to pay their debts. This fear was probably common in most
of the Greek cities, and may have been an unwanted product of the growing
cash economy. Athens was ruled by nine magistrates, the archons, all chosen
from the aristocracy, the *eupatridai* (well born), and a council of ex-archons,
the *aeropagos*. According to Aristotle:

> The many were in slavery to the few, the people rose against the upper
> class. The strife was keen, and for a long time the two parties were
> ranged in hostile camps against one another, till at last, by common
> consent, they appointed Solon to be mediator and Archon, and
> committed the whole constitution to his hands.[21]

Solon's first act was to cancel all debts and to abolish debt slavery. He then
divided the population into four classes, based purely on wealth, not on birth.
The first three consisted of those rich enough to provide their own military
equipment, either as cavalry or hoplites. The fourth class consisted of the
poor, the *thetes*. Solon restricted the magistracies to the first three classes but,
perhaps for the first time, allowed the *thetes* to attend the assembly and to be
a part of the juries for trials. Once he had completed his reforms he went into
voluntary exile for ten years to avoid becoming a tyrant.

Once Solon had departed his reforms started to come apart as:

> The mass of the people had expected him to make a complete re-
> distribution of all property, and the upper class hoped he would restore
> everything to its former position, or, at any rate, make but a small
> change.[22]

The population divided into factions and it often proved impossible to elect
people to the offices, or to remove the incumbents. Civil war again appeared
to be a real possibility. The Athenians were, like many other cities, forced to
look to a tyrant to solve their political problems. In 561 a certain Peisistratus,
a war hero, seized power. He had a reputation as 'being an extreme democrat'. Peisistratus was exiled twice but both times returned to power. He is
reputed to have ruled moderately, 'more like constitutional government than
a tyranny.'[23] Most likely he used his position to enforce Solon's reforms and

to give the people a greater share in the offices of government. In order to achieve this he was forced to exile large numbers of the more recalcitrant nobles. Following his death in 527, his family continued to rule but in 508 they were eventually forced out by an invasion of the exiled aristocrats backed by the Spartans.

The triumphant nobles, led by Isagoras, now attempted to 'drive out the pollution' and re-impose their political domination by setting up a narrow oligarchy of 'three hundred of his partisans as the supreme power' but were defeated when 'the populace flocked together . . . besieged them for two days' and 'thus obtained the command of affairs'.[24]

Over the next half century Athens underwent a thoroughgoing democratic reform. The final, residual powers of the aristocratic *aeropagus* were finally overthrown and all the political and judicial power was held by the assembly of all Athenian citizens, including the *thetes*. Many of the magistracies were allocated by lot, a process that the Greek cities would come to consider integral to the functioning of a democracy. The citizen body included all adult males with Athenian parents – women, slaves and foreigners were excluded.

It does appear that over this period of a century and a half the class struggle, *stasis*, within the Greek cities moved beyond mere resentment into a more developed political program. The driving force behind the rise of the tyrannies also appears to shift from the newly emerged wealthy to the poor. One of the more detailed descriptions we have of a tyrant seizing power and their platform is Dionysius of Halicarnassus' account of the tyranny of Aristodemus, of the Italian-Greek city of Cumae, who took power at the end of the sixth century.[25]

He too was an aristocrat by birth, as the first half of his name shows, but 'was called by the citizens Malacus or 'Effeminate' – a nickname which in time came to be better known than his own name – either because when a boy he was effeminate and allowed himself to be treated as a woman, as some relate, or because he was of a mild nature and slow to anger, as others state.' Later authors have speculated that he was a woman, a homosexual or a hermaphrodite. He rose to fame by fighting heroically in a great victory by the Cumaeans over the Etruscans in 524.

According to Dionysius, 'at this time Cumae was governed by an aristocracy but this was unpopular and a sedition arose because of this strife.' Aristodemus took the side of the *demos* and he 'seduced the mob by his harangues, improved their condition by popular measures, exposed the powerful men who were appropriating the public property, and relieved the poor with his own money. By this means he became both odious and formidable to the leading men of the aristocracy.' The ruling nobility tried to remove Aristodemus by ordering him to command a deliberately under-resourced campaign in 504. 'They enrolled no men of distinction or reputation; but choosing out the poorest and the most unprincipled of the common people from whom they were under continual apprehension of some uprisings.'

Aristodemus 'was not ignorant of the purpose of his enemies' and returned secretly to Cumae. He and his followers took power by storming the council building and killing many of the *aristoi*. He then introduced a number of measures in favour of the poor, including the two policies that were anathema to the wealthy classes of ancient Greece. 'He established two institutions which are the worst of all human institutions and the prologues to every tyranny – a redistribution of the land and an abolition of debts.' Aristodemus then promised that he should be 'appointed general with absolute power till the public tranquility should be secured and they had established a demo-cratic constitution.' He then carried out a brutal purge of the aristocracy.

Despite his promises to the people, he then continued to rule as tyrant, supported by non-Greek mercenaries and a bodyguard of 'the filthiest and the most unprincipled of the citizens'. Fourteen years later he was overthrown by the surviving aristocrats, who had been living in exile in Capua. They murdered Aristodemus, all his family and supporters. The nobles then 'restored the traditional government.'

A brief fragment of Diodorus supports Dionysius' account, claiming that:

> He established his domination by ingratiating himself with the masses and by constantly calumniating the most influential citizens . . . he continually put to the sword the wealthiest citizens, seized their posses-sions and thus maintained mercenaries.[26]

Although it is always dangerous to generalize about the politics of the Greek cities as they were so varied, and exceptions can always be found, it is neces-sary in a discussion of this scope. The newly wealthy citizens clearly wanted to break the political monopoly of the aristocracy. In this they succeeded, and by the beginning of the fifth century the majority of Greek cities were ruled by oligarchies based on wealth rather than birth. Some, such as Corinth and Cumae, were governed by very narrowly based councils. There is insufficient evidence to know the details of the constitutions of most of the Greek cities at this time. It is generally considered, however, that most cities had more broadly based assemblies, often including the entire hoplite class. Depending on one's political views, this is either referred to as a moderate (or hoplite) democracy or an oligarchy. Others allowed all citizens to attend the assembly but limited its influence by assigning many powers to the elected magistrates. A few posts, mainly ceremonial or religious, did remain exclusively in the hands of the surviving aristocrats. This form of government was the one most admired by Greek writers such as Aristotle and Thucydides. The latter claimed that when the Athenian democracy was briefly overthrown and replaced by a hoplite democracy, 'the Athenians appear to have enjoyed the best government that they ever did.'[27]

Athens was the first city to have created a democracy for which there is any detailed and continuous record. There is, however, fragmentary evidence from Polybius, Aristotle and Herodotus that other *poleis* had set up democracies prior to Athens.[28] Polybius claims that the cities of Achaea in the northern Pelopponesus had an unbroken record of democratic government going right back to the seventh century or earlier. This passage is usually rejected, but it is probable that there were democratic regimes in existence prior to that of the Athenians.[29]

The poor living under oligarchic rule appear to have had a different outlook to that of Thucydides. Although there is no direct record of their views, they are perhaps best summed up by the aptly named, but candid, writer known as the 'Old Oligarch'. Although he despises the Athenian democracy he freely admits that:

> I pardon the people themselves for their democracy. One must forgive everyone for looking after his own interests. For the people do not want a good government under which they themselves are slaves; they want to be free and to rule . . . whenever they have undertaken to prefer the upper class, it has not turned out well for them.[30]

The breaking of the political monopoly of the *aristoi* did change the nature of *stasis* in the Greek cities. Society would again be divided into two groups but now they would be the rich, *plousioi*, and the poor, *penetes*. The struggle would now be between the poor, trying to obtain admittance to the assemblies, and the rich trying to keep, or in the case of an existing democracy drive, them out. This form of political struggle became endemic during the Peloponnesian War of the late fifth century, with Thucydides claiming that:

> So bloody was the march of revolution, and the impression which it made was the greater as it was one of the first to occur. Later on, one may say, the whole Hellenic world was convulsed; struggles being made everywhere . . . revolution thus ran its course from city to city.[31]

Tyranny was a form of government that the Greek cities would sometimes turn to in order to solve crises. The early tyrannies were largely the result of political struggle between the different classes. This continual class struggle within the Greek cities would produce many later tyrants. Rather than seizing power in order to break the political power of the aristocracy, however, they would be a product of the struggle between rich and poor. Another type of tyranny would be the imposition of tyrants by outside conquerors, such as the Persians or the Macedonian kings.

The Greeks of Sicily would be, however, confronted by an additional type of crisis. This was the constant threat of invasion by the powerful and despised Carthaginians. The first major invasion in 480 would be defeated by an alliance of tyrants led by Gelon, tyrant of Syracuse. This gave the tyrants of Sicily a reputation as successful generals and saviours. This reputation encouraged the Sicilians to look for a new saviour when faced by a fresh crisis, the Carthaginian invasion of 407.

Chapter 3

The First Sicilian Tyrants

Hippokrates began the ruin of the Khalkidian cities, which was prosecuted more effectively by Gelon and Hieron. On moral grounds he appears to have been a worthy predecessor of Dionysios and Agathokles, a worshipper of power for power's sake.

Dunbabin[1]

The Greek cities of Sicily appear to have followed a similar political path to their parent cities in Greece. Those founded in the eighth century had aristocratic forms of government, although it cannot be established if these were simply transplanted from their founding cities or evolved from the colonists themselves. Given the exclusive nature of aristocracies, the former is most likely. It is known that the leader of the colonists to Syracuse was a member of the Bacchiad clan.

In Sicily, as in the rest of the Greek world, the rise in the numbers of the wealthy soon led to resentment of the political monopoly of the aristocracy. The ruling aristocrats of Syracuse were known as the *gamoroi*, 'land-holders'. Civil strife appears to have already developed by 648, with one group being exiled to Himera. By 485, at the latest, the common people had revolted, exiled the *gamaroi* and established their first democracy. Aristotle claims that 'at Syracuse the democracy aroused contempt before the tyranny of Gelon arose.'[2] It was not, however, in Syracuse that the first Sicilian tyranny arose.

Although there is evidence of earlier tyrants, the first for whom we have any detailed account is Phalaris of Akragas. In 571, only ten years after its foundation, Phalaris seized power in the city. Phalaris was most likely an aristocrat as he is recorded as holding two offices in the city: public debt collector and being in charge of the construction of a temple to Zeus. Unlike Cypselus he did not seize power through the support of the populace but supposedly by arming a gang of slaves and foreigners. Nothing is recorded of his domestic policies, although Aristotle does include him in a selection of anecdotes told about demagogues, inferring that he sided with the people against the aristocracy. Phalaris was remembered for two things. One was his notorious cruelty to his political opponents. He was reputed to have roasted his enemies alive in a bronze bull, designed so that the shrieks of the victims resembled the bellowing of a bull.

Phalaris was also renowned as a successful general and conqueror. He captured a number of Sicanian cities and extended the territory of Akragas to the borders of the city of Himera in the north and to the River Himera in the east, midway between Akragas and Gela. The people of Himera are also supposed to have chosen Phalaris as their *strategos autocrator*, literally 'general with all power', but a position that often involved civilian powers as well. The term was also used as a euphemism for tyrant. After sixteen years of rule, Phalaris was overthrown and was said to have been the last victim of the bronze bull.

Phalaris' campaigns of conquest were not unique but were part of a general movement by the Greeks in the western Mediterranean during the first half of the sixth century. The Massalians were in the process of expanding into Spain. In Africa, the Cyrenian Greeks pressed westward and reputedly defeated the Carthaginians at sea. The Phocaeans had also continued their policy of expansion. This was exacerbated by the conquest of their home city by the Lydians, sometime between 560 and 545, and its final annexation by the Persians in 546. Rather than submit to the Persians, they abandoned their city, many fleeing to their colony of Alalia on Corsica, founded twenty years before. From here they conducted a highly successful campaign of piracy against their neighbours.

The western Phoenicians must have felt themselves under pressure on a broad front. The Phoenician cities of the Levant were, however, not in a position to assist their colonies. They had been conquered by the Persians in 539 and many refugees had fled to the western colonies. Without help from the east, the defence of the western colonies would now fall to the largest of the Phoenician cities of Africa, Carthage. They had already made one unsuccessful attempt to halt the advance of Massalia. Carthage began its campaign by bringing the other Phoenician cities of Africa into an alliance under its leadership, more likely than not, by force.

Sometime during the reign of the Persian king Cyrus (559–529), the Carthaginians sent an army to Sicily for the first time. Its commander, Malchus, campaigned successfully, imposing hegemony over all the Phoenician towns in Sicily and the Elymians. He also appears to have forced Selinus into an alliance with Carthage. It is possible that he may have campaigned against Phalaris, and that it could have been a result of this expedition that the population of Himera invited Phalaris to be their general. Malchus' campaign in Sicily must have been completed sometime before his death around 550.

The Carthaginian's next target was the Phocaean city of Alalia. In an alliance with the Etruscans of Italy, they launched a combined fleet of 120 ships, fifty-oared pentaconters, the standard warship of the time. The

Phocaeans sailed out with sixty such ships and met the enemy off the coast of Sardinia. The Phocaeans won the ensuing battle but at the cost of forty of their own ships. Herodotus describes this as a 'Cadmean sort of victory, with more loss than gain', the ancient version of the modern expression 'Pyrrhic victory'.[3] (The origin of the expression comes from the myth in which the soldiers who sprang from the dragon's teeth sown by the hero Cadmus fought and killed each other until only five survived. The survivors became the legendary founders of Thebes.)

The Greek survivors of the battle collected their families and abandoned Alalia, fleeing to Rhegium. Those captured by the Etruscans were stoned to death as a punishment for their piracy. The victors divided the spoils, with the Etruscans annexing Corsica and the Carthaginians claiming Sardinia.

The Sardinians, however, put up strong resistance and defeated the Punic expedition in a battle, inflicting heavy losses on the invaders. The Carthaginians, who would show a penchant for punishing failed commanders, exiled both Malchus and his army. This force, unlike those the Carthaginians would later use once they had built their empire, appears to have consisted mostly of Carthaginian citizens. Hearing of their exile, they rebelled and sailed back to Carthage, claiming that 'they were not come to overthrow, but to recover their country; and that they would show their countrymen that it was not valour, but fortune, that had failed them in the preceding war.'[4] Malchus succeeded in taking Carthage, supposedly after crucifying his own son for siding with the city against him. He executed ten of his leading opponents but then refused to seize power as a tyrant. As well as being vindictive towards failed commanders, the people of Carthage were also suspicious of ambitious generals. They accused Malchus of plotting a coup and executed him.[5]

Carthage had been a monarchy since its foundation. Following the execution of Malchus, a new dynasty, the Magonids, took power around 550. The first of the new kings was named Mago. He is reputed to have 'been the first, by regulating their military discipline, to lay the foundations of the Punic power, and after establishing the strength of the state'. His sons, Hasdrubal and Hamilcar, would continue his policy. Hasdrubal would be killed in Sardinia, supposedly after he had 'enjoyed four triumphs' awarded for successful campaigns.[6] Hamilcar would go on to complete the conquest of the island.

It was in Spain, however, that the Carthaginians met their greatest success. Beginning with the annexation of the island of Ibiza in about 540, they brought the surviving Phoenician cities of Spain under their control. They then attacked and destroyed the Greek colonies in eastern Spain.

In Africa the Carthaginians faced another new threat when a Spartan prince named Dorieus, who had been passed over for the throne, founded a colony at Cinyps in Libya, in about 515. This foundation was well to the west of any other Greek colonies in Africa and was considered a threat by the

Phoenician city of Lepcis. The Carthaginians, in alliance with the local Libyan tribes, attacked the colony and drove the settlers out. A frontier between the Greeks and Carthaginians was then agreed upon, at the altar of the Philainoi, near modern El Agheila in western Libya.

Dorieus was not yet finished. He then launched an expedition to seize the Elymian town of Eryx in Sicily. The Greeks had long coveted this city and had already created a propaganda campaign to justify any conquest. Eryx was famous for being the site of one of the labours of the mythical hero Hercules. Hercules had, according to legend, killed the king of the Elymians in a wrestling match. He then left the inhabitants to enjoy the city until his descendants should return to claim it. A Spartan prince could claim descent from Hercules and therefore the right to rule Eryx, as could any of the Rhodian aristocrats from Akragas. The Greek belief that the Elymians were descended from the Trojans, and therefore natural enemies, could also be used to justify any attack.

Dorieus' campaign was a disaster. An alliance of the Carthaginians and Elymians easily defeated the Greeks and killed Dorieus. The survivors fled to Heraclea Minoa and seized the city. They then helped the people of Selinus to overthrow their tyrant, Peithagoras. Euryleon, the new leader of the Spartans, next tried to make himself tyrant of Selinus. The people of the city, not wishing to replace one tyrant with another, revolted and killed him, despite the fact that he had sought refuge in the temple of Zeus. From this point on Selinus tended to follow a policy of seeking accommodation with the Carthaginians rather than confrontation.

By the close of the sixth century the Carthaginians had come to dominate the western Mediterranean. So much so that the Romans referred to it as *mare clausum,* closed waters. Only the Massalians, due to their naval strength, managed to hold out by winning two naval victories over the Carthaginians. In about 490 a treaty was signed between Carthage and Massalia, fixing the boundary between the two in Spain at Artemision (Denia). The agreed frontiers in Spain and Africa would remain fixed for the next two centuries. Only in Sicily would the two peoples continue to wage war on one another.

A new wave of Greek expansionism began in Sicily in the early fifth century. In 505 Cleander had seized power in the city of Gela. In common with most other earlier tyrants he probably took measures to curb or break the power of the aristocracy, but this can only be supposition. Aristotle claims that he overthrew an oligarchy, but this may mean the aristocracy as Aristotle sometimes uses the terms interchangeably. He was murdered in 498 and succeeded by his brother Hippocrates. There is nothing recorded of Hippocrates' political program. His seven-year rule was one of continual military campaigning and he appears to have been one of the first of the tyrants to rise to power mostly on a program of military aggression and conquest. At first there was strong opposition to Hippocrates, including the assassination of his brother. This may have been a popular revolt against his rule, of which the assassination of his brother was the beginning, but it is impossible to tell for certain. Hippocrates secured his rule through the support of a popular noble named Gelon, who he made commander of his cavalry.

At this time Gela's *chora* was extremely limited, hemmed in to the north by the mountains and by the fortified settlements of the Sicels. It is not certain how the Sicels fought, but what evidence there is suggests they were lightly armoured and probably fought as skirmishers. This would give them the tactical advantage in the mountains over the more heavily armed Greeks. Like many an imperialist, Hippocrates solved this problem by hiring rival tribes as mercenaries. To ensure their loyalty he 'always gave them the largest portion in the distribution of booty; he gave them increased pay; he complimented them on being the best troops in his army; and he tried by every means to entice as many of them as possible into his service.'[7]

Hippocrates successfully seized and destroyed a number of the Sicel settlements, establishing his own forts and opening the passes to the north and west. He now embarked on a series of campaigns aimed at subjugating his fellow Greeks. First he seized the otherwise unknown city of Callipolis and then Naxos. He then advanced further north, capturing the city of Zancle, and setting up as a puppet tyrant in that city one of his officers named Scythes. While campaigning along the coast Hippocrates had bypassed the important city of Leontini, for reasons that it is now impossible to determine. This would have left his lines of communication back to Gela exposed, so it is likely that he had either come to an agreement with, or had frightened the Leontinians into neutrality, on his way past. The exact dates of these campaigns are unknown but they had certainly been completed by the end of 492.

Scythes, or more likely Hippocrates, then planned to create a new colony on the north coast of Sicily between Zancle and Himera. As luck would have it, the aristocracy of the island of Samos had already determined to flee their home and to found a new colony rather than submit to the Persians. Their determination was the result of the defeat of the Ionian Greeks by the Persians at the Battle of Lade in 494. Scythes was a native of the Ionian island of Cos and had apparently been keeping contact with his home region. He therefore invited the Samians to come to Sicily and be a part of this new foundation.

Zancle had always been on close terms with Rhegium, located on the Italian side of the Straits of Messina. The new tyrant of Rhegium, a Dorian Greek aristocrat by the name of Anaxilas was, probably wisely, alarmed by Hippocrates' ambitions, and feared that the capture of Zancle would be followed by an attack on Rhegium. For the next two centuries, successful Sicilian tyrants would display an inclination to expand their ambitions into southern Italy. What followed was a tale of deception and depopulation that would become all too common.

The Samian refugees called in at Rhegium on their way to Sicily. Anaxilas presented them with a bold plan, that rather than become colonists they should instead seize Zancle. This was possible as Scythes and the troops of Zancle were away in the west fighting the Sicels in preparation for the foundation of the new city. The Samians seized Zancle as planned. Scythes hurried back to his city and Hippocrates also brought up his army in support. Enraged at the incompetence of his subordinate, Hippocrates arrested Scythes and sent him away in chains. He then did a deal with the Samians. According to Herodotus, he:

> After an exchange of guarantees, completed the betrayal of the whole population of Zancle. The reward of his treachery was to be half of all the moveable property and slaves the town contained, and anything he could find in the open country. The greater number of the townspeople he seized and kept as slaves for himself; the three hundred leading citizens he handed over to the Samians, to have their throats cut. This, however, the Samians refrained from doing.[8]

The Samians did not long enjoy the fruits of their treachery, as they were 'driven out in their turn not long afterwards by Anaxilas, the tyrant of Rhegium and the city was by him colonized with a mixed population and its name changed to Messene after his old country.'[9] Scythes managed to escape from his imprisonment and his son would later become tyrant of Cos.

Once he had settled affairs at Zancle, Hippocrates then moved against and captured Leontini. He again imposed one of his officers as tyrant over the city. Hippocrates then attacked Syracuse, already the wealthiest and largest of the Greek cities of Sicily. Hippocrates first marched on the Syracusan fortress town of Helorus. Along the river of the same name he met and defeated the Syracusan army in battle. The courage of one of the Gelan cavalry was celebrated by the poet Pindar:

> Who armed his warrior-spirit to repel the destruction of the war-god. But few are able to conspire with hand and heart to turn back against the ranks of the enemy the cloud of slaughter that presses close upon them. Indeed men say that glory blossomed for Hector beside the flowing Scamander; and around the steep cliffs of the Helorus' banks at the place which men call 'the passage of Rhea,' this light has shone on the son of Hagesidamus, in his earliest manhood.[10]

Hippocrates then advanced on Syracuse and captured the Temple of Zeus which lay on high ground about five kilometres to the south of the city. Little remains on the site except the ruins of two columns. The hill dominates the coastal plain, with a clear view to the city. It would become a common point for invading armies to base themselves while besieging Syracuse. Here

Hippocrates captured some of the leading citizens of Syracuse. According to Diodorus, Hippocrates hoped 'that he would set the commons at variance with the administrators of the affairs of Syracuse, because men would think the latter were ruling the state to their own advantage and not that of all the people nor on the principle of equality.'[11] Hippocrates was again taking advantage of the *stasis* within a Greek city to try and conquer it from within. In this he appears to be completely driven by expediency rather than dogma. At Zancle he had done a deal with the nobles and enslaved the people; at Syracuse he attempted the reverse.

His attempt failed, however, and without a powerful fleet he was unable to capture the already strongly fortified city. He accepted the mediation of Corinth, and another of its colonies, Corcyra, and made peace with the Syracusans. Hippocrates did win one concession. He was able to trade his prisoners for the site of the abandoned city of Camarina. Hippocrates rebuilt the city and populated it with a group of his mercenaries. Camarina had previously rebelled against its founders, the Syracusans, in 552, and been destroyed in retribution.

Hippocrates then returned to the north and spent the last year of his life, 491, campaigning against the Sicels. He had already encouraged a large number of Sicels from the town of Ergetion to join his army as mercenaries. According to Polyaenus he took the town by another act of brutal treachery:

> He placed the Ergetini on the shore, and the rest of the army was encamped higher up in the country. While the Ergetini were stranded in this way by the edge of the sea, Hippocrates dispatched a body of cavalry to their abandoned city, and sent a herald to take possession of it in his name. Then he ordered the men of Gela and Camarina to fall upon the Ergetini, and cut them to pieces.[12]

Next he captured a number of other Sicel towns. Although the campaign cannot be placed exactly, it was probably carried out against the surviving Sicel settlements to the north of Leontini, which lie on the southern slopes of Mount Aetna. During this campaign Hippocrates died in battle while fighting the Sicels.

Hippocrates' rule would become a template for many of the Sicilian tyrants that followed. He died with his ambition to create a unified Greek empire in Sicily only partly achieved. His aggression had also destroyed the peaceful relations that appear to have existed with the Sicels throughout the sixth century, and laid the grounds for a later war. Hippocrates' career is perhaps best summed up by Dunbabin, who states that 'like many Sicilian tyrants after him, he seems to have had a complete lack of morality and practiced a policy of bare force.'[13]

Chapter 4

Gelon and the Battle of Himera

The monument was destroyed by the Carthaginians in the course of a campaign against Syracuse, while the towers were thrown down by Agathocles out of envy. Nevertheless, neither the Carthaginians out of enmity, nor Agathocles out of his native baseness, nor any other man has ever been able to deprive Gelon of his glory; for the just witness of history has guarded his fair fame, heralding it abroad with piercing voice for evermore.

Diodorus 11.38

After Hippocrates' death, the people of Gela rose up against his sons but were defeated by his commander of cavalry, Gelon. He then deposed the two children and seized the tyranny for himself. The usurping of power by regents would be a common practice throughout ancient Greek history. Philip II, the father of Alexander the Great, being the most famous example.

Gelon was from one of the founding aristocratic families of Gela. During the wars of Hippocrates, he was supposed to have distinguished himself above all others for his bravery. He appears to have had ambitions even greater than those of his predecessor. Although it cannot be certain, there is strong evidence in both Herodotus and Justin that he renewed Dorieus' campaign to conquer the west of the island. His aspirations appear to have stretched as a far as proposing an invasion of Carthaginian Africa by an alliance of all the Greeks. In a later speech to a group of Greek ambassadors, he asked them:

Have you the face to come here and urge me with your selfish arguments to help you resist a foreign invader? Have you forgotten that I was at war with a foreign power – the Carthaginians – and that I applied to you for help? Yes and I begged you to avenge upon the men of Segesta their murder of Dorieus, the son of Anaxandrides, and offered to free the ports which have been the source of great profits and advantage to you. But what was your answer? You refused to come either to help me or to avenge Dorieus death – for all you cared, this whole country might now be subject to foreign rule.[1]

These campaigns are unrecorded and appear to have had no lasting result. Gelon now cast his covetous eyes upon the rich prize of Syracuse. In 485, he was able to take advantage of the internal political struggles within the city. Since Hippocrates' failed attempt to take the city, the people of Syracuse had allied with the *kyllyroi*, driven the nobles from the city and set up a democracy. The exiled *gamaroi* had established themselves within the fortress town of Casmenae, to the west of the city. Gelon allied himself with the exiled aristocrats and marched on Syracuse. The new regime collapsed into anarchy and surrendered control of the city to Gelon.

With the richest city in Sicily in his possession, Gelon based himself there and made his brother Hieron governor of Gela. Apart from its wealth, Syracuse had one other great advantage: its two harbours. Although Greek ships could land by simply being dragged up upon a beach, a new style of warship had made control of a genuine port necessary for the possession of any sizeable fleet. The penteconters that had fought the Battle of Alalia had been replaced by a much larger warship, the trireme. This had three banks of oars on each side and a crew of over two hundred men. Although it could be beached, it needed to be serviced regularly on specialized slipways. The vessel had first been developed by the Phoenicians at the end of the eighth century but did not become the dominant warship of the Mediterranean fleets until the sixth century. If Gelon was serious in his ambitions to challenge the Carthaginians he would need a fleet of triremes and therefore a suitable harbour. The only two Greek cities of Sicily which possessed such ports were Messene and Syracuse.

Gelon's next ambition was to strengthen Syracuse, both by strengthening its defences and by increasing its population. To achieve the latter he embarked on a brutal series of pogroms directed against the surrounding Greek cities. He relocated half the population of Gela and the entire population of Camarina to Syracuse and granted them citizenship. Camarina was again razed to the ground. He took Megara Hyblaea by storm. Here he removed the wealthy citizens, who had opposed him, to Syracuse and made them citizens, but sold the common citizens, who had stood aloof during the siege, into slavery.

Megara Hyblaea was destroyed and never repopulated. A few survivors managed to flee to their colony of Selinus. Gelon repeated the process on another city, Sicilian Euboea. This policy appears to have been based completely on class hatred, as according to Herodotus 'in both cases Gelon's motive was his belief that the masses are very disagreeable to live with.'[2] Gelon appears to have been ensuring political stability in Syracuse by increasing the number of the rich and reducing the proportion of the poor.

This policy of mass displacements under Gelon and his successors was part of their aggressive expansionism. The selective expulsion, or selling into slavery, of all, or part, of the population of other cities allowed them to be secured by mercenaries loyal to the tyrant. Even larger mass displacements would occur under the later tyrant Dionysius the Elder. The Syracusan tyrants would become notorious for such enforced demographic movements. Generally, any transfer of populations between cities was seen by the Greeks as a bad thing, whether forced or voluntary. It was seen as undermining the unity of the state and causing instability. It was, correctly, seen as the work of tyrants attempting to strengthen their own positions regardless of the negative effects it might have on the city as a whole. Conversely the re-founding of destroyed cities was seen as a move away from tyranny.[3]

With Syracuse now firmly in his grasp, Gelon appears to have spent the following years building up his forces, particularly his fleet, in preparation for a war of conquest against the Carthaginians. At about the same time that Gelon was taking power in Gela, another local aristocrat, named Theron, seized power in Akragas, probably in 489. The two tyrants appear to have had a friendly relationship. This was strengthened by Gelon marrying Theron's daughter and Theron wedding Gelon's niece. Theron probably joined in Gelon's war against the Carthaginians, although this is not certain.

Gelon and Theron had created a strong alliance that included most, but not all, of the Greek cities in Sicily. Standing outside the alliance were Selinus, Messene and Himera. To these people any claims of Gelon to be leading some sort of Greek crusade against the barbarians – anybody who did not speak Greek but spoke *bah bah* like a sheep and was therefore uncivilized – must have appeared to be the height of hypocrisy given his treatment of his fellow Greeks. All three cities now sought to protect their independence by forming an alliance with the Carthaginians. Selinus may have already been an ally of the Carthaginians since Dorieus' defeat. The arrival of the Megarian refugees would certainly have hardened their resolve against Gelon. In Himera a *proxenos* (an individual who acted as a type of honorary ambassador for a foreign state) of the Carthaginians, named Terillos, seized power as tyrant. Anaxilas, the ruler of Rhegium and Messene, made an alliance with both Himera and the Carthaginians, and married the daughter of Terillos.

Despite these cities siding with the Carthaginians, Gelon and Theron were able to present their coming campaign as a holy war. The coming struggles between the Greeks and Carthaginians would be marred by both religious and ethnic hatred. Both sides would carry out the wholesale destruction of cities, massacres of entire populations and destruction of each other's temples. This latter act was normally considered to be a sacrilege. To carry it out was a deliberate sign that the invading army intended to destroy utterly their enemy's culture, an early form of ethnic cleansing.

The Greeks, as well as the Persians, regarded the Carthaginian rite of sacrificing children as obscene. This archaic practice had long been abandoned by most Phoenicians but for some unknown reason the Carthaginians had continued it. They also appear to have introduced it into at least some of their subject cities, as the remains of a place of sacrifice, a *topeth*, have been located in the ruins of Motya. These ruins are still visible on the western side of the island.

As can be seen by the acts of Hippocrates, Gelon and many later examples, the Greeks in their own internal wars did destroy entire cities, both for political reasons and the enormous amounts of booty that could be seized. Such acts were, however, usually viewed with distaste and considered to be barbaric by the Greeks. During the Peloponnesian War the Plataeans, having surrendered to the Spartans, argued that to destroy their city and massacre its male population would be seen as 'shocking indeed . . . to be by you blotted out from the map of Hellas' and that it would be 'a heavy task to wipe away the infamy of the deed.' They further claimed that they were 'prisoners who surrendered of their own accord, stretching out our hands for quarter, whose slaughter Hellenic law forbids'.[4] Despite the Plataeans' pleas, the Spartans destroyed the city and executed their prisoners in order to appease their Theban allies. A decade later the Athenians would similarly massacre the population of the city of Melos. Public revulsion at such an act can, nonetheless, be seen in the awarding of the first prize, by popular vote, in an Athenian festival a year later to Euripides' tragedy 'The Trojan Women'. In the introduction to the play, the god Poseidon condemns such actions:

> When the evil of desolation overtakes a city, a blight falls on the cult of the gods; they delight no more in their worship . . . The mortal is mad who sacks cities and desolates temples and tombs, the holy places of the dead; his own doom is only delayed.[5]

Despite this popular sentiment, the political leaders of the ancient Greeks, as is the case with their modern counterparts, do not appear to have had many qualms in allowing political, or military, expediency to overrule any professed moral or religious scruples. The Carthaginians must have been aware of Gelon's preparations, but this appears to have been finally brought home to them when Theron drove their ally Terillos out of Himera, probably in 483. They too now began preparations for war.

In the east the Persians had now completed their own preparations for an attack on Greece with an enormous force. The Greeks sent envoys to Gelon to request assistance against the Persians. According to Herodotus Gelon offered to provide a force of 200 triremes, 20,000 hoplites, 2,000 cavalry, 2,000 light infantry trained to support the cavalry, 2,000 slingers and 2,000 archers. He also promised to supply the entire Greek army with grain. All this was promised on the proviso that he be made commander of the Greek forces.

The Spartans refused outright to serve under Gelon. He then modified his terms allowing them to command the army while he commanded the fleet. Now it was the Athenians' turn to reject his offer. Both looked down their noses at him as being a mere provincial while they claimed they came from cities with long and illustrious histories going back to the Trojan War. Gelon then refused to send any assistance, retorting that 'it looks as if you have the commanders – but will not have any men for them to command.' Gelon, fearing that the Persians might in fact conquer Greece, decided to hedge his bets. He sent an envoy to Delphi with a large amount of money and orders to:

> Wait and see how the war would go; then, if the Persians won, he was to give the money to Xerxes together with the usual tokens of submission in the name of Gelon's dominions. If the Greeks won, he was to bring the money back again.[6]

In the end Gelon's envoy brought the treasure back to Sicily after the Greeks had won the naval battle at Salamis. The passage does show how successful Gelon had been in building his armed forces, particularly his navy. It was now the biggest of all the Greek states, east or west. The offer to supply grain also shows the wealth of Gelon, which is confirmed by the evidence of his large-scale minting of coins at this time. The minting of coins to pay both soldiers and sailors was a normal preparation of ancient states when they were planning a major war. The large numbers of cavalry and supporting missile troops also show how much more tactically advanced the Sicilians were than their kinsmen in Greece. The latter would suffer badly from their lack of such troops in their war against the Persian invasion. Diodorus records a tradition that the Persians:

> Sent an embassy to the Carthaginians to urge them to join him in an undertaking and close an agreement with them, to the effect he wage war upon the Greeks who lived in Greece, while the Carthaginians should at the same time gather great armaments and subdue those Greeks who lived in Italy and Sicily.[7]

Although this passage is sometimes dismissed as being fanciful, there appears to be no good reason to do so. As Burn points out in his defence of Diodorus' assertion, 'it would be scarcely conceivable even with no evidence whatever, that Persia and Carthage were *not* in communication.'[8] Such an arrangement would be to the benefit of both, as it would prevent the Greeks from reinforcing each other. No great planning would be involved, only a simple agreement that they both attack the Greeks in the summer of 480.

The Carthaginians made massive preparations for the war. According to Diodorus they raised an army of 300,000 men and a fleet of 200 warships and 3,000 transports.[9] The army consisted of a mixture of troops that the Carthaginians recruited from around the western Mediterranean: Campanians, Spaniards, Ligurians, Gauls, Corsicans, Sardinians and Phoenicians from the whole of Africa, including some from Carthage itself. As their empire grew, unlike the earlier expedition to Sardinia, the Carthaginians would increasingly supplement their citizen forces with mercenaries to provide the troops for their foreign expeditions. Eventually this trend would result in armies outside of Africa containing only small numbers of Carthaginian citizens, mostly serving as officers and cavalry.

Much later Polybius would criticize the Carthaginians for this practice, claiming that they 'wholly neglect their infantry, though they do take some slight interest in their cavalry. The reason is that they employ foreign mercenaries . . . rather than citizen levies whereas the Carthaginians entirely neglect their infantry, though they do pay some slight attention to their cavalry.' He does allow though that 'the Carthaginians naturally are superior at sea both in efficiency and equipment, because seamanship has long been their national craft, and they busy themselves with the sea more than any other people.'[10] Although this criticism might apply to the later wars against the Romans, it was not the case in 480 and the Carthaginians would continue to use citizen troops in Sicily at least until the end of the fourth century.

The expedition was commanded by another Hamilcar, the son of the ruling king in Carthage. The figures given for the army are impossibly high. Peter Green in his commentary on Diodorus repeats the argument that the Greeks, at least in this early period, misunderstood foreign methods of accounting, confusing the terms for 1,000 and 10,000. Therefore all estimates of barbarian numbers over 10,000 should be divided by ten, giving a more believable figure of 30,000.[11] It is also possible that the Sicilian Greek historians possibly made up this impressive sounding figure for propaganda purposes as it matches that given by Herodotus for the Persian army at Plataea. The exact size of the Carthaginian army is impossible to know but 50–80,000 is a common figure for later expeditions to Sicily, so an estimate of 30–80,000 is credible. Ancient armies usually took large numbers of servants along with them to do the work around the camp and take care of the soldiers needs. These sometimes equalled the number of the soldiers. The total number of the expedition may have been well in excess of 100,000 men, if it included the sailors of the fleet and all the non-combatants.

Despite their careful preparations the Carthaginians could not control the weather. Violent and unpredictable storms often strike the sea to the south of Sicily. One of these tempests struck a part of the Carthaginian fleet, sinking many ships. As bad luck would have it, these were the transports carrying the Carthaginian chariots and horses. A lack of mounted troops would prove to be a terrible handicap to the Carthaginians in the coming campaign.

Dunbabin argues that the story of the loss of the horse transports was a later invention. He claims that the Carthaginians always planned to recruit cavalry from their Greek and native allies in Sicily. Rather than a disaster he states that the storm was in fact beneficial to the invaders as it prevented Gelon's fleet from intercepting the invasion force.[12] On this occasion there does, however, appear to be no good reason to reject Diodorus' evidence that was certainly based on the evidence of earlier, but now lost, Sicilian Greek historians. The Greek failure to intercept the Carthaginian fleet was more likely a result of the Greeks not knowing where the Carthaginians were headed, and the difficulty that ancient fleets had in maintaining any sort of blockade.

There were a number of places in Sicily where the Carthaginians could have landed. The most obvious was Motya, followed by a direct advance along the southern coast towards Akragas. Another possible landing site was Messene, held by their ally Anaxilas of Rhegium. This was not a very promising site as Messene is surrounded by difficult hilly terrain, which funnels any advance to the south through a narrow pass. Instead, Hamilcar decided to land at Panormus, with its safe harbour. From there he could advance on Himera, where he might be greeted by any surviving supporters of Terillos and then be able to make contact with his allies in Messene.

After the storm, the surviving Carthaginian fleet made it safely into port at Panormus. With the sea crossing now safely behind him he is supposed to have encouraged his troops by boasting that the war was now as good as over. Hamilcar kept his army about the city for three days, allowing them to recover from the voyage and to repair the ships. He then marched the army along the coast towards Himera guided by the former tyrant Terillos. The fleet sailed alongside them, close to the shore. As soon as the force arrived at Himera, Hamilcar ordered two camps to be built. One was built on the shoreline for the navy. The ships were protected with deep trenches and barricades of timber. The army was encamped on hills that overlooked the city from the west. The two camps were then joined by a palisade. Only once his fortifications were complete did Hamilcar unload the provisions from the ships. He then sent some of his ships away to gather more provisions from Africa and Sardinia.

The valley between Himera and the Carthaginian camps is quite narrow at its northern point, only a few hundred metres wide. It gradually opens to about 2km wide as it stretches roughly 5km to the south. Mount Calogero, immediately to the west of Himera, has a narrow ridge of foothills on its eastern side but soon climbs steeply to become much more difficult terrain. Along the base of the mountain runs a small river, but this was, most likely, dry at the end of summer when the battle was fought. It is along these foothills that the Carthaginian army's camp and palisade must have been constructed.

The naval camp was probably located on the narrow coastal plain to the north of these hills.

Theron led the Himerians out of the city in an attempt to drive off the besiegers but was routed by Hamilcar who counter attacked with the best troops of his army. This defeat is supposed to have 'struck a great terror into the besieged.' Theron, although he had forces 'sufficient with him for the defence of Himera', panicked and fled to Syracuse to beg the support of Gelon. Fortunately for the Himerians, Gelon had already made preparations for the Carthaginian invasion. With a minimum of delay he marched out of Syracuse with a force of 50,000 infantry and 5,000 cavalry.[13] This is far more troops than Syracuse alone could have provided, so it clear that Gelon had already called up the troops of his allied cities. It is sometimes claimed that the figures for the Greek army are unreliable and exaggerated. Two centuries later, Pyrrhus of Epirus raised about 25,000 infantry troops from roughly the same cities, but this was after both Gela and Akragas had been devastated by the Carthaginians. As well as the levies from the cities, Gelon also had 10,000 mercenaries in his employment.[14] Although it is possible that proud Sicilian Diodorus has exaggerated the size of the Greek army to make it larger and more impressive than that raised by the Greeks for Plataea, an army containing in excess of 40,000 hoplites is credible.

Gelon forced-marched his army across the island to Himera. His rapid arrival revived the morale of the Himerians. He built his camp close to the city and fortified it with a wall and deep trench. Not expecting the rapid arrival of the Syracusans, the Carthaginians had sent out much of their army to forage all around the countryside. Gelon ordered his cavalry to attack the dispersed Carthaginians. The loss of the Carthaginian horses now proved decisive, for without the protection of their own cavalry the Carthaginian foragers were almost defenceless against the rampaging Greek cavalry. The Greek horsemen easily overcame the foragers, capturing 10,000 prisoners. After taking the Carthaginians captive, Gelon undertook a stratagem that was common in the ancient world when troops faced a strange enemy for the first time. He 'stripped all the feeblest, especially from among the auxiliaries, who were very swarthy, and exhibited them nude before the eyes of his troops, in order to convince his men that their foes were contemptible.'[15] This, along with the success of the cavalry enhanced the authority of Gelon and, supposedly, caused the Greeks to no longer fear the Carthaginians but instead to treat them with disdain.

Gelon now set his mind to finding a plan by which he could destroy the Carthaginian force. His first thought was to attack the enemy's naval camp and burn their fleet. With the total domination of the countryside by the Greek cavalry the Carthaginians were now totally reliant on their fleet for supplies. If the Greeks could destroy the Carthaginian fleet then the invading force could be starved into submission without the need for a battle. As Gelon was making his plans, however, fortune delivered into his hands an even greater opportunity. After losing his own mounted troops, Hamilcar had sent to his Greek ally Selinus and requested that a force of cavalry to be sent to him. Gelon's cavalry had captured the returning courier with a message that told of the date that the Selinuntians would send their horsemen to him.

Gelon, previously an experienced and daring cavalry commander, made his plans. On the appointed day he would send his own cavalry, at dawn, into the Carthaginian naval camp, pretending to be the reinforcements. At this time one Greek cavalryman would have looked much the same as another, as none carried shields or any other identifying insignia. The cavalry were given orders to seek out and kill Hamilcar once they had entered the camp, and to set fire to the Carthaginian ships. He also placed scouts upon the neighbouring hills with orders to signal the successful entry of the Greek cavalry into the camp. Gelon would draw up the main part of the army at daybreak and attack as soon as he received the signal.

Everything went as planned. At sunrise the Carthaginian guards allowed the Greek cavalry into the camp. Another stroke of luck then befell the Greeks as that day was a Punic festival and they found Hamilcar preparing to sacrifice to the god of the sea. Finding him unprepared for battle, the horsemen immediately charged the Carthaginian commander and killed him. They then set about firing the ships as ordered. Herodotus records a more dramatic version of Hamilcar's death, claiming that when:

> His army was routed, he leapt into the flames, and was burnt to nothing. But whatever explanation we adopt of his disappearance, the fact remains that he is treated with divine honours and monuments were erected to him in all the Carthaginian colonies in addition to the one – the most splendid of all – in Carthage itself.[16]

Meanwhile, the scouts had given their signal and Gelon led the already formed-up Greek army in an assault against the camp of the Carthaginian army. The Carthaginian commanders did not, however, panic but:

> Led out their troops to meet the Sicilians, and as the lines closed they put up a vigorous fight; at the same time in both camps they sounded with the trumpets the signal for battle and a shout arose from the two armies, each eagerly striving to outdo their adversaries in the volume of their cheering.[17]

Both sides were, in the manner of most ancient armies, yelling their battle cries and clashing their weapons against their shields. Later Carthaginian infantry mostly fought in phalanxes in a manner similar to the Greeks. It is unlikely, however, that they had adopted this formation by the time of

Himera. Most of their troops probably still fought in their native style, in looser formations and more lightly armoured than the Greeks. They would have thrown javelins from afar and retreated before the advancing Greek line. Unfortunately for them, the great size of the Greek army would not have allowed them to isolate any small groups of Greeks or get around their flanks. Instead, they would have been confronted by an unbroken line of shields and armour. Some of the more fierce tribesmen, such as the Spanish, may have closed and engaged the Greeks with their swords. They would, however, have been at a disadvantage, outreached by the Greek spears and out-numbered by the more closely ordered Greeks.

Despite this, the two battlelines clashed and both sides 'fought with great obstinacy' and 'great slaughter on both sides, with little or no advantage to either.' While the fighting was continuing the flames from the Carthaginian ships began to be seen over the battlefield and the Greeks received news of the death of Hamilcar. The Greeks were elated; they again gave voice to their battle cry and attacked the Carthaginians with renewed vigour. The Carthaginians, by contrast, were dismayed by the sight of their burning camp. The valley of the battle was relatively narrow at the northern end and even-tually the Carthaginian infantry was forced to make a stand or flee and abandon its camp.

Finally in close combat, the more closely ordered and better armoured Greeks held the advantage. In desperation some of the Carthaginian infantry probably emulated the Persians when faced with the same dilemma:

> At last they came to jostling; for the barbarians would take hold of the spears and break them off. Now in courage and in strength the Persians were not inferior to the others, but they were without defensive armour, and moreover they were unversed in war and unequal to their oppo-nents in skill; and they would dart out one at a time or in groups of about ten together, some more and some less, and fall upon the Spartans and perish . . . since in truth they were contending light-armed against hoplites.[18]

The Greeks hoplites were able to force a breakthrough. The demoralized Carthaginian infantry gave way and were routed. Gelon had given orders that no prisoners were to be taken and this, along with ethnic hatred, assured that the pursuit was hard pressed and the slaughter ferocious. Diodorus claims that 150,000 were slain in the pursuit alone.[19] This figure is, most likely, another exaggeration passed down by the earlier, patriotic Sicilian historians. Pausanias, the Spartan commander in the victory over the Persians at Plataea in 479, gave the same order as he feared to leave alive large numbers of armed and desperate barbarians. The same anxiety may well have influenced Gelon's order.

Many of the surviving Carthaginian troops managed to escape through the southern opening of the valley. Others took shelter in broken terrain, probably higher up Mount Calogero, whose steep slopes finally brought about a halt to the Greek pursuit. These latter refugees, however, lacked water and soon they were forced to surrender themselves to the Greeks' mercy. With their fleet also destroyed, the Carthaginians had no escape and eventually the entire force was either killed or captured. Reputedly not one member of the army escaped to take the news of the disaster to Carthage. The only survivors of the entire force were twenty ships that were at sea on various duties. These were overloaded with fugitives from the naval camp and when they encountered another storm all were lost except one small boat. This pitiful remainder was all that was left of the enormous armada that had set off from Carthage only a few weeks previously.

The battle is variously recorded as occurring on the same day as either the Battle of Thermopylae or that of Salamis. Regardless of the date, news of the victory was supposed to have greatly boosted the morale of the Greeks fighting the Persians. For before the victory at Himera the Greeks of both Sicily and Greece 'were struck with dismay before the conflict at the multitude of the barbarian armies, it was the prior victory of the Sicilian Greeks which gave courage to the people of Greece.'[20]

Nothing is recorded for certain of any part played by the Greek fleet during the campaign. Dunbabin tentatively suggests that it may have been neutralized by Anaxilas' fleet, holding the Straits of Messina.[21]

Gelon's overwhelming victory brought him great renown but also great wealth, as he was able to take the pick of the spoils for himself. The booty from such an overwhelming victory was truly enormous and there was plenty to go around. The remainder of the spoils, and all the captives, he distributed among the rest of the Greeks. Gelon used part of his spoils to construct a temple of Athena on the acropolis of Syracuse. Sixteen centuries later the Normans would build a cathedral on the same site. Many of the original columns of the temple were used in the construction of the church and are still visible both inside and outside the building.

All the Greek cities appear to have used their newly won wealth in the construction of temples and public works. The city of Akragas benefited in that many of the fugitives from the battle fled south and were captured in their territory. There was supposedly so many that some private citizens captured 500 each. The Akragantians also set them to work, building 'not only the largest temples to the gods . . . but also the underground conduits were built to lead off the waters from the city; these are so large that their construction is well worth seeing.'[22] The ruins of these temples are still able to be visited today, and, as apparently was also the case in Diodorus' time, are one of Sicily's major tourist attractions.

The terrible news they brought reputedly so terrified the Carthaginians that they fully expected Gelon to invade Africa and stood watch night and day in preparation. The enormous number of dead also had a devastating effect on the morale of the Carthaginians. As Diodorus describes:

> And because of the multitude of the lost the city went into public mourning, while privately the homes of citizens were filled with wailing and lamentation. For some kept inquiring after sons, others after brothers, while a very large number of children had lost their fathers, alone now in the world, grieved at the death of those who had begotten them and at their own desolation.[23]

Although many of the army were mercenaries, some of the soldiers, and all of the officers, cavalry and the fleet would have come from the citizens of Carthage and its subject Phoenician cities. The officers and cavalry would have come from the nobility and the sailors from the poorer citizens. The loss of the fleet alone may have accounted for around 40,000 deaths. It is little wonder that there was great mourning and fear within Carthage.

The Carthaginians sent an embassy to Gelon. In his presence they adopted the position of supplicants, crying and begging for his favour. In victory Gelon's terms were surprisingly mild, demanding only an indemnity of 2,000 talents from Carthage, enough to pay the cost of the war. The Phoenician settlements were allowed to remain. In later campaigns the Greeks would be far less sympathetic. Instead, they would be determined to drive the Carthaginians totally from Sicily. Gelon, a master of the Machiavellian world of Greek politics, possibly saw them as a useful threat to his rival tyrant, and erstwhile ally, Theron. This strategy may have succeeded as Akragas appears to have campaigned against Motya and Eryx in the years immediately following the battle. Despite this, Gelon's victory would remove any serious Carthaginian threat to the Greeks of Sicily for over seventy years.

Gelon died two years after Himera and his reign was remembered as a golden age by the Syracusans. After his victory he entered the assembly of the Syracusans and was proclaimed *basileus* (king). This probably had no real constitutional meaning but was a common appellation of honour given to winners of great victories. The years following the battle were those of peace and great plenty. Despite laws forbidding extravagant funerals the Syracusans built him a lavish tomb. This would later be destroyed by the Carthaginians in an act of vengeance. A century later, after Timoleon had liberated Syracuse from its tyrants, 'the statue of Gelon, their ancient tyrant, was preserved by the Syracusans, though they condemned the rest, because they admired and honoured him for the victory which he had won over the Carthaginians at Himera.'[24]

It would be Gelon's good fortune to be remembered as one of the saviours of Hellenism from the joint attacks of the Persians and Carthaginians. He certainly encouraged this reputation, dedicating a golden tripod at Delphi to commemorate his victory. The base of which, decorated by a bull, still stands at Delphi today. While Gelon's achievement would be remembered, memories of his treatment of Megara Hyblaea and Euboea were forgotten, but then, as now, history was largely written by the victors.

Chapter 5

The Democratic Experiment.

In Sicily, as soon as the tyranny of Syracuse had been overthrown and all the cities of the island had been liberated, the whole of Sicily was making great strides toward prosperity.

Diodorus 11.72

Gelon died in 478 after only seven years of rule. While on his death bed he anointed his brother, Hieron, to be his successor. Hieron soon came to suspect the ambitions of another surviving brother, Polyzelus, who was governor of Gela and had married Gelon's widow, the daughter of Theron of Akragas. He was also reputedly very popular among the people. Hieron, by contrast 'was avaricious and violent and, speaking generally, an utter stranger to sincerity and nobility of character. Consequently there was a good many who wished to revolt; but they restrained their inclinations because of Gelon's reputation and the goodwill he had shown towards all the Sicilians.'[1] The new tyrant quickly raised a bodyguard of mercenaries and foreigners, believing that this would be the surest way for him to keep himself in power.

Hieron used the tried and true method of attempting to remove his rival by sending him off on a foreign campaign. He gave him command of an expedition to be sent to assist Croton in their war against another Italian city, Sybaris. This was supposedly done for the same reasons that the Cumaeans had in appointing Aristodemus to a similar campaign; the hope that he would die in battle or at least be forgotten. According to one source, Polyzelus, suspecting the design, refused the command and, fearing his brother's rage, fled to Theron in Akragas. Another account has Polyzelus commanding the expedition with great success, returning to Syracuse in triumph and then fleeing to Akragas to escape Hieron's paranoia.

Hieron raised an army and prepared to march on Akragas in order to rid himself of both of his rivals. The unity of the Greek tyrants that had been created by the Carthaginian threat soon vanished once the danger had been eliminated.

Meanwhile, Thrasydaeus son of Theron, and his father's governor of Himera, had also lived up to the ancient stereotype of the tyrant's successor, making himself unpopular by his harsh government of that city. The Himerians did not dare to approach Theron for justice, as they believed that he would not be impartial. Instead they sent an embassy to Hieron, offered to betray their city to him and to assist him in his campaign against Theron. Hieron decided, however, that it would be in his best interests to come to an arrangement with the powerful Theron. He reversed his policy and betrayed the Himerians' plot to his fellow tyrant. Theron responded by reconciling Polyzelus with Hieron. He then massacred the opposition in Himera.

Hieron followed his brother's policy of mass deportation. Soon after these events he expelled the citizens of Catane and Naxos, transplanting them to Leontini. He replaced them with 5,000 fellow Dorians from the Peloponnesus and a similar number from Syracuse. Catane was renamed Aetna. Theron, once he had finished his purge of Himera, repopulated it with settlers and ordered that they be given citizenship.

In Campania the power of the Etruscans had been seriously damaged in their wars against Cumae in 524 and 504. In 474 Hieron sent a fleet to assist the Cumaeans in their continuing struggle with the Etruscans. The combined Greek fleet won a complete victory. An inscribed helmet commemorating this victory is now held by the British Museum. This victory broke the power of the southern Etruscans completely. The poet Pindar, in one of his odes, compared this victory to those won earlier against the Persians and Carthaginians, claiming that it was Hieron who had delivered 'Hellas from grievous bondage.'[2] It must be remembered, however, that Pindar made his living by writing poems for patrons.

Although this would remove the Etruscan threat to the Greeks of south-western Italy it would have dangerous long-term consequences. The lands of the weakened Etruscans would become prey to the Samnites of central Italy and later be fought over by the Samnites and Rome. These wars, lasting until 290, would start Rome along the long road to empire.

In 472 Theron died and the tyranny of Akragas passed down to his son Thrasydaeus. According to Diodorus, since Theron had 'administered his office equitably,' he had 'not only enjoyed great favour among his countrymen during his lifetime, but also upon his death he was accorded the honours which are paid to heroes; but his son, even while his father was still living, was violent and murderous, and after his father's death ruled over his native city without respect for the laws and like a tyrant.'[3]

Thrasydaeus turned on his previous benefactor, Hieron. He raised an army of 20,000, including mercenaries and the citizen levies of Akragas and Himera, and prepared to attack Syracuse. Hieron was prepared. He countered by invading Akragas, ravaging the border areas and thereby forcing Thrasydaeus to face him in battle. The battle was decided by the clash of the two phalanxes, with the Syracusans winning the day. Casualties in the battle were 4,000 dead among the Akragantians and 2,000 Syracusans killed.

The people of Akragas, as had the people of Himera earlier, rose up against Thrasydaeus, and overthrew him. At first the city was ruled by an oligarchy known as 'the thousand'. This was overthrown and replaced by a democracy three years later. Thrasydaeus fled to Megara but was put on trial and executed. One of the first acts of the democratic regime was to make peace with Hieron. Presumably the oligarchy had continued the war but no details are recorded.

Hieron's reign was noted for his patronage of the arts. The famous poets Simonides, Pindar, Bacchylides, Aeschylus and Epicharmus, and the philosopher Xenophanes were all invited to his court at some time. He was also known for his use of organized informers, an early type of secret police, to maintain control over his subjects. Hieron was also the subject of a fictional dialogue between himself and the poet Simonides, written about a century later by the Athenian aristocrat and mercenary commander Xenophon. Xenophon was a pupil of Socrates, he was an opponent of the democracy and exiled by the Athenians, although one of his sons later died fighting for Athens.

In this dialogue, the only known work of an ancient writer devoted entirely to tyranny, Hieron laments being forced to play the role of tyrant because he can no longer enjoy the simple pleasures of life: 'the fact is rather that the pleasures of the despot are far fewer than those of people in a humbler condition, and his pains not only far more numerous, but more intense.' He further goes on to complain that as a tyrant he can have no true friends and constantly lives in fear, 'to dread a crowd, to dread solitude, to dread the absence of a guard, to dread the very guards that guard, to shrink from having those about one's self unarmed, and yet to hate the sight of armed attendants.'[4]

Hieron and Simonides then go on to debate the measures that a tyrant must take in order to stay in power: the use of terror against one's subjects, the hiring of mercenaries, the use of informers and the necessity of a bodyguard. Furthermore, the autocrat needs to recognize 'the wise, the just and upright', because instead of admiring them, 'they are afraid of them – the courageous, lest they should venture something for the sake of freedom.' The tyrant, if he wished to remain in power, needed to replace men of talent with subservient followers of lesser ability. This latter need has long been recognized even by the leaders of modern, democratic regimes. For the autocratic leader to stay in power as long as possible, his or her best move is to remove any capable ministers who might be a threat, and replace them with compliant non-entities. This is a method, it is sometimes argued, that is commonly practiced by long-term Australian Prime Ministers and Premiers.

In the dialogue Hieron freely admits to the almost universal dislike of tyrants, lamenting that when one is assassinated, 'instead of aiding or avenging their despotic lord, cities bestow large honours on the slayer of a tyrant; ay, and in lieu of excommunicating the tyrannicide from sacred shrines, as is the case with murderers of private citizens, they set up statues of the doers of such deeds in temples.'

Simonides replies that if the tyrant rules well and manages to 'raise this state, of which you are the patron and supreme head, to some unprecedented height of fortune' then 'you will have won the affection of your subjects.' Given Xenophon's background and career it is tempting to see this work as an apology for tyranny, provided the tyrant rules effectively, but to see it only in that light is to do the author an injustice. It should also been seen as an expose on how such regimes not only dehumanize their victims but also the perpetrators.

Hieron died at Catane in 467, and was buried there by his supporters with heroic honours. Sometime later the exiled Catanians returned to their city and destroyed his shrine in revenge. He was succeeded by yet another brother, Thrasybulus.

Any relief that the Syracusans may have felt at the death of Hieron was short-lived. Supposedly, Thrasybulus 'surpassed in wickedness his predecessor to the kingship. For being a violent man and murderous by nature, he put to death many citizens unjustly and drove not a few into exile on false charges, confiscating their possessions into the royal treasury.'[5] Thrasybulus, fearing a revolution, raised an army of mercenaries to defend his regime. Despite his precautions the people of Syracuse rose in revolt. Thrasybulus collected more troops from the colonists of Catane. His army now totalled 15,000 men. Despite this he was forced to abandon part of the city and retreat to Ortygia and the section of the city immediately adjoining it, called Achradina, giving him control of both of Syracuse's harbours. The two sides launched constant raids on each others' areas.

The Syracusans approached the new democratic regimes of Akragas and other cities requesting aid. These cities readily sent supplies, troops and ships. Most likely they hoped to remove the constant threat of ambitious tyrants occupying Sicily's most powerful city, and anticipated that a democratic regime would make for a more peaceful neighbour.

Soon the rebels had gathered both a large fleet and army, and offered battle on both land and sea. Thrasybulus was deserted by most of his supporters and was left only with his mercenaries. The tyrant's navy fought a sea battle against the rebel fleet but was defeated. This loss caused him to abandon the mainland and retreat to the strongly fortified island of Ortygia. In desperation he launched an assault on the city but was again defeated with heavy losses. After a rule of only eleven months he was forced to come to terms with the rebels and their allies.

The Syracusans allowed Thrasybulus to go into exile in Locri and those mercenaries that so wished to march away unmolested. According to Diodorus, 'Thrasybulus had taken over a kingship which had been established on so fair a foundation, disgracefully lost his kingdom through his own wickedness, and fleeing to Locri he spent the rest of his life there in private station.' Whereas, the 'Syracusans having liberated their native city . . . from this time the city enjoyed peace and increased in prosperity, and it maintained its democracy for almost sixty years.'[6] The Syracusans then removed their garrisons from those cities that were occupied. They also helped others to overthrow their tyrants and replace them with democracies.

This description of Hieron's nature and the overthrow of the later tyrants must be placed in perspective. It was a frequent tale among ancient historians that a popular ruler would be followed by a more vicious tyrant who would rule through repression and whose brutality would force the people to overthrow him. Diodorus even repeats the same words, 'violent and murderous' when describing Thrasydaeus and Thrasybulus. The stories were, nonetheless, common enough that there was, probably, some basis to them.

The first tyrants had generally come to power with the support of the *demos* and a program to overthrow the aristocracy. Once this was achieved, the goodwill it had produced allowed them to continue to rule. After their deaths there was no good political reason for their successors to remain in power. Without the popularity of their predecessors they continued to rule, solely for power's sake, through repression. Gelon had been fortunate in that his victory over the Carthaginians had given him a basis for his own reputation. Tyrants, as usurpers, did rely heavily on the abilities and popularity of the person in power. Legitimate monarchies can survive a weak or unpopular king; tyrannies usually cannot.

Diodorus claims that the whole of Sicily benefited by the overthrow of the tyrannies and the widespread introduction of democracies:

> For the Sicilian Greeks were at peace, and the land they cultivated was fertile, so that the abundance of their harvests enabled them soon to increase their estates and to fill the land with slaves and domestic animals and every other accompaniment of prosperity, taking in great revenues on the one hand and spending nothing on the wars to which they had become accustomed.[7]

The removal of their garrisons from the other cities would have been an immensely popular move on the part of the Syracusans. The two principles that a Greek city valued above all others were their freedom (*eleutheria*) and autonomy (*autonomia*). In the cut-throat world of Greek, and particularly Sicilian, politics, such a state was often hard to maintain. Cities might have their freedom of action restricted in a number of ways, most often in an alliance led by a powerful state, the *hegemon*. Foreign conquest and the imposition of a governor, puppet oligarchy or tyranny might also destroy both their freedom and autonomy.

Perhaps the biggest threat to a city's freedom and autonomy was the

imposition of a foreign garrison. Even if the *polis* retained its own government its freedom of action was curtailed by the garrison, which would allow
immediate military action against the city if it stepped out of line. The
imposition of a foreign garrison was so hated by the Greeks that later would-
be *hegemons* would generally promise to leave their allied cities ungarrisoned,
if they wished to win their support. Diodorus claims that the removal of their
garrisons by the Syracusan democracy was so popular that they 'voluntarily
conceded the hegemony to the Syracusans.'[8]

After the overthrow of Thrasybulus, the Syracusans called an assembly to
decide on their new constitution. Little is recorded of the details of this constitution. Although the Athenian democracy was probably not the first, it is
certainly the best documented. As such most other Greek democracies are
inevitably compared to it. The most important bodies in the Athenian democracy were the assembly and the law courts. The assembly could be attended
by all citizens and was the sole legislative institution. It issued decrees (such
as deciding to go to war, elected some officials, passed laws and tried political crimes. The standard format was for speakers to make speeches for and
against, followed by a general vote by show of hands. During the fifth century
attendance at the assembly was compulsory for all citizens within the city and
those found to be absent were fined.

There was also a council, *boule*, made up of 500 members. The *boule*
served as an executive committee for the assembly and oversaw and co-
ordinated the activities of the various boards and magistrates that carried out
the administrative functions of Athens. The council was therefore responsible
for the administration of the state, but was granted little latitude for initiative as it was completely subservient to the wishes of the *demos*, the assembly.
The president was chosen by lot each day and this position could only be held
once in a lifetime. He would also preside over the assembly if one was held on
that day. In addition he held the keys to the treasury and the seal to the city,
and welcomed foreign ambassadors. Many citizens, no matter what their
station in life could hold this position and it has been calculated that one
quarter of all citizens must have held the post at some time.

The control of the courts by the people was another crucial element for a
democracy. Juries were large, at least 200 strong, and selected by lot from
a panel. Payment for jurors was introduced around 462 and was seen as
fundamental to true democracy. Verdicts were based on a simple majority
and sometimes reflected the will of the jurors, the *demos*, rather than being
based on evidence. Cases could be brought by any citizen.

Most office holders were chosen by lot from a voluntary panel. A much
smaller group was directly elected: the ten generals and those who handled
large sums of money. The election of magistrates was generally seen as
anti-democratic, as it favoured the elite, but was seen as a necessary evil
as these individuals could be prosecuted and heavily fined if found guilty

of corruption. All posts were annual. Generals were perhaps the most powerful officials as they could call emergency sessions of the assembly. This was the post usually sought by ambitious politicians.

Two things were fundamental to the whole system. One was the right of any citizen to speak in the assembly, to initiate a law suit or to propose a law. The second was that while doing so citizens were free of any review or punishment. A radical democrat would probably add that selection by lot and payment for performing government posts were also crucial as this allowed the poor to fully participate in the running of the state. Such participation was considered essential for being a good citizen. Democrats felt that those who did not participate in politics were *idiots,* and were treated with contempt for being useless to the people.

The Syracusan democracy does appear to have been similar to that of Athens but, probably, had initially some crucial differences. The magistrates appear to have been directly elected rather than chosen. It also appears unlikely that there was payment for attendance in the law courts, the assembly or the council. A truly radical Greek democrat would consider that these omissions smacked of oligarchy. The first would have had overtones of elitism. The second would have been seen as excluding the poor.

Some historians argue, however, that Syracuse was not a true democracy at all, as the rich ruled through the council and the assembly had little real power. Aristotle gives some support to this argument saying Syracuse changed its constitution from a *politaea* to a radical democracy only after their victory over the Athenians in 413. The meaning of this word is generally best rendered as 'constitutional government' but is often taken as meaning a 'limited' or 'hoplite' democracy. Diodorus simply refers to the new governments as democracies. The opinion of the contemporary historian Thucydides is perhaps most compelling. He describes the Syracusans as similar in character to Athenians and under a democracy 'like themselves'.[9] In 415 the Athenians therefore had little to offer that could win over the Syracusan democrats. On balance it would appear that the Syracusan government was a genuine democracy by Greek standards but not initially as 'radical' as the Athenian version.[10]

Ancient Greek cities, at least in Greece proper, tended to be very exclusive with their citizenship, and it was rarely granted to outsiders. In the long term this would prove to be a fatal weakness in their struggles against the later empires, as it limited the size of the citizen body unnecessarily. During the formation and consolidation of the state, however, it did create a strong and unified sense of community. The earlier tyrants in Sicily had shattered this sense of homogeneity by their transplanting of whole populations and the giving of citizenship to mercenaries and foreigners. This led other Greeks to characterize the Sicilians as fickle and unpatriotic. The Athenian politician Alcibiades, although probably exaggerating, portrayed the Syracusans as an easy conquest, on the basis that the Sicilian cities were 'peopled by motley rabbles, and easily change their institutions and adopt new ones in their stead and consequently the inhabitants, being without any feeling of patriotism, are not provided with arms for their persons.'[11] The subsequent military victories of the Syracusan democracy would show that this was a false assumption.

The mercenaries in particular appear to have been resented by the new governments, perhaps because of their association with the tyrants and their repression. Six years after its foundation the democracy of Syracuse voted to strip 7,000 former mercenaries of their citizenship. Not unnaturally, the mercenaries resented this and raised an armed revolt, seizing a strongly fortified section of the city. The citizens responded by laying siege to the rebels' stronghold. For the second time in only a few years the city had become a battleground between two factions.

The Syracusans built a wall separating the rebels from the countryside and defeated them at sea, thereby imposing a blockade over them. With the threat of being starved into submission, the rebels were forced to abandon their fortifications and offer battle outside the city. Despite the superior military skill of the mercenaries, the more numerous citizens won the victory. After the final battle the Syracusans crowned 600 men for their bravery in the battle and awarded them a *mina* in cash. This was about 4.3 kilograms of silver, or 1,000 drachmas, the equivalent of about three years of the basic wage paid to an ancient Greek labourer. Nothing is recorded of the fate of the mercenaries; perhaps they were again allowed to march away unmolested.

The antipathy of the new democracy towards the supporters of the tyrants does not appear to have been limited to those residing in Syracuse itself. The city was soon at war with Hieron's settlers of Aetna (formerly Catane) on behalf of the exiled former citizens. In this campaign they were joined by the Sicels, under their warlord Ducetius. Apparently the new citizens of Aetna had been enlarging their landholdings at the expense of the native population. The allied Syracusans and Sicels defeated the colonists in several battles and drove them out of the city. The new refugees occupied the city of Inessa and, in turn, renamed it Aetna. The former population of Catane returned to their city, which reverted to its original name.

According to Diodorus these victories inspired more cities to expel their tyrants and allow their exiles to return:

> After these events the peoples who had been exiled from their own cities while Hieron was king, now that they had assistance in the struggle, returned to their fatherlands and expelled from their cities the men who wrongly seized for themselves the habitations of others: and these were the inhabitants of Gela, Akragas and Himera. In like manner Rhegians along with Zancleans expelled the sons of Anaxilas, who were ruling over them, liberated their fatherlands. . . . and practically all cities being

eager to make an end of the wars, came to a common decision, whereby they made terms with the mercenaries in their midst; they received back the exiles and restored the cities to the original citizens . . . with almost no exceptions portioned out their lands in allotments among all their citizens.[12]

It appears from this that the Sicilians took advantage of the overthrow of the tyrants to carry out that constant demand of the Greek poor – the redistribution of the land. This does appear, however, to have been done at the expense of the mercenaries and other expelled foreigners rather than the rich. Only seven years later, Diodorus described that, due to the haphazard nature of the redistributions and enrolling of citizens, civil strife had again broken out in the cities. There were, supposedly, so many lawsuits around the contested ownership of land that later Roman lawyers, such as Cicero, claimed that forensic oratory and the first legal handbooks were developed by the Sicilian Greeks.

This civil strife was most pronounced in Syracuse. The poor in particular were disappointed by the half-hearted nature of the land reform. Many began to support a politician by the name of Tyndarides. Following the example of earlier would-be tyrants, he gathered a bodyguard and plotted a coup. In 454 his plans were discovered and he was tried and sentenced to death. His supporters rioted and tried to free him, but were defeated and executed alongside him. Tyndarides execution did not ease the situation and the unrest continued.

In an attempt to prevent the rise of another tyrant, the Syracusans copied the Athenian system of ostracism. The Athenians could vote to exile any politician they considered too ambitious from the city for five years. The Syracusan system was called *petalism*, as the names were written on olive leaves rather than pieces of pottery (*ostracon*) as in Athens. In Athens it was used successfully for many years as a relief valve for political pressure. In Syracuse, however, the poor used it simply as a system to remove the rich. This in turn caused the wealthier citizens to withdraw from public life for fear of exposing themselves to exile. As a result the law was repealed soon after its introduction. Diodorus claims that it was the *demos* that passed the law for *petalism*, evidence that the Syracusan assembly did have legislative powers.

The peace in Sicily was broken not by the Greeks but by a revolt of the Sicels. In 459, the same Ducetius who had assisted the Syracusans against Catane began to organize a rebellion of the Sicels against the Greeks. First, he founded his own city at Menae (Mineo) and distributed land to settlers. He then attacked the Greeks and took the city of Morgantina. By 452 he had united the Sicels of central Sicily and founded a new capital at Palice, about 3km from Menae, near two holy crater lakes of the same name. The city grew quickly, becoming a refuge for escaped slaves.

In 451 Ducetius launched an ambitious campaign against the Greeks. First he captured the city of Aetna, refuge of his old enemies the mercenaries from Catane. He then attacked the territory of Akragas, besieging the town of Motyum. The Syracusans, perhaps initially pleased by his destruction of Aetna, now came to the conclusion that Ducetius was a dangerous threat. They allied with Akragas and went to the relief of Motyum. Ducetius defeated the allied force in battle and captured both of their camps. After the victory Motyum capitulated to the Sicels. Winter prevented Ducetius from following up his victory. The Syracusans accused their general, Bolcon, of taking a bribe from Ducetius, found him guilty and executed him.

The following year the Syracusans appear to have taken the threat more seriously. They raised a much stronger army and attacked Ducetius near the city of Nomae. After a fierce battle the Syracusans routed the Sicels. The survivors of the defeat scattered and fled to their own strongholds. Ducetius, along with a few loyal followers, fled to Motyum. The Akragantians attacked and captured the city. Before the final assault, Ducetius, fearing that his followers would betray him, fled to Syracuse and sought refuge as a supplicants in one of the temples.

Amazed to suddenly find their enemy amongst them, the Syracusans called an assembly. Some argued for the death penalty but others, the aristocrats, declared that they should not risk the wrath of the gods but show mercy. They further argued that the people should not only consider 'what punishment Ducetius deserved, but what action was proper for the Syracusans', and that 'to spare the suppliant was an act worthy of the people.'[13] To their credit the Syracusans voted for mercy, sending Ducetius into exile at Corinth, on the provision that he never return to Sicily. They even provided him with an income. The Syracusan's motives may not, however, have been totally honourable, as Ducetius appears to have ordered the surrender of those towns that he ruled. This may have been part of a deal to save his life.[14] These towns now fell under Syracusan control, were forced to pay tribute and some were subjected to garrisons by their Greek overlords.

In about 454, in western Sicily, war broke out between Segesta and Selinus. The two cities had previously enjoyed good relations, but the cause was a traditional one, the ownership of disputed agricultural land. A bloody and indecisive battle was fought, but the outcome did not end the dispute. It is perhaps as a result of this clash that Athens made an alliance with the Elymian town of Segesta. It is difficult to know why the Athenians, who were then involved in the First Peloponnesian War, agreed to an alliance with such a distant city. It is possible that the expansionist Athenians had already cast a covetous eye upon the wealth of the island and saw any alliance as a potential future bridgehead. Whatever the immediate reason, the decision would have long-term consequences for Athens' future role in Sicily.[15]

Ducetius was, however, not finished. In 446 he broke his parole on the pretext that an oracle had decreed that he should found a city on the northern shore of Sicily. He sailed to Sicily with a group of both Greek and Sicel colonists and founded the city of Cale Acte (Caronia). If nothing else, Ducetius must have been a charismatic character. As his new foundation was so distant the Syracusans apparently decided to ignore it. The citizens of Akragas, who had suffered a Sicel invasion, were not, however, so sanguine. They had originally opposed the Syracusans pardoning him without reference to them and were outraged at his return. As a result they declared war on Syracuse.

Many of the other Greek cities of Sicily now took sides. Akragas and Syracuse were the two most powerful Greek cities in Sicily and rivalry between them was to be expected. The reappearance of Ducetius may well have been a convenient excuse for Akragas and its allies to declare war. They most likely hoped to halt the expansion of Syracusan power that had restarted with the overthrow of the tyrants and continued with the defeat and subjugation of the Sicels.

The other Greek cities of Sicily probably had bad memories of previous periods of Syracusan expansion. The goodwill that had existed for almost a generation between the cities, after the overthrow of the tyrants, had come to an end. Along with their allies both sides could probably have mustered around 20,000 troops. The two sides fought a battle at the Himera River. The Syracusans were victorious and killed over 1,000 of the enemy. After the battle the two sides concluded a peace treaty. Diodorus later records that 'affairs likewise in Sicily also were in a peaceful state' as 'the Akragantians after their defeat at the Himera River, had come to terms with the Syracusans.'[16]

Here it is likely that Diodorus, a proud citizen of the Sicilian city of Agyrium, is putting a favourable spin on events. It is more likely that after their defeat at Himera River the other cities were forced into an alliance that formalized Syracuse's leadership. Such forced alliances were the usual manner by which powerful Greek cities, such as Athens and Sparta, secured their leadership over their fellow Greeks. The other cities would be forced to cede their foreign policy and command in war to the hegemonic power. In some cases they might also be forced to pay tribute, often disguised by the euphemism 'voluntary contributions.' Unfortunately, Diodorus does not record the terms of the treaty.

In 440 Ducetius made one last attempt to unite the Sicels but died of illness before his plans could be realized. The Syracusans had made all the cities of the Sicels subject except for the otherwise unknown town of Trinace. It was, apparently, the last refuge of the most militant of the Sicels, 'full of military leaders who took an immense pride in their own manly spirit.'[17] The Syracusans, fearing that the city would take the leadership of another Sicel revolt, led a large army of their own and their allies' troops against them.

These Sicels, being the last die-hards of their rebellion, fought stubbornly, but were overwhelmed by the superior numbers of the Greeks. The last survivors committed suicide rather than submit. The victorious Greeks destroyed the city, selling the women and children into slavery. The revolt of the Sicels had now been completely crushed. Although in the future some might ally themselves with the enemies of Syracuse, they would never again pose an independent threat.

The Syracusans were able to use the extra revenue generated by their conquest of the Sicels to further increase their military power. They built 100 extra triremes, doubled their number of cavalry and increased their number of hoplites. Diodorus claims they funded this through increasing the amount of tribute that the Sicels paid. Another possibility is that they introduced the system of *cleruchies*. This involved allotting land in conquered territories to individual Syracusans, who acted as absentee landlords, collecting a share of the produce. Those allotted such lands would increase their wealth and their ability to pay for their military equipment. Diodorus argues, probably correctly, that Syracusans adopted this policy with a view to gradually subjugating all of Sicily.[18]

Little is recorded of the next thirteen years of Sicilian history. Diodorus had claimed that after the overthrow of the tyrants Sicily had enjoyed sixty years of peace and prosperity. This is obviously an exaggeration, but the forty years from the overthrow of Thrasybulus until the first Athenian invasion was a period of relative peace. There were wars against the Sicels, the Elymians, the mercenaries and one battle between Syracuse and Akragas. Despite this, war does appear to have been intermittent and at a relatively low level compared to the previous period of the tyrants. More importantly, the tyrant's practices of the widespread transplantation of populations and the total destruction of Greek cities are generally absent. It is no wonder that later Sicilians, such as Diodorus, would look back at the period as a golden age for the Greeks of Sicily.

The prosperity of these years of peace produced its own dangers. The obvious wealth of the island would make it a target of an unrelenting series of invaders hoping to avail themselves of Sicily's resources. The first of these invasions would be by their fellow Greeks, the Athenians, who had already cast covetous eyes on Sicily's wealth.

Chapter 6

The Leontine War

For some time past the Athenians had been covetous of Sicily because of the fertility of its land, and so for the moment, gladly accepting the proposals of Gorgias, they voted to send an allied force to the Leontines, offering as their excuse the need and request of their kinsmen, whereas in fact they were eager to get possession of the whole island.

Diodorus 12.54

In 480–479 an alliance of the cities of what we now call Greece, led by their two most powerful cities, Sparta on land and Athens at sea, defeated a sizeable invasion by the Persian King Xerxes. Such voluntary alliances among the Greek states were rare and soon after the Persian threat had been removed their rivalries returned. Much to the disapproval of the Spartans, the Athenians refortified both their city and its port Piraeus. The Spartans, who considered themselves pre-eminent among the Greeks, objected to a fortified harbour being so close to the Pelopponesus.

Although Herodotus claims that the war against Persia ended with the victory at the Battle of Plataea, this was only true for the threat to Greece itself. In 478 an expedition under the Spartan prince Pausanias, the victor of Plataea, began an offensive to try and liberate the Ionian Greek cities of Asia from the Persians. They quickly liberated both Cyprus and Byzantium. These victories appear to have led to personal ambitions on the part of Pausanias. He was accused of 'behaving more like a despot than a general' and of conspiring with the Persians.[1] The conservative Spartan government, fearing his ambition, recalled him. He was later condemned to death for plotting with the helots against the Spartan government. The whole episode appears to have made the already insular Spartans even more fearful of overseas adventures.

The Greeks of Asia and the Aegean islands, usually referred to as the Ionians, now looked to Athens for support. In 477 they rejected the appointment of a new Spartan commander. The Spartans now withdrew from the war, leaving the Athenians in control. Along with the Ionian Greeks the Athenians formed a new alliance, the Delian League, with its treasury in the temple of Apollo on the island of Delos. The stated purpose of the League was to liberate the Greek cities from Persian control. With the victory of the League at the Battle of the Eurymedon River (Aspendos in southern Turkey) in 469, Persian power in the region was smashed.

According to Thucydides, the smaller allies now lost interest in military service, 'making most of them arrange to pay their share of the expense in money instead of ships, and so avoid leaving their homes.'[2] This is of course the Athenian point of view, but, whatever the reasons were, the voluntary alliance of the Delian League soon changed into an Athenian Empire, where nearly all the smaller cities paid tribute to the *hegemon*, Athens. The collection of tribute enhanced Athens' power as she was able to increase the size of her fleet and military power at the expense of her so-called allies.

The total control of Athens was first demonstrated in 465 when Thasos attempted to leave the alliance. The Athenians besieged and captured the city. In retaliation, Thasos had its *autonomia* virtually destroyed by having its walls torn down, and its land, mines and naval ships confiscated by Athens. A hefty fine was also imposed. The lesson to the other allies was unmistakable; the cities of the League were now clearly subjects of Athens.

This point was made even more obvious in 454, when Athens removed the treasury from Delos to Athens and used the money to fund building projects within the city. When confronted by complaints that this high-handed behaviour amounted to tyranny, the leading Athenian politician Pericles retorted 'not a horse do they furnish . . . not a ship, not a hoplite, but money simply; and this belongs, not to those who give it, but to those who take it.'[3]

This increase in Athenian power did not go unobserved by the rest of the Greeks. Sparta, however, had its own internal problems. In 464 the city was struck by a severe earthquake which killed many of its citizens. The *helots* took this opportunity to revolt. The aristocratic Athenian commander Cimon led an expedition to assist the Spartans, as the old alliance dating from the Persian War was still in operation. The expedition was not a success as the two sides immediately distrusted one another. According to Thucydides, 'the first open quarrel between the Spartans and Athenians arose out of this expedition.'[4] The Spartans, fearing that the democratic Athenians might set a bad example to their other allies, soon sent the Athenians home. Resenting their treatment, the Athenians ended their alliance with the Spartans and instead allied with the latter's traditional enemy, Argos.

The two sides finally came to blows in the First Peloponnesian War (459–446). Sparta, fearing a further uprising of its *helots*, took little direct part in the war, leaving most of the fighting to its allies. In 446 Athens was forced to sign a thirty-year treaty with Sparta. Both sides kept their empires largely intact but Athens had lost most of its influence in central Greece.

Green argues that Athens' shortage of raw materials and particularly food, a shortage common to most of the cities of Greece, but more so to Athens with its rapidly increasing population, was the main cause of Athens' imperialism during this period.[5] The shortage of grain was solved by importations from Macedonia, Thrace and, most importantly, the Black Sea region. In order to safeguard these imports Athens was committed to building its power in Thrace, the islands of the northern Aegean and the Dardanelles. The Black Sea route was, nonetheless, insecure and costly and the Athenians were constantly looking for a more reliable source of grain. The other three major grain exporting regions were Campania, Sicily and Egypt. In 460 the Athenians sent an expedition to Egypt but this was decisively defeated by the Persians in 454. Another attempt was made in 450 but this too was defeated. With its Egyptian ambitions destroyed, the Athenian leader Pericles now looked covetously to the west to secure further grain supplies. With its loss of influence in central Greece, however, Athens' path to the west was blocked by Sparta's most important ally, Corinth.

In 431 Sparta, finally convinced that the ever-increasing power of Athens would eventually destroy its position as the most powerful Greek city, broke the thirty-year treaty and declared war. Although the major cause of the war was the fear of Athens' growing power, the two major protagonists mistrusted one another for a number of reasons. Sparta was oligarchic and a closed society. It discouraged its citizens from travelling abroad and foreigners from entering its territory. The boys of its ruling class were taken from their mothers at the age of seven and given a brutal, mostly military education. As a result they mistrusted the open society of Athens and feared its support for the spread of democracy.

The Athenians feared the Spartan preference for oligarchic rule or tyrannies. They also disliked the Spartans on cultural grounds, portraying them in their comedies as arrogant, boorish, and despite their reputation for honour, both greedy and untrustworthy. There was, however, a small but dangerous group of Athenian aristocrats who admired Sparta and its ability to keep the lower classes in their supposedly rightful, subservient position. As the war progressed this clique would become a dangerous fifth column within Athens. The conflict, known as the Second Peloponnesian War (or, more commonly, just The Peloponnesian War), would last until Athens' defeat in 404.

For the first few years the war was fought by both sides in a rather ineffective fashion. The Spartans relied on the traditional Greek method of waging war. They invaded Athens every summer, ravaging the farmlands and thereby hoping to force the inferior Athenian army to come out and fight them on the open field. The Athenian strategy, known as Periclean after its proponent, was to remain behind their fortifications and avoid battle. Athens was unique among Greek cities, as its naval supremacy and empire could continue to provide it with money and supplies. In retaliation, the Athenians would send out naval expeditions to ravage the coastal areas of Sparta and its allies. The Spartans, in turn, were able to import supplies of grain from their fellow Dorian Greeks in Sicily. As war-winning strategies, both were futile and expensive. Pericles would be voted out of office in 430, return in 429 but die soon after. He would be replaced by more aggressive leaders, the most important being the radical democrat Cleon.

Cleon was one of a new breed of politicians, without noble ancestors and whose wealth was earned from trade and not by farming, as a true gentleman's should be. Cleon based his power on his ability to sway the assembly. He was notorious for being the first to shout and use abusive speech while addressing the people. Cleon was a fervent opponent of the old aristocracy and passed a number of laws in favour of the poor. He also carried out a successful overhaul of Athens' finances, although this was largely done by increasing the rate of tribute paid by the allies. Cleon advocated a much more aggressive policy against Sparta, including the creation of fortified bases on Spartan soil. He also continued Pericles' ambition of further expansion to the west.

Not surprisingly, Cleon was hated by many of the established families. Thucydides describes him as 'the most violent man in Athens'[6] The comic playwright Aristophanes portrays him as deliberately stirring up civil strife and of being corrupt, comparing him to eel fishermen who when they 'stir up the slime, their fishing is good; in the same way it's only in troublous times that you line your pockets.'[7] Both writers were, however, prosecuted by Cleon, or his supporters, and are not unbiased observers. Thucydides' history libels Cleon by claiming that he was killed by fleeing from the Battle of Amphipolis. This accusation was disproved by the finding of an inscription listing the Athenian war dead for that year that included Cleon's name. The Athenians did not consider those who fled from battle worthy of being so remembered.

According to Thucydides, at the start of the war the Spartans:

> in addition to the existing naval forces, gave orders to the states that had declared for her in Italy and Sicily to build vessels up to a grand total of 500, the quota of each city being determined by its size, and also to provide a specified sum of money. Till these were ready they were to remain neutral and to admit single Athenian ships to their harbours.[8]

Thucydides later states that in Sicily 'all the Dorian cities, except Camarina, were in alliance with Syracuse; they were the same which at the beginning of the war were reckoned in the Lacedaemonian confederacy, but they had taken no active part.'[9] If Thucydides is to be believed then the Dorian cities of Sicily, under the leadership of their *hegemon* Syracuse, must have formed some sort of an alliance with the Spartans.

By 427 the years of relative peace in Sicily had finally broken down. The Syracusans were at war with Leontini, the immediate causes of which are not recorded. It is possible that Syracuse's motives for expansion were similar to those of Athens; the inability to feed its ever-expanding population.[10] Unlike the other cities of Sicily, Syracuse was now an importer rather than an exporter of grain. The obvious target for any expansion would be to seize control of the fertile Laistrygonian Plain. This strategy would require the conquest of the Ionian Greek cities of Leontini, Naxos and Catane.

The earlier Syracusan tyrants may have already begun this policy with their destruction of Megara and their conquest of Catane. In the initial euphoria of overthrowing the tyrants the Syracusan democracy had returned Catane to its original inhabitants. Over the next four decades they had mainly been occupied with establishing Syracuse's hegemony over the Greek cities and the subjugation of the Sicels. Now that this was complete, Syracuse was once again in a position to realize its ambition of controlling the rich farmlands to the north. In 433 Athens had sent an embassy to the west which had renewed earlier treaties with Rhegium and Leontini. This action cannot have gone unnoticed in Syracuse and would have been seen as a challenge to its hegemony over the Sicilian cities. This may have given Syracuse the justification for a war that it had long desired.

Leontini, although able to find allies in its fellow Chalcidian cities of Naxos and Rhegium, plus Camarina, was significantly weaker than Syracuse and in danger of being overwhelmed. It could, however, call on its alliance with Athens. In 427 the Leontines sent an embassy to Athens to request assistance against the aggression of Syracuse. The leader of the delegation was Gorgias. He was a famous orator, supposedly the first man to devise the rules of rhetoric, and as a teacher he charged enormous fees from his pupils. Athenian students of Gorgias included the murderous oligarch, Critias, and the amoral politician, Alcibiades, who would play a major role in the decision to invade Sicily in 415. Gorgias supposedly died immensely wealthy at the age of 100.

Gorgias and other teachers of rhetoric were despised by their contemporary, the Athenian philosopher Plato, who claimed that 'the rhetorician need not know the truth about things; he has only to discover some way of persuading the ignorant that he has more knowledge than those who know.' Plato further claimed that the rhetorician is 'as ignorant of the just and unjust, base and honourable, good and evil, as he is of medicine'.[11] He blamed them for the supposed lack of morality and wisdom of democratic politicians and governments. Plato was a bitter opponent of democracy and advocated rule by a 'philosopher king'. He would later come face to face with the unreality of this philosophy when confronted by the real politics of power while visiting Syracuse under the rule of its later tyrants.

This philosophical criticism did not have any influence over the democratic Athenians who were used to being entertained by speakers in their assembly. Gorgias' presentation apparently filled them with admiration and, supposedly, won the Athenians over to honouring their alliance. A more realistic motive for the decision to support Leontini is given by both Diodorus and Thucydides. Both claim that the Athenians wanted to realize their long-held ambition of conquering the island and exploiting its wealth.

Athens' military strength, and the desultory nature of the war with Sparta so far, meant that it could easily find the resources to mount an expedition to Sicily. They sent twenty ships under the generals Laches and Charoeades. The ancient Greeks made no distinction between generals and admirals. Their supposed orders were to assist the Leontines but their real mission was to prevent the export of Sicilian wheat to the Pelopponesus, to test how strong Syracuse was, and to decide if it would be possible to subjugate the entire island.

The expedition was most likely a compromise typical of a democratic government. The Athenians could not have expected to conquer Sicily with such a small force. It was, however, too small to worry those opposed to it being sent, and if it were able to successfully relieve Leontini, block the export of grain from the west to the Pelopponesus and redirect it instead to Athens this would be success enough. Those who dreamed of a conquest of Sicily could hope that initial success would allow them to convince the assembly to vote for a much larger force to be sent to enlarge the campaign and its aims. As Plutarch claims:

> On Sicily the Athenians had cast longing eyes even while Pericles was living; and after his death they actually tried to lay hands upon it. The lesser expeditions which they sent thither from time to time, ostensibly for the aid and comfort of their allies on the island who were being wronged by the Syracusans, they regarded merely as stepping stones to the greater expedition of conquest.[12]

It is sometimes claimed that the small nature of the expedition meant that Athens had not yet made plans for the conquest of Sicily and that this would only come later with the campaign of 415. The argument being that Diodorus, Plutarch and even the contemporary Thucydides are looking back at events with hindsight. This ignores the claim by comedic poet Aristophanes in his play, *The Knights*, performed in 420 where the triremes of the chorus claim that the bellicose politician, and supporter of Cleon, 'Hyperbolus, a bad citizen and an infamous scoundrel, asks for a hundred of us to take them to sea against Carthage.'[13] Although a satire, it does show that the idea of such extensive conquests in the west was certainly being openly discussed in Athens well before 415. As Alcibiades, and later Pyrrhus of Epirus, would claim, the conquest of Sicily was a necessary precursor to any attempted invasion of Phoenician Africa.

On normal duties an Athenian trireme carried four archers and ten marines. A trireme could, however, carry up to forty marines. For a large-scale expedition such as this it is most likely that a larger complement than usual would have been carried in order to provide a reasonably sized force of heavy infantry. Marines were armed as hoplites, but usually less heavily armoured. On board ship they would substitute their spear for javelins. Athenian marines were usually drawn from the lowest property class and their equipment, probably just a shield, spear and javelins, was provided by the state. A trireme's normal complement was 180 rowers and about a dozen sailors. If necessary the naval crew could also fight, usually as poorly-armed skirmishers, armed with a dagger and possibly a javelin, or sometimes by simply throwing rocks.

In the late summer the Athenians arrived in Rhegium and made it their main base. They were reinforced by another twenty ships from the Rhegians and their other Italian allies. The combined expedition would then have totalled forty triremes and 8,000 to 9,000 men, of whom somewhere between 400 and 1,600 would have been marines. From here they could hope to dominate the straits and intercept any grain ships from both Campania and Sicily, although it was less well situated to assist the Leontines, the supposed purpose of the expedition. This campaign is usually referred to as The Leontine War.

Syracuse, as *hegemon* of Sicily, should have been able to mobilize all of the Greek cities of Sicily against the Athenians. Such alliances were, however, only as strong as the power of the leading state to punish those who wavered. The Ionian colonies of Naxos and Catane supported Leontini, as did Dorian Camarina. Although the most powerful of the Sicilian cities, Syracuse was clearly not strong enough to exert its power over its recalcitrant allies if they were supported by an outside power. Syracuse did, however, have an important ally in the Italian city of Locri, which was an inveterate enemy of its neighbour, and Athens' ally, Rhegium.

During the winter of 427/6 the Athenians attacked the Aeolian Islands and took the main island of Lipari. They then ravaged the other islands but were unable to force them to submit, so they retired back to Rhegium, having achieved little. Although the islanders were allies of Syracuse they were also notorious pirates, preying on the Italian shipping of the Tyrrhenian Sea. Their defeat would have enhanced Athenian control of the straits.

The war continued during the summer of 426, including fighting among the Sicilians, but our sources only record those actions in which the Athenians took part. Presumably the Syracusans were concentrating their efforts on maintaining their blockade of Leontini and had few resources to spare to aid their allies in the north.

At some stage, probably in the spring of 426, Charoeades was dispatched south on a diplomatic mission to make contact with the enemies of Syracuse. One of those cities contacted was Segesta, and the fateful treaty was either renewed or initiated. On his return journey his squadron was intercepted and defeated by the Syracusan fleet, and he was killed during the battle. This left Laches in sole command of the expedition.

While the Syracusans concentrated on the war against Leontini, the Athenians were apparently more interested in their operations to the north than with assisting their Sicilian allies. Laches led an expedition to attack the city of Mylae (Milazzo) on the northern coast. The neighbouring Greek city of Messene, another ally of Syrcause, sent aid but the force was ambushed and heavily defeated, losing 1,000 dead and 600 prisoners. As a result of their victory the Athenians soon captured Mylae and forced them into an alliance. The Athenians, along with their new allies, then marched on Messene, which surrendered and gave hostages. Control of both Messene and Rhegium gave Athens complete domination over the straits. The Athenians followed up this victory by attacking Locri. They defeated the Locrians in battle, sinking five ships and taking one of their coastal forts.

With their control of the straits now complete, the Athenians decided to directly intervene in the fighting in eastern Sicily. Somehow the Leontines had managed to hold out over the summer, perhaps with the assistance of many of Syracuse's Sicel subjects who had taken the opportunity of the Athenians' presence to revolt. Early in the winter the Athenians, along with their allies, marched against the Sicel city of Inessa, which was occupied by a Syracusan garrison. The assault failed and the Athenians withdrew. During the retreat the Syracusans sallied out and caught the Leontines and Sicels by surprise, inflicting heavy losses on them. The Athenians ended the year by again raiding the territory of Locri.

During the winter the Athenians, along with the Sicels, raided Himera and the Aeolian Islands before the fleet returned to its base at Rhegium. While this was going on their Sicilian allies had sent another embassy to Athens requesting more aid, claiming that the Syracusans were building extra ships and the current Athenian fleet would not be able to dominate the sea much longer. They perhaps also came to complain of a strategy that appeared to favour Athens' strategic interests while providing little real assistance to them. The Athenian assembly, now under the sway of Cleon, was convinced to reinforce the expedition and the following spring sent out another forty triremes. This fleet, however, was diverted to Pylos on the western coast of the Pelopponesus. Most of it remained there but a few ships continued on under the command of Pythodorus.

On his arrival at Rhegium, Pythodorus replaced Laches as commander. His tenure got off to a poor start when he launched another raid on Locri but was defeated. These constant raids on Locri appear to have been a diversion, but the Athenians probably undertook them both to keep the fleet in training and to prevent any Locrian attack on their base at nearby Rhegium.

In the summer of 425 the Messenians revolted from Athens and a fleet of twenty Locrian and Syracusan ships came to their assistance. The Locrians supported this expedition by a diversionary land attack on Rhegium. Here they were assisted by an outbreak of civil strife within the city which prevented any opposition and allowed the Locrians to ravage the countryside before withdrawing unmolested. The Locrians placed a garrison in Messene to aid in its defence after the Messenians' heavy losses of the year before. The Syracusans sent another ten of their newly built boats, along with a land force, to reinforce the squadron they had guarding Messene. According to Thucydides, they wished to break the Athenian stranglehold over the straits because it 'afforded an approach to Sicily, and [they] feared that the Athenians might hereafter use it as a base for attacking them with a larger force.'[14]

The Syracusans hoped to bring on a battle at sea against the much-reduced Athenian squadron, which now only numbered sixteen Athenian and eight Rhegian triremes. They were clearly going on the offensive against the depleted Athenians, directly threatening their main base. This effort was in concert with, and at the suggestion of their Locrian allies, who supported it with another attack from the land. Late one day the Syracusan fleet of thirty ships sallied out to attack a merchant vessel. The Athenians came out boldly to meet them. Once again the Athenians demonstrated their superiority at sea, sinking one Syracusan vessel before nightfall allowed the rest to escape to the shelter of Cape Pelorus, just north of Messene. Seeing the defeat of the naval attack, the Locrian land forces withdrew from Rhegian territory.

The next day the Syracusans brought up their land forces to support their fleet. They then sailed south to Messene. The emboldened Athenians attacked but in a running battle lost two ships to the Syracusans, who then were able to reach the safety of the harbor of Messene. This victory, albeit minor, must have been a great morale boost for the inexperienced Syracusan fleet.

Ancient Greek warfare was often conducted in a manner that would have modern military theorists tearing their hair out. The concept of maintenance of aim was rarely adhered to, and usually ignored due to the result of political events. The major powers were often forced to change their plans in order to save an important ally or to take advantage of an opportunity for a quick victory, usually as the result of political turmoil within an enemy city. As Thucydides claims, 'in war, with an alliance always at the command of either faction for the hurt of their adversaries and for their own corresponding advantage, opportunities for bringing in the foreigner were never wanting to the revolutionary parties.'[15]

Just such a situation now diverted the Athenians. The city of Camarina was about to be betrayed to Syracuse by internal political dissidents and the Athenians sent a force to support their allies. The Messenians took advantage of their absence to attack another Athenian ally, the city of Naxos. They invaded Naxian territory and in the usual manner ravaged it in attempt to force the enemy to abandon their walls and fight. The neighbouring Sicel tribes came to the rescue of Naxos and attacked the Messenians while they were dispersed. The Naxians sallied out to assist their allies and between them they routed the Messenians, killing 1,000. More were killed by the Sicels as they withdrew along the only road through the mountainous terrain back to Messene. It had so far been a costly war for the Messenians, losing at least 2,000 dead in two years.

The Leontines now arrived and, along with their Sicel allies and the newly returned Athenians, attempted to recapture the seriously weakened Messene. The Messenians, reinforced by their Locrian garrison, attacked bravely and defeated the Leontines. The Athenian fleet intervened to save their routed allies. They landed troops and drove the dispersed Messenians back into their city.

The Athenians claimed to have won the battle and set up a trophy claiming the victory. This was a common practice amongst the ancient Greeks. The trophy was usually a tree trunk decked out in a captured enemy suit of armour. The side that held the battlefield at the end of the day was considered to be the victor, whatever the later strategic consequences of the battle were. Although the Locrians and Messenians had defeated the Leontines and saved the city, the fact that the Athenians held the field at nightfall allowed them to set up a trophy.

The Athenians, once again, withdrew to Rhegium and then took no further part in the war. The promised reinforcements had still not arrived and the remaining Athenian forces were impotent against the combined might of Syracuse, its Sicilian allies and Locri. Finally, in the autumn, the Athenian reinforcements arrived but they continued to do nothing other than patrol the straits and ensure their alliance with Rhegium. As Green astutely observes 'the Sicilian dream had come up against a touch of harsh reality. This island was not a fruit ripe for the plucking, but a collection of rich and powerful city-states both willing and able to defend their own interests.'[16]

The Sicilian Greeks continued to make war on each other by land, but again neither Thucydides nor Diodorus record any further details of the fighting. Diodorus' account only describes the Athenian invasion up to the capture of Mylae. The final withdrawal of the Athenian fleet is placed within the same chapter, but should be seen as an addendum. Thucydides' more detailed account has the war dragging out for four years, 427–424, and is more likely to be accurate.

In 424, most likely tired of war, the cities of Gela and Camarina agreed to an armistice. Following this, all the other Sicilian cities, similarly exhausted, sent embassies to Gela in order to discuss peace. This conference is perhaps the first example of the Greek cities attempting to conclude a 'common peace'. Such agreements would become common in the next century as the smaller cities looked to protect their autonomy from the ever-increasing interference of the hegemonic powers. The so-called King's Peace of 387 is usually considered to be the first such peace, when the Persian King Artaxerxes asserted that 'the other Hellenic cities both small and large should be autonomous . . . and whoever does not observe this peace, against them I shall make war, both by land and sea, with ships and money.'[17] The peace did not last long, and Persia was not strong enough to enforce its threats, but the tradition had been established. Over the next half-century there are at least six more known attempts to create a 'common peace'.

At first it appeared that the conference would collapse as the cities swapped accusations and grievances. It is at this point that a Syracusan politician named Hermocrates first appears. He would play a major role in Syracusan politics over the next two decades. Hermocrates was clearly a member of the Sicilian aristocracy. He is recorded as visiting Athens in two of Plato's dialogues. While in Athens, Hermocrates was a guest of the Athenian aristocrat Critias.

This association infers that Hermocrates mixed in political circles that were hostile to democracy and favoured oligarchy. The Critias that Hermocrates visited was probably the grandfather of another Critias. The later Critias was an Athenian oligarch who led the overthrow of the democracy and set up the dictatorial rule of 'The Thirty' after Athens' defeat in the Peloponnesian War. The rule of The Thirty was begun with the mass executions of leading democrats and later they 'put people to death in large numbers, some because they were personal enemies, some for the sake of their money'. Xenophon, himself no friend of democracy, records the claim, probably exaggerated, that The Thirty in their eight months of rule 'come close to killing more Athenians than the Peloponnesians did in ten years of war.[18] That Hermocrates sympathized with their views would be clearly demonstrated over his subsequent career.

Despite Hermocrates' political leanings, or more likely because of them, Hermocrates was greatly admired by the historians Thucydides and Polybius. Thucydides describes him as 'a man who with a general ability of the first order had given proofs of military capacity and brilliant courage in war'.[19] The Syracusan people appear to have recognized his ability, often electing him as general and appointing him as ambassador. Nonetheless, they never trusted him fully, fearing correctly that he harboured ambitions to overthrow the democracy and become the next tyrant. Although willing to use his talents, they were always quick to remove him from office when the opportunity arose.

Just as the conference was about to collapse in acrimony, Hermocrates rose to give a final address which Thucydides records. Speeches in Thucydides, even though he is considered to be one of the more reliable of the ancient historians, should not be taken literally, as he admits to fabricating his accounts: 'So my habit has been to make the speakers say what was in my opinion demanded of them by the various occasions.'[20] Thucydides does claim to report accurately the general content of the speech. They are, nevertheless, a device used by Thucydides, and other ancient historians, to present their own interpretations of the motives of the protagonists.

In this speech, Hermocrates argued that Sicily should be for the Sicilians, and that the cities should not ally themselves with outside powers, in this case Athens. Hermocrates admitted that as the most powerful city in Sicily, Syracuse, would benefit most from the adoption of this principle, but promised that they are ready 'to give up anything in reason'. He ended his speech with the promise that by adopting this policy the Sicilians will be ridding the island 'of the Athenians, and of civil war, and in future shall live in freedom at home, and be less menaced from abroad.'[21]

After Hermocrates' speech the Sicilians agreed to make peace on the basis that each would keep control of what they currently possessed. Camarina would keep control of Morgantina, which it had captured, after paying compensation to the Syracusans. This is probably one of the concessions that Hermocrates' promised. Hermocrates claimed to be protecting the freedom and autonomy of all states, but in reality he was attempting to safeguard the continuing power of the existing *hegemon*. The 'common peace' had been made, but, like many others to follow, it would collapse as soon as the *hegemonic* power was incapable of enforcing its provisions.

Hermocrates' speech also gives an interesting insight into the Machiavellian attitude of many ancient Greek politicians towards war. Early in the speech he mouthed the platitude: 'that war is an evil proposition is so familiar to everyone that it would be tedious to develop it.' Later in the address he more candidly admitted that 'as sensible men, if we call in allies and court danger, it should be in order to enrich our different countries with new acquisitions, and not ruin what they possess already.'[22] Here there is no cant about self-defence, war is portrayed as right provided that one wins and gains benefits, but wrong only if one loses.

As in every society, not everyone agreed with this view of war. A year before Hermocrates delivered his speech, the Athenian playwright Aristophanes won first prize for his anti-war play *The Acharnians*. In this work the main character Dicaeopolis, the 'honest citizen', comes to the 'assembly fully prepared to bawl, interrupt and abuse the speakers, if they talk of anything but peace.' Of course they do not make peace and as a result he makes his own separate treaty with Sparta. This allows him to enjoy the good things in life free of fear. At the end of the play Dicaeopolis is compared with the experienced general Lamachus, who elsewhere is described as 'a good soldier and a brave man.'[23] Aristophanes, instead of portraying him as brave and noble, makes him look shallow and corrupt when compared to the hedonistic Dicaeopolis. Lamachus would later be made one of the commanders of the next expedition to Sicily, where he would die in battle. The main theme of the play is to highlight the benefits of peace over the vainglory of war.

The allies of the Athenians informed the commanders of the expedition of their decision and the fact that they had been included in the treaty, without their agreement. The Athenian generals, believing that nothing further could be done, took their forces back to Athens. The Athenian assembly was outraged; they were so used to success that they believed that the generals must have taken bribes. Two were exiled and the other was fined. Such prosecutions by the democracies of ancient Greece are often seen as vexatious and politically motivated by many modern historians.

In a later prosecution of their generals by the citizens of Gela, Brian Caven asserts that such accusations were made 'no doubt quite falsely' and motivated by 'tension between the governing class and demos'.[24] Such claims ignore the fact that the non-democratic Spartans often punished their generals, including Pausanias the victor of Plataea, for similar behaviour. In ancient Greek politics the concept of conflict of interest was less important than it is now, and accepting gifts from friends or acquaintances, even from the enemy, was a normal part of political life. This left nearly all politicians open to such accusations. Success or popularity would usually protect one from such charges, whereas failure would often lead to prosecution and punishment.

The 'common peace' of the Syracusans did not last long. Soon after the peace was concluded, Leontini appears to have come under the control of the extreme democratic faction. They enrolled many new citizens and planned to carry out that most revolutionary of all policies, the redistribution of land. The upper classes, in an attempt at self-preservation, came to an agreement with Syracuse. They allied themselves with the Syracusans, drove out the *demos* and laid waste to their own city. They were then granted citizenship in Syracuse. With little effort, the Syracusans had realized their ambition to control Leontini. Some of the Leontine aristocrats later came to regret their treason and returned to the now-desolate city. They were joined by most of the exiled *demos* and, setting themselves up in fortified positions, began a guerrilla war against the Syracusans. Technically the Syracusans could claim not to have breached the peace, but their behaviour towards Leontini must have been viewed with some anxiety by the other cities, especially Naxos and Catane.

Despite the withdrawal of the fleet, the Athenians were not yet ready to abandon their designs on Sicily. In 422, after learning of the new outbreak of hostilities between Leontini and Syracuse, they sent a delegation, headed by Phaeax, to Sicily. The purpose of the mission was to see if they could build a new alliance against Syracuse on the pretext of saving the people of Leontini. Phaeax met with success in only two cities, both old enemies of Syracuse, Akragas and Camarina. Gela completely rejected his advances. Sensing that the rest of the Greek cities were also not interested in breaching the peace he headed north through the country of the Sicels. Next he stopped at Leontini, giving encouragement but nothing more. Finally he sailed back to Athens from Catane, having achieved nothing of consequence in Sicily.

Supposedly, the original Athenian expedition had been sent out with orders to assist the Leontines, prevent the export of Sicilian grain to the Pelopponesus and to ascertain if it would be possible to subjugate the entire island. They could claim in 424, after the congress, that they had met the first part of their orders. Whether they succeeded in their second task is not recorded, although it is likely that the war would have interfered with both wheat production and export. The commanders certainly would have been able to make an assessment of the military strength of the Sicilians, but whatever conclusions they reported were hotly disputed nine years later.

If, however, Diodorus, Thucydides and Plutarch were correct in claiming that the real aim of the expedition was the conquest of Sicily then it was a total failure. The end result was to leave Syracuse even more firmly in control of the eastern part of the island than it had been before the invasion.

Chapter 7

The Athenian Decision to Invade Sicily

Men were quite amazed at the boldness of the scheme and the magnificence of the spectacle, which were everywhere spoken of, no less than at the great disproportion of the force when compared with that of the enemy against whom it was intended. Never had a greater expedition been sent to a foreign land; never was there an enterprise in which the hope of future success seemed to be better justified by actual power.

Thucydides 6.31

The first ten years of the Peloponnesian War, from 431 to 421, are usually referred to as the Archidamian War, derived from the name of the Spartan king who led the invasions of Athenian territory. Although the war was fought over a widespread area, the initial strategies of pillaging both sides' territories had proved to be ineffective. In both Athens and Sparta, younger and more belligerent politicians began to demand more aggressive policies. Pericles died in 429 of a plague that had ravaged the beleaguered Athens for a number of years. The plague had mainly affected the wealthier classes and may have killed possibly as many as a third of the city's hoplites and cavalry. Pericles' place as the dominant Athenian politician was taken by the radical democrat Cleon.

In 425, the Athenians, under Cleon's leadership, seized and fortified a headland on the western coast of the Pelopponesus known as Pylos. It was to here that the relief fleet for Sicily had been briefly diverted. The Athenian goal was to provide a refuge for dissident Spartan helots and hopefully to provoke a revolt. The Spartans, realizing the threat, sent a force to occupy the island of Sphacteria, just off the headland, in order to blockade Pylos. The naval dominance of the Athenians ensured that the would-be besiegers instead became the besieged. The Spartan force included 120 of the Spartan ruling class and military elite, the Spartiates. The whole survival of the Spartan system relied on this group and their ability to militarily suppress the helots. They were, however, declining in numbers, from a population of around 5,000 in 479 to one of about 3,300 by 418.

Traditionally a Spartan was expected to 'come home with their shield or on it', that is to fight bravely to the death, being carried home dead on one's shield, rather than throwing it away and fleeing the battlefield. Cowards in Sparta were usually deprived of their citizenship and shunned by their peers. Nevertheless the Spartiates on Sphacteria did surrender, much to the astonishment of the rest of Greece. Their surrender gave the Athenians not only a base on Spartan territory but also a useful group of hostages.

Despite this the Spartans adopted their own offensive strategy, sending one of their best generals, Brasidas, to the north to attack Athens' subjects along the Thracian coast. Athens had come to rely heavily on wheat from the Black Sea to help feed the city. Although it could not have been known to the Athenians, it was probably a fungal infection in these wheat imports that had caused the plague. The reason it had affected the rich so heavily was that the poor could not afford wheat and instead ate barley. Control of the Thracian coast was essential for the security of the grain fleets as they sailed south to Athens.

Brasidas captured a number of cities, including the strategically important Amphipolis. At a battle near its walls in 422, Brasidas defeated the Athenians who were led by Cleon. More importantly, the two generals, both leaders of the new aggressive factions within their cities, were killed.

With the death of the leading pro-war proponents on both sides, the growing peace movements in both cities were able to gain control. The Spartans sought peace as their fifty-year peace treaty with their main Peloponnesian rival, Argos, was about to end. They also wanted to recover Pylos, which was becoming a haven for dissident helots, and to repatriate the captured Spartiates. The Athenians wanted time to allow both their revenues and population time to recover. They also wanted to recover their control of the Thracian coast.

The Peace of Nicias, named after its main Athenian proponent, was signed in 421. It immediately ran into problems. Two of Sparta's main allies, Corinth and Thebes, refused to ratify the treaty. Corinth refused to sign because it had lost many of its overseas possessions to Athens during the war and wished to recover its position. Thebes refused because it had done well during the conflict and did not want to give up any of its gains. Both threatened to ally themselves with Argos. Sparta, fearing isolation, surprisingly made an alliance with Athens.

This new alliance was doomed from the start. The newly liberated Thracian cities refused to be handed back to Athens, and the Spartans were unable, or unwilling, to force them. Although the Athenians returned the Spartan prisoners they refused to hand over Pylos until they had recovered the Thracian cities. Athens soon denounced the treaty and instead made an alliance with Argos. Things looked grim for Sparta, but in 418 it recovered its dominance with a complete victory over Argos and its allies at the Battle of Mantinea.

After the death of Cleon, the two dominant Athenian politicians were his opponent Nicias and Alcibiades. Nicias was the older of the two, being born about 470. Unlike Alcibiades he was not an aristocrat; instead, his family was newly rich. He made most of his money by owning more than 1,000 slaves and hiring them out to the state-owned silver mines. This was a particularly vicious form of earning income as conditions in the mines were brutal and the life expectancy of the slaves was short. In common with other rich men, Nicias spent his money conspicuously to gain the favour of the masses. He sponsored religious processions and theatre performances. Like many others who did the same, he became popular and was elected to important state offices.

After 427, Nicias was often elected as general, *strategos*. He had a consistent record of victories, albeit mostly in minor campaigns as he 'tried to evade commands which were likely to be laborious and long.'[1] His successes, and the fact that his name had its root in the Greek word for victory, *nike*, caused him to be considered as a lucky general by the Athenians, and a good luck charm for any expeditions he accompanied. He also cultivated an image of a hard-working official in Athens' interests, always staying back late and having little time for socializing. In creating this image Nicias made use of perhaps the world's first spin-doctor, his attendant Hiero, who not only instructed him in rhetoric but, 'was forever putting forth among the people moving tales about the life of severe hardships which his patron led for the sake of the city.'[2]

According to Plutarch, Nicias' career so far had been as the leader of 'the party of the rich and notable. These made him their champion to face the disgusting boldness of Cleon.' Plutarch does, nonetheless, portray him in a largely unflattering light:

> Timid as he was by nature, and distrustful of success, in war he managed to succeed in hiding his cowardice under a cloak of good fortune, for he was uniformly successful as a general; while in political life his nervousness, and the ease with which he could be put into confusion by accusers, actually tended to make him popular, and gave him in high degree that power which comes from the favour of the people, because they fear men who scorn them, but exalt men who fear them.[3]

One noted character trait of Nicias was that 'he was one of those who are excessively terrified at heavenly portents, and was addicted to divination, as Thucydides says. And . . . it is recorded that he sacrificed every day to the gods, and that he kept a diviner at his house'.[4] His excessive superstition would later have terrible consequences for the Athenians under his command.

Nicias had been the main proponent of the policy of an alliance with Sparta, believing Athens should concentrate its diminished resources in recovering its losses from the war.

Alcibiades, although also incredibly wealthy, was different in almost all other aspects to his rival. He was much younger, born about 450, and was an aristocrat from one of the oldest noble families in Athens, the Alcmaeonidae. In contrast to Nicias, he was flamboyant, a brilliant orator and supposedly physically beautiful. In a society where physical beauty was so valued that the word for it, *kalos*, was also the word for good, his appearance gave Alcibiades a huge advantage over his rivals. He was courageous in battle and would later prove to be possibly Athens' best general of the war. Like most of the aristocrats of the period he 'was naturally a man of many strong passions, the mightiest of which were the love of rivalry and the love of pre-eminence.'[5] After the death of Cleon, he became the leader of the faction that wanted to continue the war against the Spartans. With the failure of this policy after the Battle of Mantinea, he temporarily lost influence to Nicias.

Although he was constantly looked to by the *demos* for leadership in times of crisis he was never trusted by them, perhaps because according to Plutarch he 'was the most unscrupulous of men'.[6] The Athenians twice voted to send him into exile. As Aristophanes described, the people's attitude was one where 'she loves, and hates, and longs to have him back.'[7] Thucydides blamed his character for this as, 'his habits gave offence to everyone, and caused them to commit affairs to other hands.'[8] He believed that Alcibiades' second exile was one of the main causes of the final Athenian defeat.

The two were different in age, temperament and foreign policy aims. The comic poets make much of the growing differences between the generations in Athens. The young, growing up with war, were considered to be belligerent and adventurous. The older generation were portrayed as cautious and inclined to peace. Nicias and Alcibiades were the archetypes of these two stereotypes.

One of the few times the two joined together was to arrange the ostracism and exile of the new radical democratic leader Hyperbolus. This affair was viewed as so sordid, even by the politically robust Athenians, that the process of ostracism was never used again. This made the popular and flamboyant Alcibiades temporarily the *de facto* leader of the people, but it was never an easy relationship. They always suspected him of aspiring to become the next Athenian tyrant. Nicias and Alcibiades would play crucial roles in the decision to go to war against Syracuse.

In 416 the simmering border dispute between Segesta and Selinus broke out into full-scale warfare. The Segestans attacked Selinuntian settlers on what they believed to be their side of the border. Both sides mobilized their armies and a battle was fought, with Selinus being the victor. The Segestans now looked around for allies, approaching Akragas, Carthage and Syracuse. All refused to assist. They did, however, find a friend in the Leontines, as both were allies of Athens.

A joint embassy was sent to Athens in the winter of 416/5. The sources constantly emphasize Athens' ambitions toward conquering Sicily, and the two found ready supporters among a large section of the Athenians, particularly Alcibiades. The Segestans emphasized the Syracusans' crimes against Leontini. They also tried to frighten the Athenians with visions of a Sicily united behind Syracuse sending an expedition to assist their Dorian brothers, the Spartans. More importantly, they offered to pay the cost for an expedition of sixty triremes to come to the island. The promised amount would have been sixty talents of silver per month. Such a figure was extremely high; perhaps half, or even all, of the revenues of a city of Segesta's size for a whole year. The Segestans claimed that they held much accumulated wealth in their temples which they could use. Although the cities of Sicily were proverbially rich, even the optimistic Athenians were sceptical. They voted to send a delegation to Segesta that same winter, to check out their claims.

The Segestans succeeded in hoodwinking the embassy. They filled their temples with money borrowed from their citizens and other friendly cities. They also richly entertained their guests, moving the gold dinner sets from home to home. The embassy returned to Athens the following spring, with the first sixty talents payment and glowing reports of Segesta's supposed wealth.

Meanwhile, Alcibiades and his supporters had been doing everything to convince the Athenians of the benefits of the campaign. Once Sicily was captured, they claimed that the Athenians could then use its resources to capture Carthage, Libya and Spain, or to conquer the Pelopponesus. Plutarch gives us an engaging image of the armchair strategists of Athens:

> The youth in their training-schools and the old men in their work-shops and lounging-places would sit in clusters drawing maps of Sicily, charts of the sea about it, and plans of the harbours and districts of the island which look towards Libya. For they did not regard Sicily itself as the prize of the war, but rather as a mere base of operations, purposing there from to wage a contest with the Carthaginians and get possession of both Libya and of all the sea this side of the Pillars of Heracles.[9]

The Athenian assembly now met and voted to send an expedition to Sicily of sixty triremes commanded by three of their generals: Alcibiades, Nicias and Lamachus. Their orders were to assist Segesta against Selinus, restore the Leontines to their city if possible, 'and to order all other matters in Sicily as they should deem best for the interests of Athens'.[10] As with the earlier expedition, these orders allowed the generals a free hand to annex as much of Sicily as they thought possible. Diodorus gives some idea of what the best interests of Athens were, 'that they would enslave the Selinuntians and Syracusans, but upon the other peoples they would merely lay a tribute which they would pay annually to the Athenians.'[11] Thucydides claims that the Athenians only made such grandiose plans because they were always overly optimistic of success, and where it came to Sicily, 'most of them being ignorant of its size and the number of its inhabitants'.[12]

Nicias was, nonetheless, still strongly opposed to the campaign and to playing any part in its command. Five days later another assembly was called to plan the expedition. Nicias used this as an opportunity to have the decision reversed. He argued that it was foolish to embark on any overseas adventure while still engaged militarily closer to home. At this time Athens was still giving assistance to Argos against Sparta, although it was not openly at war with the latter. It was also engaged in a campaign, at Nicias' instigation, against Macedonia in an attempt to regain its losses in Thrace. Nicias pointed out that so far the Syracusans had done little to assist Sparta and were unlikely to do so unless provoked by the Athenians.

Alcibiades then addressed the assembly, defending the expedition. He dismissed the military strength of the Sicilians, claiming it was exaggerated and that they were unwarlike and unpatriotic. Alcibiades also claimed that the subject Sicels would also join the Athenians to free themselves from their hated Syracusan masters. He further argued that the conquest of Sicily and its resources would allow them to become the masters of the entire Greek world. Plutarch has the further conquest of Carthage and the entire western Mediterranean as the ultimate goal.

Nicias replied with a different argument, claiming that the planned expedition was too small to achieve anything against the wealthy, numerous and well-armed Sicilians, and that few of the Sicilian cities would side with Leontini against Syracuse. He offered to resign his command as he could not, in all conscience, support such a futile campaign. Nicias claimed that for Athens to achieve anything in Sicily it would have to send a much larger expedition, and would have to supply the bulk of the funding. Nicias' goal was to try and dissuade the Athenians from mounting such a large-scale and costly invasion.

He had, however, totally misjudged the mood of the assembly. One speaker called his bluff, asking exactly how large a force he would need. Nicias, now cornered, answered that he would need at least 100 triremes, 5,000 hoplites and large numbers of light infantry. The assembly then voted to supply the expedition with these forces. They also voted to give the generals full powers, allowing them to make decisions on the spot rather than constantly having to refer back to the assembly in Athens.

The selection of the three generals was again the type of compromise that democratic regimes were forced to make. The assembly probably thought that by appointing both Alcibiades and Nicias as commanders they would be able to keep check on one's ambition and the other's reticence. In order to prevent deadlocks they also appointed the bluff, no-nonsense soldier Lamachus to share command. In reality it would mean that, initially at least, no coherent strategy could be followed. In addition to his opposition to the campaign, Nicias had another reason for wishing to be relieved of his command: he was suffering from a disease of the kidneys. The side-effects of his illness included lethargy and the inability to make decisions, traits that would further exacerbate his limitations as a commander. Furthermore, Nicias was *proxenos* in Athens for Syracuse, and therefore must have had many connections within that city. The Athenians may, however, have thought this to have been an advantage rather than a drawback.

The planned invasion was so popular in fact that people were competing with one another to provide ships and to volunteer as hoplites. In Athens, and most of Greece, triremes were funded by assigning the cost to one wealthy individual on a rotational basis, a form of taxation. If times were hard this could be varied by having several people combine to meet the costs. Hoplites were usually conscripted. The state would call them up by year of birth and tribe. This latter division could have a historic origin based on place or ethnicity, or could be, as in the case of the ten tribes of Athens, a later, artificial political grouping.

To many modern observers it seems amazing that Athens would so recklessly embark on such an ambitious campaign of conquest. This view ignores, however, the reality of the dog-eat-dog nature of power politics in the ancient world. It was believed that the only way to remain a great power was to continually expand and stay ahead of one's rivals. These ambitions are perhaps best described by Pyrrhus of Epirus, who, according to Plutarch, planned that after annexing all of Italy, he desired to conquer Sicily, Carthage, Libya, Macedonia and all of Greece.[13] At least Pyrrhus' grandiose schemes had a limit. The poet Alkaios of Messene claims that after conquering the land and the sea Philip V planned to march on Olympus itself. Pyrrhus' wish list is very similar to that of Alcibiades, who described the reality of empire to the Athenian assembly:

> Moreover, we cannot fix the exact point at which our empire shall stop; we have reached a position in which we must not be content with retaining what we have but must scheme to extend it for, if we cease to rule others, we shall be in danger of being ruled ourselves.[14]

Once the decision to sail had been made, the Athenians prepared for the campaign with great enthusiasm. A number of evil omens are recorded but the Athenians either disbelieved them or preferred other, more favourable, forecasts. One evil omen, however, could not be ignored. In the early June of 415 the Athenians awoke to find that their stone statues of the god Hermes had been mutilated. Their faces had been ruined and their erect penises smashed off. Every home in Athens had such a statue for good luck.

Hermes was also the god of travellers and the desecration was obviously aimed to produce an evil portent for the coming expedition. Religion and the state in ancient Greece were closely intertwined and such a sacrilege would have been seen as an act of treason. Most Athenians considered, correctly as it turned out, that the desecration was part of an oligarchic plot against the democracy.

Alcibiades, due both to his aristocratic background and an earlier prank where he had profaned some sacred rites, was suspected of being involved. He denied this and asked that any charges be brought against him, in order to clear his name, before he sailed for Sicily. Alcibiades believed, rightly, that his enemies would use his absence to bring charges against him. His request was ignored.

In July 415, with a cloud still hanging over the head of one of its commanders, the Athenian fleet sailed out of harbour. Supposedly, the entire population of the city turned out to watch the spectacle. It was the largest naval expedition that the city had ever sent out and the best-equipped. The commanders of the triremes and the soldiers had vied with one another to obtain the most ornate and expensive equipment. When describing the departure, Thucydides is clearly playing up the magnificence of the spectacle, and the hopes of the Athenians, in order to later enhance the pathos of the final destruction of the expedition.

The fleet sailed to Corcyra where it was joined by the allies. The final invasion force numbered 134 triremes, 100 of which were Athenian and 34 allied. Of the Athenian ships, 60 were outfitted to carry troops. The land force was made up of 5,100 hoplites, of whom 2,200 were Athenians, plus 1,300 light infantry and 30 cavalry.[15] In addition, the fleet also included 30 merchant ships carrying equipment and tradesmen, and 100 smaller vessels. Tagging on behind the fleet were large numbers of other vessels owned by private traders. These merchants were essential to any ancient Greek force, as they sold supplies to the army and/or fleet. The pay of a Greek soldier or sailor traditionally consisted of two parts: a cash payment for attending, and the supply of provisions – usually grain, but any sort of food would suffice. As time went by, it was found more convenient to replace the provisions with an additional cash payment. By the time of the fifth century, a single, combined cash payment was the norm. Soldiers were then expected to buy their own food, and other necessities, from a local or accompanying market.

The Syracusans, having received reports of the Athenian fleet, called an assembly to discuss what to do. Hermocrates spoke first. He was remarkably well informed with regard to the Athenian expedition, including the reluctance of one of its commanders. No doubt he had been in contact with his aristocratic friends in Athens. He advised sending envoys to the Sicels and their Greek allies. Hermocrates even recommended that they send an embassy to their old enemy the Carthaginians, claiming that they had long feared an Athenian invasion. He also advocated an aggressive defence, sending a fleet to Tarentum to confront the invaders and catch them unawares while their ships were still heavily laden. Few in the assembly supported Hermocrates' plan and it is not hard to deduce why. The first part of the plan was sound but the sending of a fleet to Tarentum was extremely foolhardy. The biggest fleet recorded for Syracuse since Himera was the thirty ships it had sent to Messene during the last Athenian invasion. In the coming war the largest would be the eighty ships that were easily defeated by sixty Athenian vessels. Any force the Syracusans sent would be bound to be defeated by the seventy-four battle-ready triremes of the Athenians.

Athenagoras, the leader of the popular party, spoke against Hermocrates' proposal, claiming that the reports were only rumours and that even if true the Athenians could not possibly bring a force large enough to threaten Syracuse. He claimed that the reports had been exaggerated by the oligarchs, who wished to frighten the *demos* and have themselves appointed to positions of extreme power. He then goes on to defend democracy and condemn oligarchy in harsh terms, a speech certainly only possible if Syracuse was a functioning democracy. Thucydides uses the debate to contrast the apparent wisdom of his hero, Hermocrates, to the supposed paranoia and lack of judgement of his democratic rivals.

Athenagoras, although he would be proven wrong in regard to the fleet, was perhaps politically wiser in his opposition than he is often given credit for. If a fleet had been sent, the crews would have consisted mostly of the poor. Even if only thirty ships had been sent this would have meant that about 6,000 of Athenagoras' supporters would have been absent from the city at the time of a possible military crisis. Only those citizens actually present could vote in a Greek assembly. These were exactly the times that would-be tyrants often emerged, using the emergency to have themselves voted extraordinary powers. Later, in 411, the Athenian oligarchs would use the absence of their fleet to allow them to gain the numbers in the assembly and to overthrow the democracy.

Generals were elected officials; the Athenians elected ten annually and the Syracusans fifteen. In most Greek states they had the power to call assemblies in emergency situations. On this occasion the generals were presiding over the assembly and brought the discussion to a close. They decided against Hermocrates' plan, but to take measures to prepare the city and to send out agents to determine the truth of the reports. Here we see a possible example of the limitations of Syracuse's democracy. The generals take matters into their own hands with no record of a vote of the assembly being taken. It is, however, also possible that Thucydides simply did not mention a vote, thinking it too obvious to record.

From Corcyra the Athenian fleet sailed along the southern coast of Italy, hoping to win new allies, but they were to be disappointed. Tarentum, a Spartan colony, and Locri, both long-term friends of Syracuse, refused to even let them land on their territory. The other cities provided them with water and markets but refused to ally with them, or even allow them into their cities. The biggest set-back came at Rhegium, a long-standing Athenian ally and the base for the earlier campaign. The Rhegians refused to ally with the Athenians or to allow them to use their city as a base. They claimed that they would do as the other Italians had, a diplomatic way of saying that they too would remain neutral. The Athenian commanders now waited for the return of ships which had gone on ahead to Segesta in order to determine the real situation in regard to the promised money, before deciding what to do next.

While they waited, the Syracusans received confirmation from their own spies, and others, that the Athenian fleet was at Rhegium. They now began serious preparations, inspecting their arms and garrisoning the forts around Syracuse and many of the cities of their Sicel subjects. The latter measure would also have been taken to ensure the Sicels' loyalty during the coming conflict

The ships that had gone to Segesta now returned to the Athenians at Rhegium with a report that no more money would be forthcoming. The Athenian expedition had not got off to a good start. The expected funds were not there. The Italian Greek cities were remaining neutral. Especially disappointing was the response of the Rhegians, who might have been expected to join them because they were kinsmen of the Leontines and had been, up to that point, faithful allies of the Athenians. In low spirits the Athenian generals had now to plan their coming campaign.

With major parts of their planned campaign in disarray, the disadvantages of generalship by committee, especially when two members were bitter political rivals, now began to show. The political and personal beliefs of each of the three would influence their decision making.

Nicias proposed that they should sail against Selinus, demand the funds for sixty ships from the Segestans, and bring about an agreement between Selinus and Segesta, either through negotiations or by force if necessary. They should then sail along the coast and display the power of Athens. If they could obtain more support in this way they could then assist the Leontines. If not, they should sail back to Athens and not risk the fleet any further. Nicias, who had always opposed the expedition, was proposing that they undertake the bare minimum that the assembly had ordered and go home as soon as possible.

Alcibiades claimed that it would be disgraceful to return to Athens without achieving anything. Instead, they should send embassies seeking allies to every city of Sicily, except Selinus and Syracuse. They should also try to persuade the Sicels to revolt from the Syracusans. These new allies could provide supplies and reinforcements. Most importantly, they should try to win over the Messenians, as their city possessed a fine harbour. Future events would show that Alcibiades had already made contact with a pro-Athenian faction within the city. As has already been noted, such groups were never hard to find, given the vicious nature of Greek intra-city politics. Only once these cities had come over to them should the Athenians then attack Selinus and Syracuse, unless they too agreed to the Athenians' demands.

Lamachus, who as far as can be deduced had little political support or ambition, presented a third option. He proposed that they sail directly to Syracuse and fight as soon as possible under the walls of the city. This would take the Syracusans by surprise. They would be forced to fight unprepared and be defeated, or, if they chose not to give battle, the Athenians could ravage their territory and collect provisions. Either result would encourage the other Sicilian Greeks to come over to them.

Lamachus' strategy was considered by Thucydides, another Athenian general, Demosthenes, and most modern commentators to be the best option. He lacked, however, the prestige of the other two commanders, being far less wealthy, less well-born and a political nonentity. Neither of the other two would support such a risky plan. Lamachus then broke the deadlock by supporting Alcibiades' scheme rather the do-nothing strategy of Nicias. This plan was, however, clearly self-serving on Alcibiades' part. It would rely heavily on his skills as a negotiator and provide him with a network of allies throughout Sicily. Once he had built his own power base in this way he could then embark on his more ambitious plans of conquest.

Chapter 8

Nicias' First Attack on Syracuse

Instead of this, while Lamachus urged that they sail direct to Syracuse and give battle close to the city, and Alcibiades that they rob the Syracusans of their allied cities first and then proceed against them, Nicias proposed and urged in opposition that they make their way quietly by sea along the coasts of Sicily, circumnavigate the island, make a display of their troops and triremes, and then sail back of Athens, after having first culled out a small part of their force to give the Segestans a taste of succor. In this way he soon relaxed the resolution and depressed the spirits of his men.

Plutarch, *Nicias* 14

The first and most important part of Alcibiades' plan was to win over Messene. He sailed across the straits and proposed an alliance. The Messenians followed, however, the same policy as the Italian cities, refusing the Athenians admission to the city but allowing a market for them outside the walls. The pro-Athenian faction within the city obviously had not been able to win over the rest of the population. The sheer size of the Athenian force may have been a negative factor in the attempt to convince the cities of Sicily and Italy to ally with them. It gave credence to the Syracusans' claims that the Athenians had come to subjugate all the Greeks of the west.

The Athenians now sent sixty ships to Naxos, while the rest of the fleet remained in Rhegium. The Naxians, not unexpectedly, allowed them into their city. Next they sailed to Catane but here the pro-Syracusan party had gained control and denied them admission into the city. On the following day they sent a squadron of ten ships right into the Great Harbour of Syracuse to determine the preparedness of the Syracusan navy and defences. On board one of the ships a herald proclaimed artfully that the Athenians had come to restore the Leontines to their city, and that any Leontines within the city should abandon Syracuse and join with them. Meeting no resistance, the fleet then made a reconnaissance around the harbour, most likely surveying the best landing places.

The fleet returned to Catane and this time met with greater success. The Catanians held an assembly and invited the Athenian generals to address it.

While Alcibiades was speaking, the Athenians broke into the city, through a poorly guarded and maintained section of the walls, occupying the *agora*. With the Athenians within the walls, the pro-Syracusan faction fled the city. The remaining citizens, no doubt intimidated by the Athenians, voted for an alliance. The whole incident appears to have been stage-managed with the help of a fifth column within the city. The Athenians then moved their entire force to Catane and built a fortified camp outside the walls. After a false start at Messene, Alcibiades' strategy had finally brought results, although not unexpected ones. Naxos and Catane were fellow Ionians and had been long-standing allies of the Leontines. The Athenians now had a secure base within one day's sailing of Syracuse.

Meanwhile, reports came that the Syracusans were preparing their fleet. News also came from Camarina, another old enemy of Syracuse, that if the Athenians would send a force they too would ally with them. The entire Athenian fleet set sail. First they went to Syracuse, where they found that the tardy Syracusans still had not prepared their fleet. Next they sailed to Camarina but the citizens there declared that a previous oath had bound them not to receive the Athenians if they came with more than one ship. Again the size of the fleet had possibly frightened potential allies and Alcibiades' strategy had once more been thwarted.

On the return voyage to Catane, the Athenians decided to ravage Syracuse's territory. As well as intimidating the enemy, plundering their territory was also a useful method of raising much-needed funds. A unit of Syracusan cavalry, however, caught a unit of Athenian light infantry and destroyed them. The Syracusan superiority in cavalry would quickly become a severe problem for the Athenians during the first year of the invasion.

Meanwhile, in Athens, Alcibiades' fears had been realized. Charges of impiety had been brought against him. When the fleet returned to Catane it found the official trireme of Athens, the *Salaminia*, waiting. They had a summons for Alcibiades, and others, to return to Athens and stand trial. The delegation had, however, been ordered to conduct the arrest quietly so as not to alarm their own troops and particularly the allies, many of whom had close ties to Alcibiades. He was allowed to return in his own ship, sailing alongside the *Salaminia*.

The unsecured Alcibiades used the opportunity to escape at Thurii. He was unwilling to trust in Athenian justice, claiming 'in the matter of life I wouldn't trust even my own mother not to mistake a black for a white ballot when she cast her vote.' Alcibiades, now an exile, crossed from Thurii to the Peloponnesus. The Athenian assembly condemned him and his companions to death. Hearing this he threatened to 'show them . . . that I'm alive.' Alcibiades soon deserted to the Spartans and gave them advice on how to bring 'ruin and destruction to his native city.'[1] His first act of betrayal was to denounce the Athenian sympathizers in Messene. It is little wonder that the Athenian *demos* never fully trusted him, nor other Greek democracies their own aristocrats. Their inflated egos and sense of self-importance tended to be more important to them than any sense of patriotism.

With Alcibiades gone there were now only two Athenian generals in Sicily. Lamachus' lack of wealth and prestige meant that in reality Nicias was now in supreme command of the expedition. Despite the obvious lack of preparation of the Syracusans, Nicias chose to follow his own strategy, rather than attack Syracuse directly, as proposed by Lamachus. The fleet now sailed along the north coast of Sicily towards Segesta and Selinus. Plutarch condemns Nicias thus: 'always using his forces in a cautious and hesitating manner, he first gave the enemy courage by cruising around Sicily as far as possible from them, and . . . won their utter contempt.'[2]

During the voyage the Athenians were refused entry at Himera. They then took Hyccara, a small Sicanian city to the west of Panormus, which was at war with Segesta. They handed the city over to the Segestans and sold the population into slavery for 120 talents. The Segestans provided the Athenians with a small force of much-needed cavalry and another thirty talents. With this minor success achieved, Nicias abandoned his intention of sailing against Selinus. The troops now marched overland through the land of the Sicels, trying to win over allies. They assaulted one town, but failed to take it, and returned to Catane. Nicias' campaign had achieved little of note except collecting enough cash to keep his force paid for another month. With this the summer ended.

The mild Sicilian winter does not, however, prevent military operations. The Syracusans, emboldened by Nicias' failure to attack them, now sent their cavalry to harass the Athenians and ravage the countryside of the Catanians. The raiders taunted the Athenians with the accusations that they had only come to occupy Catane rather than liberate Leontini.

Nicias, spurred by the sneers of both his enemies and friends, finally decided to take direct action against Syracuse. First, he devised a stratagem to draw the Syracusans away from their city. He sent an agent to pretend to be a friend of Syracuse and to tell them that he and his friends were prepared to betray the Athenian camp. With the Syracusan forces away, Nicias would land the Athenian fleet in the Great Harbour and occupy the Temple of Zeus, to the south of the city, as a base. This site is the main high point on the plain south of Syracuse. It stands about 1km from the coast, and is well protected on its northern side by steep slopes.

Nicias' strategy worked as planned; the now over-confident Syracusans took the bait and marched their whole army against Catane while he landed his forces unopposed. According to Plutarch:

This was the best generalship that Nicias displayed in Sicily. He brought his enemy out of their city in full force, thereby almost emptying it of defenders, while he himself put out to sea from Catane, got control of the enemy's harbours, and seized a spot for his camp where he was confident that he would suffer least injury from that arm of the service in which he was inferior, the cavalry, and meet no hindrance in fighting with that arm whereon he most relied.[3]

At dawn the Athenians disembarked, close to the temple and south of the River Anapus. At the same time the Syracusan cavalry, scouting ahead of the army, discovered that they had been tricked and that the Athenian army had sailed. The Syracusan commanders immediately turned their army around and marched home. The march from Catane to Syracuse is a long one, about 60km by road. Although the infantry had not made the entire march, the return trip would require hard marching and would result in many of the hoplites straggling.

Rather than land close to the city, build a camp near to it, and attack it while still having the element of surprise, the ever-cautious Nicias landed 5km south of the city. The Athenians then spent their time building a camp and preparing for battle in a location where the Syracusan superiority in cavalry would be neutralized. Thucydides describes the Athenian preparations and positions as:

Being flanked on one side by walls, houses, and trees, and by a marsh, and on the other by cliffs. They also felled the neighbouring trees and carried them down to the sea, and formed a palisade alongside of their ships, and with stones (which they picked up) and wood, hastily raised a fort at Dascon, the most vulnerable point of their position, and broke down the bridge over the Anapus.[4]

This strategy of course relied on the supposition that the Syracusans would come and fight; fortunately for the Athenians they did. Nicias' continuing tentative approach to the war had caused him, and the Athenians, to be held in contempt by their enemy. This disdain was expressed by Hermocrates who claimed 'as he sought to encourage the Syracusans, that Nicias was ridiculous in manoeuvring so as not to give battle, as though it was not for battle that he had crossed the seas.'[5]

The first of the Syracusans to return were the cavalry, followed by their infantry. Despite their exhausting march, the now-confident Syracusans marched right up to Athenian position and offered battle. Nicias again refused to fight and ordered the Athenians to retire to their camp. Finally, on the next day, the Athenians marched out to give battle. There is some dispute among modern historians about whether the battle was fought north or south of the river, with some claiming that the Athenians crossed to the north of the river to form their battle line. From having walked the area I am convinced that the topography to the south of the river closely matches the description in Thucydides. The Athenians would have been able to guard their left flank against the hill of the Temple of Zeus and their right on the marshy ground near the coast. The land to the north of the river is open plain, with nowhere for the Athenians to guard their exposed left flank. Arguments that the Syracusans would not have crossed the river due to Nicias destroying the bridges ignore the fact that the river is no great obstacle and can be easily waded.

The Athenians formed up with only half their hoplites in the front line in the traditional eight ranks. The rest formed a hollow oblong behind them defending the baggage and servants, with orders to advance if any part of the line was under pressure. The Athenians had received a few reinforcements from the Sicilians and Sicels, so their front line would have contained about 2,500 to 3,000 hoplites. They formed up with the Argives and Mantineans on the right, Athenians in the centre and the other allies on the left.

Thucydides describes the Syracusan dispositions as follows:

> The Syracusans, meanwhile, formed their hoplites sixteen deep, consisting of the mass levy of their own people, and such allies as had joined them, the strongest contingent being that of the Selinuntians; next to them the cavalry of the Geloans, numbering two hundred in all, with twenty horse and about fifty archers from Camarina. The cavalry, full twelve hundred, was posted on the right, and next to them the darters [javelin-men].[6]

As the Syracusan hoplites matched the length of the Athenian line, this would have meant that they numbered from five to six thousand hoplites. This number included some allied hoplites from Selinus, but as they too were a target of the invasion, and at war with Segesta, they were unlikely to have sent more than a token force. Although Thucydides states that it was the whole Syracusan army, it is unlikely that this could have been the full levy of Syracuse's hoplites, which had numbered substantially more than 7,000 in 462. Many were probably still straggling their way back from Catane. Others showed a lack of discipline and 'not expecting an immediate engagement . . . some had even gone away to the city, which was close by; these now ran up as fast as they could, and though late, took their places here or there in the main as they joined it.'[7] This lack of discipline among the Syracusans is a constant theme in Thucydides. It is hardly surprising, as the Syracusans had probably not fought a serious battle since they had defeated the Sicels in 440. This victory, it is claimed by Diodorus, had ushered in a lengthy period of relative peace, broken only by the Athenian invasion in 427 and the war against Leontini.

Just before the battle began, Nicias, in the normal manner of ancient generals, went along the line and addressed his troops. This was usually done to rouse the troops' spirits. He started by emphasizing the superior skill of the Athenian army but finished with the negative thought that 'we must conquer or hardly get away, as we shall have their horse upon us in great numbers. Remember, therefore, your renown, and go boldly against the enemy, thinking the present difficulty and necessity more terrible than they.'[8] This was hardly an inspiring message to give under the circumstances.

The battle began with the usual exchange of missiles by the skirmishing light infantry in front of the main battle lines, and the taking of omens by the priests. As the lines advanced, Thucydides gives us an interesting insight into the possible attitude of Athens', and perhaps most other, conscripted allies: 'the subject allies owed most of their ardour to the desire for self-preservation which they could only hope for if victorious and as a secondary motive, for the chance of serving on easier terms after helping the Athenians to a fresh conquest.'[9]

Eventually, the light infantry retired and the two lines of hoplites clashed. Xenophon gives us some idea of the nature of such fighting when two phalanxes 'crash front to front . . . with shields interlocked they shoved and fought and fought and shoved, dealing death and yielding life. There was no shouting, nor yet was there even silence, but a strange and smothered utterance, such as rage and battle vent.'[10] The Syracusans at first fought well, but during the battle a storm broke out, and with it came thunder, lightning and heavy rain. The inexperienced troops of the Syracusans considered this to be a terrible omen, whereas the veteran Athenians and their allies were more used to this type of event and thought it not unusual if one fought in winter.

The Argives, on the Athenian right, first gained the ascendancy, routed the Syracusans in front of them and made a hole in their line. The rest of the Syracusan army, losing heart, also broke. Thucydides speaks well of the courage of the losers, stating that 'lack of zeal or daring was certainly not the fault of the Syracusans, either in this or other battles, but although not in-ferior in courage' it was their lack of military experience that proved inadequate.[11]

The Athenians were unable to press their pursuit of the defeated infantry too far as the uncommitted Syracusan cavalry intervened and 'wherever they saw hoplites advancing from the ranks attacked and drove them back.'[12] The Athenians advanced as far as was prudent and then returned to their camp and claimed the victory by raising a trophy. Due to the lack of pursuit losses on both sides were relatively light, 260 dead on the Syracusan side, and 50 on the Athenian.[13]

Once the pursuit came to an end the Syracusans rallied. It is at this point that Nicias committed another of his many serious errors during the campaign. Although the Athenians held the field, he delayed in sending any troops to hold the important hill of the Temple of Zeus. This allowed the Syracusans to send a detachment to occupy and barricade the hill. Plutarch claims that 'Nicias purposely delayed operations until it was too late, and allowed a garrison from Syracuse to enter in, because he thought that if his soldiers plundered the temple's treasures the commonwealth would get no advantage from it, and he himself would incur the blame for the sacrilege.'[14] If true, this would not be the only time that Nicias' superstitious nature would hinder Athenian operations. Whatever the reasoning, not occupying the hill was a terrible oversight. The Syracusans would later use the temple as a base from which to conduct continual cavalry raids to harass the Athenians.

The next day, the Syracusans, as was customary in the aftermath of battles between the Greeks, received their dead for burial under a truce. The Athenians then, having secured the victory, gathered any booty they had stripped from the Syracusan dead and sailed back to Catane to spend the winter. Both Diodorus and Thucydides explain this remarkable decision by emphasizing that the lack of Athenian cavalry put the army at a huge disadvantage when facing the Syracusans. Thucydides also states that the Sicilian cities would be more likely to ally with them after the victory. The Athenians intended to return in the spring after they had received reinforcements of money and cavalry from home and from the Sicilians.

Nicias' decision to retire has been roundly condemned by historians both modern and ancient, including Thucydides himself. Thucydides uses the later Athenian commander Demosthenes to deliver his verdict that Nicias 'by wintering in Catane instead of at once attacking Syracuse had allowed the terror of his first arrival to evaporate in contempt and had given time for Gylippus to arrive with a force from the Peloponnesus.[15] By placing the Syracusans immediately under siege he could have prevented them from receiving outside aid.

Plutarch, no admirer of Nicias, supports this verdict, claiming that 'Of his victory, which was so noised about, he made no use whatever, but after a few days had elapsed withdrew again to Naxos.'[16] Only a few months after the battle, in March 414, Aristophanes, in his play *The Birds*, was making fun of Nicias' timid leadership: 'by Zeus! it's no longer the time to delay and loiter like Nicias; let us act as promptly as possible.'[17]

Donald Kagan makes an attempt to explain Nicias' withdrawal and refusal to immediately besiege the city. He defends him by writing that the significance of the Syracusan superiority in cavalry 'has been greatly underestimated', and that 'any detachments sent out to dig trenches or build encircling walls, however, would be vulnerable to attack by the Syracusan cavalry'. Despite this, he too concludes that by not taking the risk to immediately lay siege to Syracuse, while the defenders were demoralized by their defeat, he committed 'a strategic error that was probably the main cause of the expedition's failure.'[18]

If there was no intention of besieging Syracuse, then the mounting of this expedition appears to have been largely pointless and foolhardy. Nicias already had plenty of evidence of the Syracusan superiority in cavalry from their raids on Catane. If he did not intend to besiege the city then the most likely reason for the action, as Thucydides states, appears to be an attempt to lift Athenian morale and demonstrate Athenian superiority in arms, in order to impress the so far uncommitted Sicilian and Italian Greek cities. If this is correct, it does not appear to have brought any success worthy of the risk, that of being defeated and trapped in hostile territory. Nicias, in his speech to his troops, demonstrated that he was well aware of this danger. Although daring and well carried out, the whole operation appears to have been ill-conceived from the beginning. It seems to have been done merely for the sake of appearing to do something.

If the desired result was to impress the Sicilians, then events over the rest of the winter showed that it had made little impact. After departing from Syracuse the Athenians sailed to Messene, expecting that the city would be betrayed to them. Here, however, Alcibiades' treason began to influence events. The pro-Syracusan party seized power and executed the partisans of Athens. They placed the city on an armed footing and refused the Athenians admission. Next they sent a delegation to win over Camarina, which had been allied to them during the previous war. The Syracusans despatched Hermocrates, suspecting that the Camarinians would not be willing to assist them any longer now that the Athenians had gained a victory. The two embassies addressed the assembly but in the end the Camarinians decided to remain neutral, fearing both sides' motives. 'They sympathized with the Athenians, except insofar as they might be afraid of their sub-jugating Sicily, and they had always been at enmity with their neighbour Syracuse.'[19]

The Athenians also approached the Sicels. A few of those that remained independent joined the Athenians and supplied them with food and money. Expeditions were sent against those who refused; a few were forced into submission but most were protected by their Syracusan garrisons. In addition to their diplomacy in Sicily they sent a trireme back to Athens asking for money and cavalry, and embassies to the Etruscans and Carthaginians. The Etruscans, old enemies of the Greeks, would send a few ships and troops but the Carthaginians stood aloof. Plutarch perhaps best sums up the lack of success over the winter period, claiming that Nicias had spent the time 'making large outlays on his vast armament, but effecting little in his negoti-ations with the few Sicels who thought of coming over to his side.'[20]

The Syracusans, by contrast, would spend the winter much more productively. Immediately after the defeat they called an assembly. Hermocrates addressed the people and encouraged them to continue their resistance. He too blamed the defeat on a lack of experience rather than courage, suggesting that they should also increase the number of hoplites by providing arms for the poor and spend the coming winter improving their drill and discipline. Hermocrates also claimed that they had too many generals and should elect fewer but give them full powers. He also implied that with fewer generals 'their secrets would be better kept'.[21] This last statement was surely a veiled accusation that some within the city, by implication the democrats, were in contact with the enemy.

These brief passages in Thucydides are some of the very few descriptions we have of the debates within the Syracusan assembly. They do demonstrate that, in common with other Greek democracies, internal politics in Syracuse were a constant struggle for power between the oligarchs and the democrats. Hermocrates' proposal was of course the very concept that the democratic leaders had earlier opposed vigorously. Defeat appears, however, to have made the people more amenable to his motion. Stung by their loss, the *demos* were now prepared to accede to his suggestions. They chose only three generals for the coming year: Hermocrates, Heraclides and Sicanus. The last two are generally regarded as democrats and were, perhaps elected to keep a watchful eye on Hermocrates. They also sent ambassadors to Corinth and to Sparta, both to request aid and to urge them to renew full-scale war against the Athenians. As Green points out, the Syracusans had voluntarily suspended their democracy and appointed an 'authoritarian junta . . . However the average citizen body is liable to vote for surprising things in an emergency, especially if the emergency is war.'[22] This tendency would later be exploited to the full by other would-be tyrants.

The Syracusans also used the winter to construct further defensive works. They extended the walls of the city on the side that faced the plateau of Epipolae to the north. The remains of Megara Hyblaea were fortified and garrisoned. The Temple of Zeus, which they had seized after the battle, was also fortified and stockades built at the likely landing places along the shore. Finally, again emboldened by the inactivity of the Athenians, they marched out their entire army to Catane, ravaged the countryside and burnt down the camp of the Athenians, while most were away on their expeditions against the Sicels or involved in various other distractions. The Athenians were now forced to retreat to Naxos.

The first nine months of the Sicilian expedition had achieved little other than the capture of Catane. At first the Athenians had been hamstrung by disunity of command and later by the timid leadership of Nicias. Plutarch claims that everyone blamed Nicias for the lack of success:

since, as they said, by his excessive calculation and hesitation and caution he let the proper time for action go by forever. When he was once in action no one could find fault with the man, for after he had set out to do a thing he was vigorous and effective; but in venturing out to do it he was hesitating and timid.[23]

Chapter 9

The Athenian Siege Begins

And Nicias himself, contrary to his nature, was straightway so emboldened by the present momentum of his good fortune, and, most of all, by the secret messengers sent to him from the Syracusans, was so fixed in his belief that the city was just on the point of surrendering conditionally, that he made no sort of account of Gylippus at his approach. He did not even set an adequate watch against him.

Plutarch, *Nicias* 18

The embassy that the Syracusans had sent out over the winter had met with some success. Firstly, they had persuaded the Italian Greeks that they too were threatened by the Athenians and should continue to remain neutral. Next they had convinced their mother city, Corinth, to support them and to send a joint delegation to Sparta to propose that they should resume the war with Athens in Greece, and to send aid to Sicily. In Sparta the delegation met with Alcibiades and won his support. Up to this point the Spartans had planned to send envoys to Syracuse to encourage them to continue the war against the Athenians, but had no intention of assisting them directly.

After the Syracusans and the Corinthians had appealed to the Spartans, Alcibiades also addressed them. He repeated the claim that the Athenians had 'sailed to Sicily first to conquer, if possible the Sicilians and after them Italians also, and finally to assail the empire and city of Carthage' and using the resources of these conquests to 'then to attack the Peloponnesus.'[1] Kagan argues that this proposed conquest of Carthage was 'never part of the public discussion in Athens, much less a part of any of the formal decrees' and later claims that the plan was a creation of Alcibiades to enhance his own reputation and impress the Spartans.[2] He is most likely correct in the latter statement but the contemporary evidence of Thucydides and, more importantly, the poets from before the expedition; demonstrate that such an ambition was being discussed openly in Athens. There probably was not an official policy to conquer Carthage after Sicily; it was almost impossible for an ancient democracy to make long-term plans given that their magistrates were elected for a one-year term, but as has already been discussed, ancient empires rarely put limits on their ambitions. An invasion of Africa would have been a possible, and obvious, option for further conquest after Sicily.

Alcibiades further argued that to avoid this fate the Spartans must send a force of hoplites and, more importantly, a *Spartiate* to take command and to instil discipline into the Syracusan forces. He also advised the Spartans to take and fortify Decelea, a strongpoint in Athenian territory, as a permanent base to more effectively carry the war to the Athenians.

After listening to the delegation, the Spartans decided to both attack the Athenians and to send immediate assistance to the Syracusans. They appointed Gylippus to take an expedition to Sicily and to take command of the Syracusan forces. Despite Alcibiades urging, Gylippus was not a *Spartiate*, a full citizen, but a *mothax*. The exact meaning of this term is not certain, but most likely means the son of a Spartan man and a helot mother, or the child of an impoverished *Spartiate* no longer able to contribute to the common mess. In either case, a *mothax* would not have had full citizenship status. Gylippus' rank was even more questionable as his father had been exiled for accepting an Athenian bribe during the First Peloponnesian War. The rest of the expedition was also miserably small, originally only four ships. None of the force was a true *Spartiate*; in effect Sparta was sending a token and largely expendable force. The impact that Gylippus' leadership would have was, as Kagan rightly points out, 'greater than anyone had a right to expect.'[3]

At the beginning of spring the Athenians left Catane, sailed to Megara Hyblaea, attacked the small Syracusan fortress but failed to take it. They then ravaged the farmlands of the enemy. Next they marched with their whole force against the Syracusans' Sicel subjects, capturing one town and burning more crops. Returning to Catane they received from home 300 talents of silver, and the much-needed reinforcement of 250 Athenian cavalry and thirty mounted archers, most likely Scythians from the Black Sea region. When not fighting in the field, these archers served as a police force back in Athens, a job which, like many low-level public service positions, was generally considered to be unworthy of a citizen.

Now that the Athenians had received the reinforcement of cavalry, Nicias no longer had this as an excuse not to attack Syracuse directly. After nearly a year of indecision the Athenians had finally decided on a course of action; they would besiege and capture the city. Whether this decision was taken by Nicias and Lamachus, or was as a result of a directive from the impatient assembly at home, is not recorded. The Athenians landed to the north of the city near a place called Leon, not visible from the city due to the intervening heights of Epipolae. The fleet retired to Thapsus, a peninsula with a narrow isthmus, about five kilometers further north. Meanwhile, the troops, advancing by way of the pass of Euryalus, the easiest access to the plateau from the west, gained the summit before the Syracusans were aware that they had arrived. Once more, the total naval supremacy of the Athenians had allowed them to surprise the Syracusans.

The key to the defence of the city was the dominating heights of Epipolae. According to Thucydides, the Syracusans were well aware of the importance of holding the Epipolae, but as Green astutely observes, they had so far made no effort to fortify the heights. He concludes convincingly that 'however extraordinary we may find it in retrospect, the Syracusans were utterly oblivious to the strategic importance of Epipolae until it was thrust upon their notice at the last possible moment.'[4]

Once the importance of the high ground above their city had dawned upon them they immediately sprang into action. The very morning that the Athenians had arrived, the Syracusans marched out their whole army to the fields near to the River Anapus and held a review of their forces. They picked a select unit of 600 of their best hoplites, commanded by Diomilus, an anti-Athenian refugee from the island of Andros, as a mobile force to guard Epipolae. Orders were given for this force to guard the paths leading to the summit, but they were too late by a matter of hours. The Athenians had already arrived.

On learning that the Athenians were already in possession of the heights, the army rushed to attack the Athenians with Diomilus and the 600 in the lead. The distance, however, was over 5km, with the last part uphill. As a result they were tired and disordered as they closed with the Athenians. They were, as a consequence, easily defeated as they arrived piecemeal, losing 300 dead, including their commander. The remainder of the army retreated back to the city. As was customary, the Athenians erected a trophy and gave the Syracusans the bodies of their dead under a truce. The next day the Athenians marched against the city, but the Syracusans refused to come out to fight. The Athenians then withdrew and built a fort at Labdalum on the edge of the northern cliffs of Epipolae to serve as a store for their baggage and property.

Soon after they had established their bridgehead, the Athenians were joined by 300 cavalry from Segesta and another 100 from the Sicels and other Greeks, bringing their total up to 650. Leaving a garrison in Labdalum, they advanced south to a position known as Syca where they built a circular fort. Now that they had firmly established themselves on the Epipolae, the Athenians finally began to besiege Syracuse in earnest, beginning to build walls north and southeast from the Syca. The Syracusans realized that they must prevent these walls from being built and led their army out to fight. The poor discipline of the Syracusans again let them down. As they advanced they fell into disorder. Not being able to form a battle line, their exasperated generals were compelled to lead them back into the city, except for a detachment of the cavalry who remained to harass the Athenians as they gathered stones for their walls. The Athenians then advanced with both hoplites and all their cavalry, driving off the Syracusan horse. The newly-arrived Athenian cavalry had immediately shown their value.

The next day, the Athenians continued with the building of their walls. To the north they laid out wood and stones along a course towards Trogilus, the shortest distance from the Great Harbour to the outer sea. It was to the south-east, however, that the real building commenced, from the Syca to the Great Harbour. If completed, this wall would cut the Syracusans off from the shore-line of the harbour and allow the Athenians to bring their fleet safely into the bay. The Syracusan commanders were understandably reluctant to engage the Athenians in the open field. Instead, they planned to build a wall west-wards, across the line of the Athenian wall and thereby prevent it from reaching the harbour. If attacked by the Athenians, they could fight from the protection of their fieldworks. So began a race to see who could build the fastest. The Athenians also destroyed the underground water pipes which supplied Syracuse, but, as the city was well supplied by springs, this was a nuisance rather than a disaster.

Using the wood taken from the groves of the temple of Apollo, the Syracusans quickly completed a section of their cross-wall and leaving a part of the army to guard it they withdrew the rest back into the city. The Athenians again took advantage of the slackness of the Syracusans and attacked the wall at noon, while many of the guards rested in their tents and others had snuck away to enjoy the pleasures of the city. They attacked with 300 selected hoplites and some light troops equipped as hoplites, ordering them to run quickly to the cross-wall. The rest of the army was split into two divisions, one commanded by Nicias and the other by Lamachus. One division advanced on the city to prevent a Syracusan sally and the other supported the attack on the walls. The advance guard took the dozing guards by surprise, drove them off and captured the further end of the wall. The now over-confident Athenians pursued the routers right up to the city wall but were driven off. The whole army then turned back and destroyed the cross-wall, carried the wood back to their camp and raised another trophy.

The Athenians continued building their wall, bringing it down from the cliff, and intending to continue it through the marshes to the south of the city, the shortest line to the harbour. The Syracusans began to build a second cross-wall through the middle of the marsh, this time protecting it with a ditch. Such work must have been horrible for both sides, being carried out in oozing mud under the hot Sicilian sun while being tormented by leeches and insects.

The Athenians planned to launch an attack on the new Syracusan wall. Nicias was ill with his kidney complaint, a condition which would continue to get worse as the campaign continued, and the attack was commanded by Lamachus. They brought their fleet into the Great Harbour while the army built a path of planks across the bog. Attacking at sunrise, they soon captured the entire wall. The Syracusans came out to defend their barricade but were again defeated in battle. Most escaped back to the city but a part of the Syracusan army, cut off from the city, fled along the river. The 300 chosen Athenian troops pursued at full speed towards the bridge, hoping to cut off their escape. The Syracusan cavalry again proved its worth, riding down the scattered pursuers and charging into the right wing of the Athenian battle line, routing a part of it.

Now it was the Athenians turn to panic. Lamachus, realising the danger, took a few archers and some Argive hoplites from the left wing and rushed to the rescue. As he crossed the ditch he and a few others were cut off from the rest. The now-isolated Lamachus was attacked by Syracusan cavalry. One of these, Callicrates, a man renowned for his courage, challenged Lamachus to single combat. The two fought and struck each other fatal blows. The Syracusans carried off both bodies. Lamachus may have been portrayed as a swaggering clown in Aristophanes' plays but had shown himself to be no coward in the face of death. His loss would deprive the expedition of its most dynamic commander.

Those Syracusans who had fled back to the city, seeing the rout of part of the Athenian line, gathered their courage and again marched out to confront the enemy. The Syracusan generals, observing that the Athenian wall on the heights had been left unguarded, sent a detachment to destroy it. The rest of the army was sent to distract the Athenians and prevent them from returning to save their fortifications. The detached force managed to capture and destroy nearly a kilometer of the wall. They then attacked the fort of the Athenians at Syca. Nicias was forced to rise from his sick bed. He had few troops with which to defend the fort, so in desperation he ordered the camp attendants to set fire to the timber which had been stored in front of the wall. The resulting blaze forced the Syracusans to give up the attack. The smoke from the fire also succeeded in attracting the attention of the Athenian army, which now hastened back from the plain. The Syracusans on the heights, seeing the Athenians returning, quickly retreated back to the city, as did the rest of the army. The Athenians, holding the field, now erected another trophy. Under a truce, they restored the Syracusan dead, and received back the bodies of Lamachus and his companions. Nicias was now left as sole commander of the expedition.

Although they had destroyed part of the Athenian wall, the Syracusans had once again been driven back into the city. Their counter-walls had been destroyed and there appeared to be no way to prevent the construction of the Athenian siege walls. The situation looked far more encouraging for the Athenians. They were able to draw plentiful supplies from Italy. Their successes also won over many of those Sicels who had previously stood aloof.

By contrast, the Syracusans despaired of winning militarily; they had suffered a string of defeats and no help had reached them from the Peloponnesus. They feared that soon they would be completely cut off and starved into submission. Many within the city began to discuss openly making peace while reasonable conditions might be granted. Approaches were made to Nicias to discuss terms but with no result. Their lack of success also brought out old suspicions and enmities. The usual accusations of treachery were circulated. Political division appears to have split the city. There is a dubious tale in Polyaenus (1.43.1) of a slave revolt within the walls. Hermocrates is supposed to have broken the rebellion by offering to free and arm the slaves as hoplites, and to pay them at the same rate as citizens. Inviting the leaders of the slaves to a conference he betrayed and imprisoned them. The rest of the slaves then surrendered. This tale is usually considered doubtful as the ruse is one often repeated throughout ancient history.

Despite Hermocrates' supposed military abilities, the *demos* took the first opportunity they could to depose him, blaming him for their lack of success. Of the three generals only Heraclides was re-elected and two new generals, named Eucles and Tellias, were chosen. Events after the campaign would show that Heraclides and Eucles were radical democrats. Green sees this election, the lack of discipline within the army and the slave revolt as the work of Athenagoras and his democratic supporters in an attempt to force the city to submit to the Athenians. They could then, with Athenian assistance, carry out a radical democratic reform of the government.[5]

This accusation is, however, based on no direct evidence whatever. Instead, it is made on the premise that it was usually the democratic faction within a city that favoured alliance with the Athenians. It ignores the direct statement of Thucydides that the Athenians had nothing to offer the democratic regime of Syracuse. The land-owning rich of the Greek cities were usually those in favour of peace as it was their estates, outside of the city walls, that suffered from the ravages of invading armies. They also bore the burden of most of the taxes needed to pay for the war. It ignores the close ties of Hermocrates with the rich of Athens. As *proxenos,* Nicias would also have had many friends within the city, mostly from the upper layers of society. Nor did the Athenians have any problem in allying themselves with the Dorian oligarchs of Thessaly. Thucydides never tells us who from within the city was in contact with Nicias. It could quite reasonably have been either side of politics or disgruntled individuals from the full spectrum of Syracusan society.

False reports that the Athenians had actually completed their walls and isolated Syracuse reached Gylippus, who had only travelled as far as the island of Leucas, off the western coast of Greece. He reportedly despaired of saving Syracuse and planned instead to prevent the Italian cities from going over to Athens. Gylippus sailed to Tarentum as fast as he could with only four ships and then continued on to Thurii. Another squadron of fifteen ships under the Corinthian Gongylus followed. Gylippus' father had spent part of his exile in Thurii and had taken a leading part in an anti-Athenian coup. Despite this connection, Gylippus failed to get any aid from Thurii or any other of the Italian cities. He was further delayed by being caught in a violent storm and forced to return to Tarentum.

Nicias received word of his approach but because of the small number of his ships did not take the threat seriously, believing him to be most likely on a plundering raid. Whatever the reason, Nicias' decision not to set a watch and try to prevent him from landing in Sicily was totally inexcusable.

Gylippus, arriving at Locri, now learned the truth that Syracuse was not yet completely surrounded, and might be approached overland from the west. He determined that an attempt to arrive by sea would be too dangerous while the Athenian navy still dominated the approaches. Instead, he decided to land at Himera and to gather any allies that could be persuaded to join him. Belatedly, after he heard that Gylippus was at Locri, Nicias sent out four Athenian ships to intercept them, but even this token effort was too late. Gylippus arrived safely, persuaded the Himeraeans to join him and to supply arms to all his unarmed sailors. The arrival of a Spartan commander convinced many who had previously waited to watch events that the Peloponnesians were now serious about assisting Syracuse. The Selinuntians, the Geloans and some of the Sicels sent troops to join the relief expedition. Gylippus now marched towards Syracuse with a force of about 3,000 men, consisting of 700 of his armed sailors and marines, allied contingents from Himera, Selinus, and Gela, and about 1,000 Sicels.

In the meantime, Gongylus had risked the Athenian blockade and arrived in Syracuse with a single ship. He found the Syracusans about to call an assembly in order to discuss the terms for an offer of peace. Gongylus, as fortune would have it, arrived at about the same time as a message was received from Gylippus. He was therefore able to convince the Syracusans that a land force and more ships were on their way. Now reassured that help was finally about to arrive, the Syracusans dismissed any talk of peace. Learning from his message that Gylippus was approaching the pass at Euryalus they advanced out with their whole army to meet him. Gylippus marched through the pass unopposed. It is impossible to know whether Nicias' failure to guard the pass was caused by exhaustion from being in sole command, illness, or as Plutarch claims, overconfidence. Whatever the cause, it was another inexcusable lapse in judgment on the part of Nicias, as the Athenians had used the very same route to capture the heights only a few months earlier. If it was overconfidence, then it was just this type of hubris that the ancient Greeks believed would inevitably lead to disaster.

Kagan accurately sums up Nicias' lack of precautions as follows:

> A great general would have taken any number of steps to guarantee success. He would have hurried to complete the circumvallation of Syracuse, sent a squadron of ships to the straits or to Italy . . . instituted a strict blockade of both Syracusan harbors to prevent access . . . and

guarded or even fortified the approaches to Epipolae, especially Euryalus . . . A general who was even prudent would have done some of these things, Nicias did none of them, and the results, contrary to any reasonable expectation at that time, were disastrous for Athens.[6]

Gylippus had arrived at the proverbial last minute. The Athenians had almost completed their double wall, over a kilometer and a half long, leading down to the Great Harbour. Only a small portion, near the shore, was still not complete. The northern wall, extending towards the sea, was nearly finished, with the necessary stones laid out along the route. As Thucydides observes 'so near was Syracuse to destruction.'[7]

Chapter 10

The Syracusan Counterattack.

After this the Syracusans plucked up heart . . . Nicias therefore fell back again upon those views of the undertaking which he had held at the outset, and, fully aware of the reversal which it had suffered, became dejected, and wrote a dispatch to the Athenians urging them to send out another armament, or else to recall the one already in Sicily, begging them also in any case to relieve him of his command because of his disease.

Plutarch, Nicias 19

As soon as he reached the heights, Gylippus joined forces with the advancing Syracusans. Intent on making a statement, he immediately advanced against the Athenian lines. Although surprised by the appearance of a new enemy, the experienced Athenians quickly drew up their forces. Gylippus now attempted a piece of psychological warfare, probably meant to inspire his own forces. He sent a herald to the Athenians offering a five-day truce and safe conduct if they were willing to quit Sicily. The still-confident Nicias simply ignored his offer, not even bothering to send a reply. Some of his more assertive soldiers mocked the Spartan, asking if 'the presence of a single Spartan cloak and staff had made the prospects of the Syracusans on a sudden so secure that they could afford to deride the Athenians, who had restored to the Lacedaemonians, out of prison and fetters, 300 men far sturdier than Gylippus, and longer haired.' The Athenians were reminding both Gylippus and the Syracusans of their earlier triumph over the supposedly invincible Spartans at Pylos. They were also mocking the archaic habit of the Spartans of growing their hair long. This attitude was also shared by some of the Syracusans themselves, as the historian Timaeus claims 'that the Sicilians also made no account of Gylippus . . . as soon as they set eyes upon him they jeered at his cloak and his long hair'. [1]

These jibes may also have had a political basis as long hair was often associated with the aristocracy.[2] Many of the anti-democratic rich in Athens emulated the Spartans by growing their hair and/or beards long, and wearing their short, red military cloaks. It is of course possible that many of the

Syracusan democrats were not happy to serve under a general from a state that had a strong antipathy towards democracies. Even Nicias, a proponent of the alliance with Sparta, had warned that the Athenians needed 'to defend ourselves most effectively against the oligarchic machinations of Sparta.'[3] That such mistrust existed is recorded in another of Polyaenus' stratagems. The Syracusan generals, at least two of whom were democrats, refused to accept him as overall commander. Gylippus is supposed to have betrayed one of their positions to the Athenians and then blamed them for the breach of security. Although the story is generally dismissed by modern historians, its survival does infer that there was strong resistance to Gylippus' supreme command within the city. Others, most likely the oligarchic faction, 'flocked to him, with ready offers of military service.'[4]

Both armies now formed up in order of battle. Gylippus, seeing that the Syracusans were once again having difficulty in forming a line of battle in the broken terrain, retreated to the more open ground. Nicias remained close to his own wall. When Gylippus observed that the Athenians were content to remain on the defensive, he led his army away to a height near to the city called Temenites, where they passed the night. The next day he positioned most of his army to threaten the Athenian wall and then, having pinned down the Athenians, he sent a detachment to assault the fort of Labdalum. This position was not visible from the Athenian lines. The attackers stormed the fort and killed all the defenders. The negligence of Nicias' command on land also appears to have spread to the fleet; on the very same day the Syracusans captured an Athenian trireme that was on picket duty near the mouth of the harbour.

The Syracusans next began to build another counter-wall to run alongside the Athenian northern wall and then cut across it at an angle. If the Syracusans could succeed in crossing the Athenian wall it would be impossible for the Athenians to then complete their blockade of the city. The Athenians had completed the section of the northern wall nearest to the sea and those involved in its construction had come up to the high ground. Gylippus, learning that a section of the wall was weak, planned to launch a night attack against it, even though this was always a risky operation. Although it could achieve surprise, troops could easily become disoriented, lose their way, or even end up attacking their friends. The Athenians were once again alert, however, and marched to oppose him. Gylippus wisely withdrew. Warned by this aborted attack, the Athenians strengthened the weak portion of their wall and increased the guard.

Nicias, now that the land operations became stalemated, looked for ways to use his naval superiority to gain some advantage over the enemy. He decided to fortify Plemmyrium, a headland opposite Ortygia near to the narrow entrance of the Great Harbour. This would place his supplies, so he reasoned, outside of the reach of the Syracusan land forces. From here the fleet could more easily blockade the mouth of the harbour. He built three forts on the site and placed most of the Athenian stores there. The position was, however, poorly chosen. Water and food were scarce and those sent out to forage came under constant attack from a large squadron of Syracusan cavalry stationed at the Temple of Zeus. According to Thucydides these horsemen were 'masters of the country, a third part of the enemy's cavalry being stationed at the little town of Olympieum expressly to prevent plundering excursions on the part of the Athenians.'[5] Nicias, having learnt from his failure to intercept Gylippus, also sent off a squadron of twenty ships to Italy to intercept a Corinthian fleet that had been reported as on its way to Sicily.

Gylippus was, however, still actively carrying out the campaign on land. He continued to build his counter-wall and constantly drew up the Syracusans in front of the wall to threaten the Athenians. With the reinforcements he had brought the Syracusans now would have had a considerable superiority in hoplite numbers over the Athenians. Eventually, he offered battle to the Athenians in the confined space between the walls. In this restricted battlefield the Syracusan superiority in cavalry and light infantry was negated, as it had been at Anapus, and again the Athenians won the battle, setting up yet another trophy. According to the Athenian poet, Euripides, 'These men at Syracuse eight times were triumphant as victors; heroes they were while the gods favoured both causes alike.'[6]

Gylippus assembled the army and admitted that the defeat was due to his generalship and not to their courage. He attempted to raise their spirits by reminding them that they, being Dorians, were naturally braver than the enemy, 'Ionians and islanders with the motley rabble that accompanied them.'[7] In this appraisal of their courage he proved correct, as despite their constant defeats at the hands of the Athenians the Syracusans had not lost heart and soon allowed themselves to be led out to battle once again.

The Syracusans had continued building their counter-wall and brought it to the point where it was almost across the Athenian wall on the Epipolae. If it succeeded, the Athenians would have no chance of effecting a land blockade of the city. As Thucydides claimed, the campaign would then be lost as 'if it went any further it would from that moment on make no difference whether they fought ever so many successful actions, or never fought at all.'[8] Nicias was now forced to once again lead the Athenians out to do battle for control of the heights.

Gylippus this time led his army further out from the walls, into more open countryside where his cavalry and skirmishers would have room to operate effectively. Now having greater room to manoeuvre, the Syracusan cavalry managed to outflank and rout the left wing of the Athenians. With their flank exposed the whole Athenian army lost heart and was driven back by the Syracusan phalanx. It was the first major victory by the Syracusan hoplites over their Athenian opponents. They were finally able to set up a trophy of their own. As the Athenians fled, Gylippus, as was the habit of Spartan commanders, quickly halted the pursuit. Instead, the victors seized the building materials of the enemy. The next day he used the captured supplies to carry the Syracusan wall beyond that of the Athenians. The campaign on land had now been effectively won by the Syracusans. The Athenians could no longer hope to complete the encirclement of the city and the Syracusan superiority in horsemen meant that they could raid the Athenian lines at will.

Soon after the battle, there was more good news for the Syracusans, as a new fleet from the Peloponnesus had managed to elude the Athenian blockade and arrive in the harbour. Gylippus made use of the propaganda value of his victory to travel Sicily in order to raise more reinforcements from Syracuse's allies and to win over the neutrals. The victory, and the arrival of the reinforcements, lifted the Syracusans' morale and they now planned to take the war to the sea. They manned their ships and began training in earnest for the coming battle. This was no light undertaking as modern trials have shown it takes several months to train the rowers to operate together effectively. Such training would have occupied the Syracusans for most of the winter.

Nicias' defeat and illness caused him to become dejected. It was nearly winter, so he determined to keep his army on the defensive and to run no risks. He abandoned the heights and withdrew to the south of the city. In the meantime, he wrote a letter to the Athenians urging them to send out reinforcements or to recall the force already in Sicily. In the dispatch, he also requested to be relieved of his command because of his illness.

Thucydides reproduces Nicias' letter in detail. It described the dismal situation on land where the Athenians have been 'forced by the numbers opposed to us to discontinue the work of circumvallation and to remain inactive . . . unless this cross wall is attacked by a strong force and captured. So the besieger in name has become, at least from the land side, the besieged in reality; as we are prevented by their cavalry from even going for any distance into the country.'

Nicias claimed that the Syracusans were about to receive reinforcements from the rest of Sicily. He accurately forecast that, with these extra troops, they planned to 'make a combined attack upon our lines with their land forces and with their fleet at sea.' So far the letter appears to accurately describe the situation on land and predict future enemy actions. Nicias then, however, goes on to describe how the fleet has deteriorated during the cause of the campaign, with the timbers of the ships being soaked, as they had no means of drawing up the vessels and airing them. He blamed this condition on the activity of the enemy fleet, which because it 'is many more than our own, we are constantly anticipating an attack.'[9] Desertion had also ravaged the fleet, with many of the allied sailors having fled to the Sicilians in search of higher pay.

This first problem that Nicias describes was a common one amongst ancient fleets. If left too long in the water the hulls of the ships would become waterlogged, making the ship heavy and therefore slower and less manoeuvrable. The best way to repair this was to take the ship right out of the water onto specially made slipways in order to dry them out. The hulls would also be stripped of marine growth such as barnacles. Major naval powers such as Athens and Carthage had specially-built sheds with hundreds of slipways, and most naval ports would have had a few. The ruins of those at Syracuse can still be seen, just to the north of the Little Harbour. When such slipways were not available triremes could simply be dragged up onto a beach and allowed to dry out. This method was not as efficient, or thorough, but was still acceptable. It is also possible that Nicias was exaggerating the damage. If he had been doing his job efficiently, ships could have been sent in relays to Catane or Naxos to be dried out. From Thucydides' description the Syracusan navy had mostly remained close to harbour and we hear of only one Athenian ship being lost to enemy action. Nicias' description of the naval situation was clearly disingenuous. If not, he had certainly been unforgivably lethargic in his command.

Nicias completed his description of the situation with a gloomy précis of the supply and political situation. He claimed that their only allies, Naxos and Catane were unable to supply their needs and that if their main suppliers, the Italian Greeks, went over to Syracuse then they would be starved into submission. Again this is less than honest. Athens did have other allies in Sicily; Segesta for one and also various Sicel communities. Nor was there any indication that the Italians had any inclination to ally themselves with Syracuse. The last two parts of the letter are clearly overstated. It is difficult to escape the conclusion that Nicias was hoping that the expedition, which he had always opposed, would be withdrawn, or at the very least that he would be recalled.

Again, however, he had underestimated both the ambitions and the determination of the Athenian people. Plutarch claims that 'even before this the Athenians had made preparations to send another force to Sicily, but the leading men among them felt some jealousy of the preliminary good fortune of Nicias, and so had induced many delays.'[10] The assembly refused to recall Nicias from his command, but instead promoted two officers who were already in Sicily, Menander and Euthydemus, to be acting generals until others could be sent out. They also voted to send a second fleet and army to Sicily. As commanders they elected Demosthenes and Eurymedon who had served in Sicily previously. Eurymedon was immediately dispatched with ten ships and 120 talents. Demosthenes remained behind to organize the remainder of the new expedition to depart in the spring. The Athenians concluded their preparations by sending twenty ships to blockade the Peloponnesian coast and intercept any vessels trying to cross to Sicily.

After an initial defeat in 426, Demosthenes had been one of Athens most innovative and energetic, although not always successful, generals during the

Archamidian War. Later that year, while fearing to return to Athens as a result of a defeat, he had landed in Ambracia and successfully ambushed a Spartan army, killing their general. In 425 he had been ordered to Sicily but had been driven ashore by a storm at Pylos. It had been his initiative to fortify the headland. Although Cleon had claimed the credit, it was also his use of light infantry against the Spartans on Spachteria that had led to their defeat. He was clearly a leading politician within the city as he had been one of the signatories of the peace of Nicias.

The Corinthians and Spartans, learning of the Syracusans' success, decided to send further reinforcements. Most likely this was an attempt to keep the Athenians busy in Sicily, as the war in Greece had now recommenced in earnest. In the spring of 413 they sent 1,600 hoplites to Sicily in troop transports. These included 600 from Sparta itself, although, as before, none were *Spartiates*. The Corinthians sent twenty-five triremes to attack the Athenian squadron stationed at Naupactus in order to prevent them from intercepting the troop convoy.

In the same spring, Gylippus returned to Syracuse, bringing from the Sicilian cities more reinforcements. He ordered the Syracusans to man as large a fleet as possible in order to attack the Athenians at sea. Gylippus claimed that a decisive victory could destroy the Athenian expedition before more reinforcements arrived and therefore justified the risk. This was not the whole of his plan. While the Athenians were distracted by the naval attack he would march the army out at night to attack the Athenian base at Plemmyrium. This would have been a considerable feat of arms, as it involved a very long march in darkness right round the Athenian army. Such marches often led to armies getting lost or falling into disarray. It was probably only successful as it was on the Syracusans' home territory and they would have been familiar with the terrain.

Once the Syracusan army was in position they gave a signal to the fleet, which then sailed out to attack. There were forty-five triremes in the Little Harbour and the plan was for them to unite with the thirty-five already stationed in the Great Harbour. Then, along with the army, they would make a combined attack on Plemmyrium. The Athenians responded quickly and manned sixty ships. Twenty-five were set to engage the thirty-five of the Syracusans in the Great Harbour, and the remaining thirty-five to attack the Syracusans sailing round Ortygia from the Little Harbour. These two squadrons met at the mouth of the Great Harbour while a second sea battle was being fought out within the harbour itself. At first the greater numbers of the Syracusans gave them the advantage and the larger squadron forced its way into the Great Harbour. Again, as was the case on land, the inexperience of the Syracusans let them down. The ships of the two squadrons fell foul of one another and the Athenians were able to counterattack and defeat the now-disorganized Syracusans. The Syracusans lost eleven ships, along with most of their crews, and the Athenians three.

. The Bay of Naxos, location of the first Greek colony in Sicily, founded about 734. The city was located at the far, southern end of the bay. Its position as the founding city was honoured by the Greeks of Sicily. Ambassadors departing or returning to Sicily would always offer sacrifice at the temple of Apollo in Naxos. The city was destroyed by Dionysius in 403. (*Author's photograph*)

. The Aeolian Islands looking down from the island of Volcano towards the main island of Lipari. The islands were settled by the surviving Greeks of Penthalos after their failed attack on Phoenician Sicily in 580. It was here that the Greek colonists set up what is sometimes referred to as the world's first socialist state. Lipari was a loyal ally of Syracuse, but was captured by the Carthaginians in 396, after which it became an important Carthaginian naval base. (*Author's photograph*)

3. A hoplite helmet of the Corinthian style. Such helmets would often have been decorated with brightly-dyed horse-hair crests. This type of equipment became common from the start of the seventh century. Now in the Museo Regionale Archaologico, Gela. (*Author's photograph*)

4. A relief from the treasury of Siphnos at Delphi circa 525. Although supposedly depicting scenes from the Trojan War, the frieze clearly shows hoplites fighting in close order with overlapping shields. This shows the hoplite phalanx was being used at least by the end of the sixth century. Now in The Delphi Museum, Delphi. (*Author's photograph*)

5. Fourth-century tomb relief showing an Athenian soldier. Only the wealthy could afford such memorials. This and the expensive muscled cuirass would indicate that the owner was probably a cavalryman or a general. The relief is held in the National Archaeological Museum, Athens. (Author's photograph)

6. The view from Himera, looking towards the Carthaginian position at the base of Mount Calogero. The Carthaginian naval camp destroyed by the Greek cavalry would have been located between the foot of the mountain and the sea. (*Author's photograph*)

7. The Temple of Victory built at Himera to commemorate the victory of the Greeks over the Carthaginians in 480. The temple was later destroyed by the Carthaginians when they sacked the city in 409. (*Author's photograph*)

8. A vase painting depicting a Greek hoplite circa 500. Such heavily-armed infantry won the Battle of Himera when they 'pressed with greater boldness upon the barbarians'. The vase is held in the Museo Regionale Archaologico, Palermo. (*Author's photograph*)

9. A fourth-century vase painting of an infantryman. From the equipment and dress it is probably a representation of one of the Campanian mercenaries who fought for both sides during the wars. They were renowned for their courage, fractiousness and treachery. The vase is held in the Museo Archaologico, Agrigento. (*Author's photograph*)

10. The inside of the cathedral of Syracuse. The cathedral stands on the site of the Greek Temple of Athena built by Gelon to commemorate the victory at Himera. Columns from the original temple can clearly be seen and still support the cathedral roof. (*Author's photograph*)

11. The Euryalus Pass leading up to the Epipolae, with the remains of part of the Walls of Dionysius in the foreground. It was the failure of Nicias to guard the pass that allowed Gylippus to gain access to Syracuse and turn the direction of the Athenian campaign. (*Author's photograph*)

12. The Temple of Zeus, which occupies a hill to the south of Syracuse. The hill dominates the coastal plain, with a clear view to the city. It was captured by Hippocrates in his failed attempt to take Syracuse. Nicias' refusal to secure this hill allowed the Syracusans to use it as a base to harass the Athenians. The Carthaginians occupied it and used it as a command-post during their siege of the city. (*Author's photograph*)

13. The quarries outside Syracuse. It was here that more than 7,000 survivors of the Athenian expedition were worked and starved to death. The tyrants would also use the quarries to imprison their enemies, including the poet Philoxenus. (*Author's photograph*)

14. A vase relief circa 395 showing a Greek cavalryman leaving home to go to war. This sight would have been repeated in 250 homes throughout Athens in the spring of 414 as they departed for Syracuse. Few returned. Now in the National Archaeological Museum, Athens. (*Author's photograph*)

15. A vase painting showing the tyrant Peisistratus with his bodyguards, who carried clubs instead of spears and accompanied him wherever he went. Such bodyguards were a common device used by tyrants to seize power and terrorize their subjects. The vase is held in the National Archaeological Museum, Athens. (*Author's photograph*)

16. A fourth-century vase showing a victory parade of a Greek general, with the goddess Nike (Victory) carrying his crown of victory. It is possible that it depicts one of the Sicilian tyrants. The vase is held in Museo Archaologico, Agrigento. (*Author's photograph*)

17. The remains of the walls of Akragas on the southern side of the city. It was against these walls that the Carthaginians launched most of their attacks. From here the Greeks would have witnessed the flight of the defeated Carthaginians to the safety of their camp. The Akraganian generals were executed for their failure to attack the routers. (*Author's photograph*)

18. The northern gate of Motya. It was against this gate that Dionysius successfully breached the walls in the first recorded use of siege-towers by a Greek army. (*Author's photograph*)

Meanwhile, Gylippus had achieved complete surprise with his night march as most of the Athenians on Plemmyrium had gone down to the shore to watch the sea fight. The Syracusans made a sudden attack on the forts. They quickly captured the largest, and, seeing this, the garrisons of the two smaller forts abandoned their posts and fled. Two of the forts they repaired and garrisoned and one was demolished. Athenian losses were heavy in both dead and prisoners but, perhaps more importantly, they had lost much of their stores. These losses included grain, three beached triremes and the sails and fittings of another forty. According to Thucydides:

> Indeed the first and foremost ruin of the Athenian army was the capture of Plemmyrium; even the entrance of the harbour was no longer safe for the carrying of provisions, as the Syracusan vessels were stationed there to prevent it, and nothing could be brought in without fighting; besides the general impression of dismay and discouragement produced upon the army.[11]

By contrast, and despite their loss in the sea battle, the Syracusans were triumphant. The elated Syracusans erected three trophies, one for each fort. The Athenians raised one on an island off Plemmyrium for their victory at sea. Diodorus has a slightly different version of the events of the naval battle. He claims that the Athenian ships broke off the fight to come to the relief of the forts but were too late. The Syracusans chased them and became disorganised in pursuit. This allowed the Athenians to turn and defeat them while they were in disarray. Either way, both writers agree that it was the superior seamanship of the Athenians that led to their victory.[12]

At the same time as these events were happening, Demosthenes had finished collecting the new Athenian force. It consisted in total of sixty-five triremes, 1,200 Athenian hoplites plus others from the allies. He cruised along the coast of the Peloponnesus, ravaging Epidaurus and Sparta along the way. At Corcyra, while engaged in recruiting light infantry, he heard that while he had been dallying the Syracusans had captured Plemmyrium. Finally, he sailed with all haste to Sicily.

The Syracusans, made more confident by their recent successes, now expanded the war beyond Sicily and into Italian waters. Hearing that supply ships were on their way to the Athenians, they sent out eleven ships to Italy to intercept them. They attacked and destroyed most of these ships and burnt a quantity of Athenian ship timber at Caulonia. The Athenians attempted to intercept them off Megara Hyblaea on their way home but only managed to capture one ship.

Back in Syracuse, skirmishing continued in the harbour around where the Syracusans had built a palisade of stakes in the sea, so that their ships might ride at anchor in safety. The Athenians brought up a large merchant ship, which they had fortified with wooden towers and bulwarks to act as a strong-point. From boats they tied ropes to the stakes and tore them up. They also sent divers to saw through them from underwater. The Syracusans retaliated with a shower of missiles from the shore which was returned by the men on the ship. Eventually, the Athenians succeeded in pulling up most of the palisade. This fighting dragged on for days, as the Syracusans replaced the stakes and the Athenians tried to stop them.

The capture of Plemmyrium had persuaded even more of the Sicilian cities to join Syracuse and to send contingents. Nicias, learning of this, organized his Sicel allies to attack some of them while they were on the march. They succeeded in ambushing one force, killing about 800 of them, and all the envoys except one Corinthian who escaped the disaster and brought 1,500 survivors into Syracuse. In addition, another 1,700 troops and five triremes arrived from Gela and Camarina, the latter finally throwing its lot in with the Syracusans. According to Thucydides, up until then many Sicilian cities 'had only watched the course of events, but now the whole island, with the exception of Akragas, which was neutral, united with the Syracusans against the Athenians.'[13]

Demosthenes was, however, finally on the way, collecting troops and ships from southern Italy as he came. At Thurii he drove out the anti-Athenian faction that had seized the city in a coup. From Thurii he received another 700 hoplites and 300 javelin-armed light infantry.

The newly-reinforced Syracusans, hearing of the approach of Demosthenes, decided to make one more effort to defeat Nicias, on both land and sea, before he arrived. According to Plutarch, the irrepressible Syracusans believed that they had previously lost at sea 'not through any superior strength in their enemy, but by reason of their own disorderly pursuit of that enemy. Accordingly, they were making more vigorous preparations to try the issue again.'[14]

The Syracusans had learnt the lessons of their previous defeat and made improvements to the construction of their vessels. They shortened and strengthened their prows, and made the beams which projected from them longer and thicker. These modifications were certainly copied from the Corinthians. The fleet they had earlier sent to the Peloponnesus in order to protect the troop ships had been modified in the same way. The reasoning behind these modifications was to negate the Athenian superiority in seaman-ship. One of the main tactics of the Athenians was the *diekplous*, which involved using their superior skill to sail through the enemy line, turn quicker than their opponents and then ram them from the rear. This was by far the preferred position for ramming, as triremes were quite fragile and ramming a moving vessel from in front, or from the side, could result in the aggressor's prow being damaged or even ripped completely off. The Corinthian theory had turned this tactic on its head.

At a battle off Erineus, in the Gulf of Corinth, they had deliberately used their reinforced prows to smash into the bow of the Athenian vessels as they tried to penetrate their line. The Corinthians lost three ships but their new device succeeded in crippling seven enemy vessels. Such had been the superiority of the Athenians up to this time that the Corinthians claimed a victory on the basis that 'they were conquerors, if not decidedly conquered, and the Athenians thinking themselves vanquished, because not decidedly victorious.'[15] The confined waters of the Syracusan harbour would be ideal for such tactics. The restricted space also negated the other favourite Athenian tactic, the *periplous*, swinging round the flanks of the enemy to hit them from the rear.

'With these contrivances to suit their skill and ability, and now more confident after the previous sea fight, the Syracusans attacked by land and sea at once.' Gylippus first led the army out of the city against that part of the Athenian wall which faced Syracuse, while the garrison from the temple attacked from the opposite side. The Athenians believed that they were facing a land attack only and were caught by surprise when the Syracusans brought out their entire fleet, eighty ships. Despite this, the Athenians responded quickly, 'forming upon the walls and in front of them against the advancing enemy, and some marching out in haste against the numbers of cavalry . . . others manned the ships or rushed down to the beach to oppose the enemy.'[16] The Athenians soon led out seventy-five ships to confront the Syracusan fleet. Plutarch claims that Nicias did not want another sea fight and wished to remain on the defensive until Demosthenes arrived. His new colleagues, Menander and Euthydemus, however, 'who had just been appointed to their offices, were moved by an ambitious rivalry', and were keen 'to anticipate Demosthenes in some brilliant exploit, and to eclipse Nicias.'[17] They badgered Nicias into allowing them to sail out and confront the Syracusans.

The sea battle went on for the greater part of the day, and despite the supposed keenness of the Syracusans, both sides limited themselves to skirmishing and were not able to gain a decisive advantage. The Syracusans did manage to sink one or two of the enemy vessels. On land the Athenians were able to hold their walls and beat off the Syracusans. The following day was quiet and Nicias used it to repair his vessels and strengthen the palisade in front of the Athenian moorings with anchored merchant vessels.

The next day, the Syracusans renewed their attacks on both land and sea. The fighting at sea was again limited for most of the day to indecisive skirmishing. The deadlock was broken by a stratagem proposed by one of the Corinthian captains, Ariston, who was reputedly the best pilot in the fleet. He convinced the authorities to have the food market moved down to the harbour so the Syracusan crews could disembark for their lunch close to the ships. The purpose was to allow them to quickly re-embark, renew their attacks and catch the Athenians unprepared.

The Athenians, seeing the Syracusans withdraw, took this as a sign of defeat and retired, thinking that there would be no more fighting that day. The plan worked to an extent, with the Syracusans suddenly manning their ships and catching the relaxing Athenians in disorder. Surprise was lost, however, when, for some reason, the Syracusans failed to engage immediately and the two fleets simply observed one another. The Athenians, who had not had the advantage of a meal or rest, decided that prolonging matters would only make them more tired and 'giving a cheer they went into action. The Syracusans received them and, charging prow to prow as they had intended, stove in a great part of the Athenian outriggers by the strength of their beaks.'[18] The Syracusan advantage in numbers also told with their javelin-armed men on the decks, and others who rowed about in light boats, doing great damage. The light boats were also able to foul the oars of the Athenian vessels. These boats were largely manned by the youth of Syracuse, those under the normal military age. One of these may have been a young Dionysius, the next tyrant of Syracuse.

The Syracusans, gradually gained the upper hand and the Athenians, retreating between the merchant vessels, took refuge at their own moorings. The Syracusans pursued them as far as the palisade but they were prevented from following further by the threat of leaden weights, which were suspended from beams placed on the merchant ships. Two of the pursuing triremes followed too far and were crippled by these devices. The Syracusans damaged many of the Athenian ships and sank seven. They then retired and raised a trophy of their own, their first for a sea battle. Their performance over the last three days had made them confident that they were now superior to the Athenians at sea. They prepared to renew the attack on both elements. By contrast, but not unexpectedly, Nicias was overcome by despair.

It was at this point that Demosthenes arrived with the Athenian reinforcements. He brought a fleet of seventy-three triremes, 5,000 hoplites, 3,000 light infantry and plenty of supplies. Although the second fleet had been expected, the sheer size of it was a shock to the Syracusans. Their high hopes had been dashed as they realized the enormous resources of the Athenians and their empire. Despite being again at war at home, they could still send another force as large as the first. As Thucydides observed 'the Syracusans and their allies were for the moment not a little dismayed at the idea that there would be no term or end to their dangers, seeing . . . a new army arrive equal to the former and the power of Athens proving so great in every quarter.'[19]

Chapter 11

The Syracusan Victory

He made a spectacular display, and one which smote the enemy with dismay. Again, then, as was natural, fear reigned among the Syracusans. They saw before them no final release from their perils, but only useless toils and vain self-destruction.

Plutarch, *Nicias* 21

The arrival of Demothenes' fleet caused great consternation amongst the Syracusans and their allies. It appeared that all their efforts of the last year were for nothing. In contrast, the survivors of the Athenian first expedition, whose morale had badly deteriorated, regained their confidence as they witnessed the arrival of so large a force. With Demosthenes' arrival it is estimated that the Athenian force before Syracuse now numbered over 40,000 men: 9,500 hoplites, 4,800 light infantry and about 27,000 naval personnel.[1]

Demosthenes' first move was to assess the situation. He came to much the same conclusion that Lamachus had two years earlier, that the Athenians should strike hard while the Syracusan morale was still brittle from the arrival of the new fleet. Having viewed the Syracusans' defences, he observed that the cross-wall was still only a single line of fortifications. If he could capture the Syracusan forts that supported this wall, then the rest of the fortifications could be taken easily. Demosthenes resolved to make the attempt immediately. He believed that if he succeeded, Syracuse would fall into his hands, or if he failed, he would withdraw immediately 'instead of frittering away the lives of the Athenians engaged in the expedition and the resources of the country at large'[2]

Demosthenes proposed this course of action at the very first conference he held with the other Athenian commanders. Nicias, of course, opposed the proposal and begged him to do nothing rash. He claimed to be in secret communication with people within the city. They had told him that delay would work against the Syracusans as the city was nearly out of money, many were worn out by the war and tired of taking orders from Gylippus, and their allies were wavering. Nicias could only hint at these things, providing no evidence and thereby made the other generals think he was simply lacking in courage. They sided with Demosthenes, claiming that it was 'the same old story over again with him . . . delays, postponements, and hairsplitting distinctions.'[3]

Despite his call for an immediate attack, Demosthenes began by ravaging the fields of the Syracusans south of the city, an operation designed to help the Athenians regain their confidence. The Syracusans no longer came out to oppose them at sea and on land they limited themselves to raids from the temple. Demosthenes began his assault on the counter-wall by bringing up siege engines, probably rams. The Syracusan defenders succeeded in burning these and defeating the accompanying attacks by the Athenian infantry.

With his opening attack beaten, Demosthenes determined that he must now go ahead with the planned assault on the forts. He decided that it would be impossible to climb the heights undetected during daylight and therefore resolved on the highly risky stratagem of a night assault. Thucydides claims that this was the only night attack carried out during the entire twenty-seven years of the Peloponnesian War. Although Gylippus had carried out a night march to Plemmyrium, he had prudently waited for daybreak before launching his successful attack. Unlike Gylippus, the Athenians would not have the advantage of local knowledge of the terrain.

Demosthenes collected all the supplies necessary for the siege works and five days' provisions. He led out most of the army, 10,000 hoplites and 10,000 light infantry. Presumably their numbers had been augmented by arming some of the naval personnel. True to his word, Demosthenes was risking the entire effective infantry component of the Athenian force in this one attack. Once again Nicias was left behind to guard the Athenian fortifications.

Demosthenes used the Euryalus pass to gain access to the heights. Advancing under the cover of night, he took the garrison of the Syracusan fort by surprise and easily captured it. Most of the guards, however, managed to escape and raised the alarm. The Syracusans had an advance guard of 600 men stationed on this part of the Epipolae. They quickly advanced to meet the enemy, but were driven back by the superior numbers of the Athenians. The Athenians immediately pressed forward, determined not to lose the benefit of surprise caused by their unexpected attack. One detachment captured the end of the Syracusan wall and began to tear it down. Meanwhile, more Syracusans were hurrying forward from their positions. Surprised by the boldness of this night attack, and outnumbered by the Athenians, they too were driven back.

Not wishing to lose the momentum of their attack or give the enemy time to rally, the Athenians continued the advance. The inherent dangers of a night attack now manifested themselves as the Athenians fell into disorder. A group of the Syracusans' Boeotian allies were first to rally. They turned, reformed their ranks into a solid phalanx and charged the vanguard of the disordered Athenians, putting them to flight.

Both sides were now in total confusion. For as Thucydides states even in the daytime a soldier could not determine:

> much of anything that does not go on in his immediate neighbourhood; but in a night engagement . . . how could anyone know anything for certain? Although there was a bright moon they saw each other only as men do by moonlight, that is to say, they could distinguish the form of the body but could not tell for certain whether it was a friend or an enemy.[4]

Large bodies of hoplites on both sides were moving about in a confined space, some fleeing some advancing. Much of the Athenian army was still unengaged but those at the front were already defeated. Their units constantly asked each other the password and thereby revealed it to the Syracusans. The now-rallied Syracusans were in a more compact group and therefore more easily able to recognize one another. They used their knowledge of the Athenian watchword to ambush some of the Athenian units. Another problem for the Athenians was the diverse nature of their army, which include Dorian Greeks from Argos and other cities. When they gave their battle cry, their *paean*, in their own dialect it caused even more confusion and ended with allied units 'coming into collision with each other in many parts of the field, friend with friend . . . actually fighting hand to hand'.[5]

The Syracusans now gained the upper hand and counter-attacked, routing the Athenians. The Athenians' only safe means of escape was back through the Euryalus pass, but this was blocked by the rear of the army still advancing through it. Many of the refugees were killed by falling over the cliffs as they fled in the darkness. Others wandered about lost until daybreak. They were then cut off and slaughtered by the Syracusan cavalry. It was an overwhelming victory to the Syracusans. The Athenian dead amounted to 2,000, so far their worst single loss of the entire war. Many of the survivors were effectively disarmed, having thrown away their shields and armour in their panicked flight. The Syracusans showed their jubilation by raising two trophies, one on the summit of the heights and one where the Boeotians had made their decisive stand.

Their success restored the Syracusans' confidence. They sent fifteen ships to Akragas on learning that a pro-Syracusan revolt had broken out. Gylippus once again went out to collect more reinforcements. The morale of the Athenian army, briefly revived by Demosthenes' arrival, had now hit its nadir. First there had been the defeat and then a plague had broken out in their camp. This illness was possibly malaria, as the Athenians were camped in the marshy territory to the south of the city.

Demosthenes, in keeping with his plan, now advocated the Athenians immediately withdraw while they still had command of the sea. He argued that it would be a better use of the city's resources to return to fight the Spartans, rather than employ more time and valuable resources against the Syracusans with little hope of victory.

Nicias was totally opposed to a retreat back to Greece. He still held out hope that there was 'a party within Syracuse who wished to betray the city to the Athenians and kept sending him messages'. In addition, he argued that he had information that the cost of the war, 2,000 talents so far, was bankrupting the Syracusans. Therefore he argued they ought to continue the siege as they were richer than the enemy. Time would show that Nicias' hopes here were in vain. For as Thucydides later described:

> These were the only cities which they had yet encountered similar to their own character, under democracies like themselves, which had ships and horses, and were of considerable magnitude. They had been unable to divide and bring them over by holding out the prospect of changes in their governments.[6]

As discussed earlier, it is not known what factions from within the city were in correspondence with him. Whoever the traitors were, they were clearly in a tiny minority, especially now that the Syracusans were winning. The time for terms, before Gylippus' arrival and again after Demosthenes' appearance, had now vanished.

The sources are less flattering about Nicias' motives for refusing to leave. As with Alcibiades before him, he feared to face an Athenian court. Thucydides claims that he was scared to return to Athens defeated, as he would be denounced as a traitor, as 'the soldiers on the spot, who now were loudly proclaiming the danger of their position would say that their generals had been bribed to betray them'. Nicias therefore, 'sooner than perish under a dishonourable charge and by an unjust sentence at the hands of the Athenians, he would rather take his chance and die, if die he must, a soldier's death at the hand of the enemy.'[7] This attitude of placing one's personal honour above the greater benefit to the state was common, as Alcibiades had already shown, but not universal. Plutarch compares his conduct unflatteringly to one 'Leon of Byzantium, who, at a later time, said to his fellow citizens: "I would rather be put to death by you than with you."'[8]

Demosthenes was still totally opposed to continuing the siege but agreed to a compromise. He stated that if the army must remain, then they should retire to Catane. From there they could ravage the countryside and maintain themselves at the expense of the enemy. They could fight their naval battles, not in a confined space but on the open sea, where their skill give them the advantage. Eurymedon agreed with Demosthenes, but Nicias resisted, and without universal agreement the divided command was incapable of taking decisive action.

Meanwhile, Gylippus had returned with more reinforcements, including those from Sparta who had been sent out in the spring but had been driven south to Africa by bad weather. They had eventually arrived in Selinus with the assistance of the Carthaginians, after having helped one of the Greek cities of Africa to defeat an attack by the Libyans. That the Carthaginians had allowed their passage to Sicily would imply that although neutral, they favoured the Syracusan cause. Perhaps they too had learned of the expansionist ambitions of Alcibiades and others in Athens. Sicanus' expedition to Akragas had been less successful, with the pro-Syracusan party having been driven into exile.

With the arrival of even more troops, the Syracusans prepared to renew their attacks upon the Athenians, both by land and sea. Observing these preparations, and with the Athenian army continuing to be weakened by disease, even Nicias now realized the futility of remaining before Syracuse. The Athenians made plans to withdraw to Catane in great secret, but just as they were about to depart, on 27 August 413, there occurred a lunar eclipse. According to Plutarch, some Greeks understood the natural causes of eclipses but the knowledge was not widely known. Generally it was considered a bad omen and as such:

> This was a great terror to Nicias and all those who were ignorant or superstitious enough to quake at such a sight. The obscuration of the sun towards the end of the month was already understood, even by the common folk, as caused somehow or other by the moon; but what it was that the moon encountered, and how, being at the full, she should on a sudden lose her light and emit all sorts of colours, this was no easy thing to comprehend. Men thought it uncanny — a sign sent from God in advance of diverse great calamities.[9]

The superstitious Nicias now insisted that the Athenians wait for twenty-seven days, until the next full cycle of the moon, before withdrawing. The Syracusans learned of the delay through the constant stream of deserters that were now leaving the Athenian camp. With victory now so close, the last thing the Syracusans would have wanted was for the Athenians to withdraw to another part of Sicily and to continue the war from there. They resolved, therefore, to attack the Athenians before they departed and to bring the issue to a final conclusion. With the knowledge that the enemy would remain in place for a month the Syracusans prepared their forces by further drilling their fleet.

All the initiative had passed to the Syracusans. So demoralized were the Athenians that Plutarch claims that Syracusan boys 'on board of fishing smacks and skiffs, sailed up from every side with challenges and insults for the Athenians.'[10] The Syracusans began their offensive by attacking the

Athenian walls by land. They managed to cut off and defeat a small number of hoplites and cavalry that had come out to meet them. The Athenian cavalry were forced to abandon their mounts in order to escape back through their gates, losing seventy horses to the enemy. The Syracusans then sent out their fleet, seventy-six triremes plus numerous small boats full of young men armed with various missiles. The Athenian fleet numbered eighty-six and therefore its line was longer than that of the Syracusans. Plutarch claims that the battle was accidentally brought about by the Athenians responding to the taunts of the above-mentioned boys, but Thucydides merely states that two sides deliberately sailed out to do battle.

Eurymedon, who commanded the right wing of the Athenians, attempted to perform a *periplous* and turn the Syracusan line. In the close waters of the harbour this proved impossible and he extended his own line too close to the land. The Syracusan centre, who had driven back their Athenian opponents, were able to outflank him in turn and trap him in an inner bay of the harbour, where, unable to manoeuvre, he was defeated. Eurymedon was killed and the vessels which were under his command were destroyed. After Eurymedon's destruction the rest of the Athenian fleet gave way and the Syracusans began to force them back onto the shore.

Gylippus, observing that the Athenians were being driven onto land outside of their fortified camp, advanced with an infantry force along a causeway which ran along the harbour. He intended to kill all those who landed and to assist in capturing the enemy ships. A force of Etruscans, who were guarding this part of the Athenian lines, attacked the vanguard of Gylippus' force and routed it. This did not deter the Syracusans, and the rest of the force continued the advance. The Athenians, in turn, fearing for their ships, advanced to the support of the Etruscans. A large engagement now took place and the Athenians routed the enemy. Most of the Athenian ships were saved, but the Syracusans still managed to capture eighteen and to kill their entire crews. Hoping to destroy the rest, they filled an old merchant vessel with combustibles, set it alight and, with the wind behind them, they aimed the ship at the retreating Athenians. The Athenians, however, managed to hold the vessel off until the flames could be extinguished and saved their ships.

The Syracusans raised two trophies, the most important one for their naval victory. It was a great feat of arms, as for the first time in decades an Athenian fleet been defeated by a smaller force. The Athenians also raised two trophies, one for the victory of the Etruscans and another for their subsequent victory on land. These would be the last trophies the Athenians would raise before Syracuse. They were also a forlorn gesture, as the minor victories on land could not offset the crushing defeat at sea. Any advantages the Athenians had regained with the arrival of Demosthenes had now been completely lost.

With the naval battle won, the Syracusans were determined that there would be no escape by sea for the Athenians. Now that the danger from the

Athenians had passed, the extremely competitive nature of ancient Greek society encouraged them to win great glory for their city. They believed that if the Athenian expedition was destroyed it would lead to a widespread uprising by their subjects and 'they, the Syracusans, would be the authors of this deliverance, and would be held in high admiration, not only with all men living but also posterity.'[11] The Syracusans now closed off the mouth of the Great Harbour, which was just over a kilometre wide, by mooring broadside a collection of damaged triremes, merchant vessels, and small boats. They also began preparing for another naval battle.

The Athenians, seeing the closing of the harbour, held a council of the surviving generals and officers. The most pressing need was for food, as they had already cancelled supplies from Catane when they had intended to depart. With the mouth of the harbour closed they could no longer get provisions by sea, and the Syracusan superiority in cavalry made it difficult to obtain them by land. They decided, therefore, to abandon their outer walls and hold only those that were absolutely necessary to defend their ships, baggage, and their sick and wounded. Leaving a guard to defend the camp, they planned to put on board every available man and to launch all their ships, no matter how damaged, and fight a decisive battle at sea. If they won they would retreat, as originally planned to Catane, but if they lost they would burn their ships and retreat by land to the nearest friendly territory.

As the fight was to be in confined waters, the Athenians emulated the enemy and loaded their vessels with extra marines, archers and javelin-men, most of whom had never fought at sea before. This, and the neglect of the fleet under Nicias, meant that the tables were turned and for once 'they fought against light and nimble ships, which bore down upon them from different directions at once, while their own were heavy and clumsy.'[12] The Athenians were admitting that their superior skill at sea was now lost, or of no value, and were copying the tactics of their previously despised enemies. As Nicias declared, they would use their superior numbers in 'a land fight that we are forced to make from shipboard'. To this end the Athenians had

> discovered the changes in construction that we must make to meet theirs; and against the thickness of their cheeks, which did us the greatest mischief, we have provided iron grappling irons, which will prevent an assailant backing water after charging, if the marines on deck here do their duty; since, we are absolutely compelled to fight a land battle from the fleet, and it seems to be our interest neither to back water ourselves, nor to let the enemy do so, especially as the shore, except so much of it as may be held by our troops is hostile ground.[13]

The Syracusans and their Corinthian allies were, however, more experienced in this style of close fighting. At the suggestion of Ariston many threw stones rather than javelins as their 'blow is just as effective however they light' and were easier to throw from a moving ship. Whereas those Athenians newly attached to the fleet found that their fire 'was disturbed by the tossing water, so that they did not all fly head on to their mark.'[14] The Syracusans also took precautions against the grapnels of the Athenians by covering the prows of their ships with hides, so that they might be deflected and fall harmlessly away.

Prior to the battle Gylippus addressed the Syracusans. He reminded them that the Athenians had come not only to conquer Sicily, but to destroy their city, kill all the men and to enslave the women and children. Instead, they had found men who could not only defend their city by land but also face their all-conquering navy and defeat it. He predicted that by defeating 'the greatest empire yet known . . . among the Hellenes' they would win for 'all Sicily her ancient freedom strengthened and confirmed'[15] and achieve a great triumph. As luck would have it, the battle would be fought on the same day that the Syracusans would celebrate a festival of their national hero Heracles. The entrails of the sacrificial victim were supposed to have foretold 'a splendid victory for them if only they did not begin the fighting, but acted on the defensive. Heracles also, they said, always won the day because he acted on the defensive and suffered himself to be attacked first.'[16] The Athenians obliged by attacking.

Despite making the opening speech, Nicias was once again left ashore while Demosthenes, Menander, and Euthydemus, led out the fleet. They proceeded straight to the palisade at the mouth of the harbour, hoping to force their way through to the open sea. The Syracusans left a detachment of ships to guard the entrance to the harbour while the rest attempted to surround the Athenian fleet from all sides. They had the advantage in that if in trouble their ships could generally retire to the shore and be assisted by their army. Python commanded the Corinthian ships in the centre of the line, while Sicanus and Agatharchus commanded the two Syracusan wings. For this battle the Syracusans had seventy-four triremes plus the usual flotilla of small boats manned by the boys of the city. By manning most of their ships, no matter what their condition, the Athenians put to sea 115 triremes and, with the extra fighting men crammed aboard, over 25,000 men.

The massed attack of the Athenians on the barrier met with initial success and they managed to break through the boom, but soon the Syracusans' wings came into contact and the battle was being fought throughout the entire harbour. Both sides knew what was at stake and fought with 'great zeal in bringing up their vessels.' The space was so crowded that each side, as the Athenians had planned, 'had no opportunity of backing water or breaking the line.' The fighting was at close quarters and brutal, where 'the men on the decks rained darts and arrows' on the enemy and 'the marines tried to board each other's vessel, fighting hand to hand.'[17]

The whole battle was in plain sight of the Syracusan population, who massed on the city's walls and hills, 'for wives and maidens and all who, because of age, could not render the service war demands, since the war was coming to its decision, were eyeing the battle with the greatest anguish of spirit.' This was not the ghoulish battlefield tourism of the nineteenth century but a matter of life and freedom for the spectators. Such a view could often be heart rending for the families as 'some Syracusan triremes would be destroyed along the walls and their crews slain before the eyes of their kinsmen, and parents would witness the destruction of their children, sisters and wives the pitiable end of husbands and brothers.'[18]

Finally, after a long struggle, the Syracusans routed the already demoralized Athenians, and drove them back onto the shore. Nicias ordered part of the army to run down and save the ships, while leaving others to defend what remained of the wall. Most, however, began to look to their own safety and fled their positions. Thucydides claims that 'the panic of the present moment had never been surpassed,'[19] as they knew that after the rout of their fleet, they had little hope of saving themselves by land. The victorious Syracusans gathered up the wrecks and the bodies of the dead, gave them a public funeral and erected a trophy. Whereas the defeat had so shattered Athenian morale that they did not even bother to:

> ask the privilege of taking up their dead. These, sooth, could go unburied; the survivors were confronted with a more pitiful sight in the abandonment of their sick and wounded, and thought themselves more wretched still than their dead, since they were sure to come with more sorrows than they to the same end after all.[20]

Losses had been heavy on both sides; the Athenians had lost sixty ships, and the Syracusans had eight destroyed and sixteen badly damaged. One of the last casualties was Ariston, who had done much to achieve the Syracusans' victories at sea. He was killed in the last stages of the battle, after the victory had already been assured.

With the defeat of the Athenian fleet, the safety of Syracuse was certain. What was still to be determined was the fate of the Athenian expedition.

Chapter 12

The Destruction of the Athenian Expedition

This was the greatest Hellenic achievement of any in this war, or, in my opinion, in Hellenic history; at once most glorious to the victors, and most calamitous to the conquered. They were beaten at all points and altogether; all that they suffered was great; they were destroyed, as the saying is, with a total destruction, their fleet, their army – everything was destroyed, and few out of many returned home. Such were the events in Sicily.

Thucydides 7.87

After the defeat, Demosthenes remained calm; he proposed to Nicias that as the barrier had been broken they should once again man their remaining vessels and attempt to escape the harbour at daybreak. He claimed that they had more ships fit for service than the enemy, the Athenian having sixty, but the enemy less than fifty. These numbers do not tally exactly with the totals and losses given by Diodorus above, but are close enough. Nicias agreed, and the orders were given, but the Athenians refused to embark, as their morale had been totally shattered. They surrounded the tents of their generals and demanded that they abandon the ships and flee by land. Seeing that it would be impossible to force the Athenians back onto their ships, the generals conceded.

While these deliberations were going on in the Athenian camp the Syracusan commanders had problems of their own, although of a less dangerous kind. Gylippus and Hermocrates both feared that the Athenians would slip away that night and continue the war from another part of Sicily. The Athenians still numbered about 40,000 men. They wished to send out the army to block the roads and passes but could not get anyone to obey their orders. Not surprisingly, virtually the entire population of the city 'in their rapture at the victory had fallen to drinking . . . and would probably consent to anything sooner than take up their arms and march out at that moment.'[1]

Hermocrates came up with his own plan to delay the Athenians. With a few friends he rode to the Athenian camp and pretended to be a part of the pro-Athenian faction from within the city. He passed on a message to the Athenian generals that they should not withdraw in darkness as the Syracusans were already guarding the roads. As it eventuated, this ruse probably was not necessary as the Athenians spent the entire next day packing their baggage. Although the sources give credit to their hero Hermocrates' trick, it is unlikely the Athenians would have been capable of marching that night. The Syracusans used the next day to much better effect. Despite their celebrations of the previous night, they marched out of the city at daybreak, no doubt hung over, and occupied the roads and passes, fortified the river fords, destroyed the bridges, and posted their cavalry in the smooth open spaces along the routes that the Athenians might use. Their fleet rowed out and dragged away those ships that the Athenians, in their panic, had neglected to burn.

It was not until the third day after their defeat that the Athenians finally completed their preparations and the army began its retreat. They were in a dreadful state, leaving their dead unburied and abandoning their wounded along the way. Those forsaken would call out the names of any friend or relation who they saw passing, begging to be carried along. Soon the whole army was in despair. The hoplites and cavalry, who were usually accompanied by a servant while on campaign, had to carry their own food and kit, for their attendants had long ago deserted. Food was also short as supplies had already failed.

Despite the fact that he was seriously ill himself, Nicias joined Demosthenes in attempting to lift the spirits of their army, riding along the ranks and encouraging the men. Nicias reminded them that they were still strong in numbers and they only had to break through to the territory of the Sicels, who still favoured them because of their hatred of the Syracusans.

The Athenians marched in an oblong, with the hoplites on the outside protecting the baggage carriers on the inside. Nicias commanded the vanguard and Demosthenes the rear. When they arrived at the ford of the River Anapus they found it guarded by the Syracusans. The foremost of the Athenian hoplites charged and dispersed the enemy. The army crossed but from then on was harassed by the Syracusan cavalry and light infantry. The Athenians made about seven kilometres on the first day before making camp on a hill. The next day they made only three kilometres before camping on an inhabited plain where they hoped to forage for food and water. The pace so far had been slow and this had allowed the Syracusans to get past the Athenians and they had 'fortified the pass in front, where there was a steep hill with a rocky ravine on each side of it, called the Acraean cliff.'[2]

The next day, the Athenians attempted to advance to the pass, while still being constantly harassed by the Syracusan cavalry and light troops. The constant attacks of the enemy forced the Athenians to return to their camp. Their supplies had now totally run out. The following morning they set out with the determination of desperation and succeeded in reaching the pass. They found that the Syracusans had completed their wall and were drawn up behind it, many ranks deep. The Athenians assaulted the barrier, but the enemy had the advantage of the steep slope and threw missiles down upon them, driving them back. During this battle another thunderstorm struck, but this time it was the Athenians who were disheartened, for they thought that even the gods were conspiring to their destruction. Such had the situation and experiences of both sides radically changed since the battle at the River Anapus.

While the Athenians rested from their first assault, a unit of Syracusans attempted to build another wall behind them. The Athenians, however, learnt of the attempt and retired with their whole army back the way they had come and camped for the night. On the following day they again advanced. The confident Syracusans, no longer feeling the need of defensive walls, surrounded and attacked them on every side. They did not confront the Athenians' line directly, but instead launched repeated attacks on their rear while skirmishing with the rest of the column. These hit and run tactics continued all day, limiting the Athenian march to about a kilometre.

There is much debate among scholars as to the exact route and destination of the Athenian retreat up to this point. Diodorus simply states that they were headed for Catane, and that this was their final destination is confirmed by Thucydides. If this was the case then the shortest and easiest route was not to cross the Anapus but to march around the Epipolae and follow the route of the modern highway S114 north to Catane. The Athenians never attempted this route; instead, they marched west and crossed the river. Clearly, they had a different, short-term objective in mind. The need to gather supplies, and put a barrier between themselves and the Syracusan cavalry, is the most likely explanation of their western route.

Nicias' declaration that they were aiming to escape to the territory of Sicels combined with the statement by Thucydides that the Athenians were heading for a point where the road ascends a steep hill called the Acraean height, has caused many historians to conclude that the Athenians were marching west towards the town of Acrae. Here they would meet and receive supplies from their Sicel allies. If the plan was to join up with the Sicels then Acrae would, on the surface, appear to be a strange rendezvous. The town was a satellite city of Syracuse built for the express purpose of dominating the Sicels and the plains to the east. There were, however, still many communities of Sicels in the mountains surrounding the town. After being supplied by the Sicels, the Athenians probably planned to move further west beyond Acrae and then follow the route of the modern S194 northeast to Catane.

A number of modern historians propose a different route. They claim that the Athenians were not aiming at Acrae but intended to swing north after crossing the Anapus and escape through the passes of the limestone cliffs of Monte Climiti and then onto Catane. They claim that this location more closely resembles Thucydides' description of the location.[3]

This alternative route does appear to be unnecessarily complicated. From personal observation, the modern road to Palazzolo Acreide (Acrae) does climb up a steep slope, with river valleys to either side. It is highly unlikely that Thucydides ever visited the site, and this location does resemble the described topography if a less dramatic translation of his text is used. Any survivors that Thucydides met may well have exaggerated the difficulties of the terrain to excuse their defeat. The traditional site would appear to be a more likely location for a site known as the 'Acraean height'. There is further evidence that the region around Acrae was the initial Athenian target of the retreat. After their defeat, the Athenians headed south and planned to follow the River Cacyparis inland. This path would also have taken them into the hills around Acrae. On balance, it is my opinion that the traditional route towards Acrae is the more likely.

The Athenians had not received any supplies for two days and were now out of food. The continual assaults of the Syracusans also meant that large numbers had been wounded. The Syracusan forces were now massed to the north and west, blocking any immediate retreat to Catane. Thucydides claims that the Athenians had now despaired of reaching that city, but instead planned to march southwest, towards Camarina and Gela, and seek refuge in the cities, either Greek or barbarian, of that region. Camarina and Gela had eventually thrown in their lot with Syracuse so it is unlikely they were the final target of the retreat. Perhaps they hoped to reach safety at one of the inland cities of their allies, perhaps Sicel-controlled Enna, where they might rest before continuing onto Catane, or possibly even to march further west to Segesta.

Nicias and Demosthenes resorted to the well-used but effective ruse of departing at night while leaving their camp fires burning. The Athenians, however, marching in the darkness in hostile country and with the enemy close by, again fell into confusion. The vanguard of Nicias kept reasonably good order, but that of Demosthenes lost contact and fell badly behind. At daybreak Nicias had succeeded in reaching the sea and struck south along the road to Helorus. The plan was to turn to the west at the River Cacyparis and to follow its course to the interior of the island. The Sicels, with whom they already made arrangements for supplies, would still be well placed to meet them on this new route.

When they reached the river, they found that the Syracusans had already barricaded the crossing. The Athenians fought their way across but then, crucially, continued south rather than turn west. They were supposedly misled by their guides, but whether this was an intentional betrayal is not recorded. Continuing south, they reached the River Erineus, near to the modern town of Noto. It had been a considerable march. In the course of one night the Athenian vanguard had covered nearly 20km, including the forcing of a defended river.

When morning came and the Syracusans realized that the Athenians had departed, many accused Gylippus of letting them go on purpose. Now that the war was nearly won the resentment and mistrust many felt towards the Spartan was being expressed more and more openly. The Syracusans easily found the line of retreat and made contact with the straggling troops of Demosthenes around midday. The Athenians of his command were still in disarray and the Syracusans immediately attacked. The Syracusan cavalry surrounded them and forced them to seek refuge in a walled olive grove. Nicias' division was now more than 8km away, for he had marched fast, thinking that their safety depended on opening up as big a gap as possible between themselves and the enemy. Isolated and crushed into a confined space, the troops of Demosthenes were easy targets for the Syracusans. They again preferred to stand off and shower the Athenians with missiles. In common with troops in victorious armies throughout the ages, none of the Syracusans wished to risk their life in hand-to-hand fighting with the desperate Athenians, and to be the last to die in the final moments of the war.

With the destruction of Demosthenes' force now assured, Gylippus and the Syracusans offered terms. They tried to split the enemy by offering freedom to any of their allies who surrendered. Few took up the offer and eventually an agreement was made that included the entire force. They were to surrender their arms but their lives would be spared and guaranteed from future mistreatment. Demosthenes tried to kill himself with his own sword but was prevented from doing so and captured by the Syracusans. The prisoners numbered 6,000 and the money taken from them filled the hollows of four hoplite shields.

While Demosthenes' force had been destroyed, Nicias and his troops crossed the River Erineus, and camped on a hill. The following day the Syracusans caught up with his force as well and informed him of Demosthenes' surrender. Nicias did not believe them and instead agreed to a truce while he sent a scout to check the truth of the matter. Upon the return of the horseman bringing the bad news, he sent a herald to Gylippus and offered, on behalf of Athens, to pay the expenses which the Syracusans had incurred in the war, on condition that the Athenians were allowed to depart in safety. The Athenians would leave hostages until the indemnity was paid at the rate of one talent for one man.

These terms were completely unacceptable to both Gylippus and the Syracusans. Gylippus would not have wanted such a large force of Athenians to return to the war against the Spartans at home. The triumphant Syracusans were also not interested and responded with angry insults. They attacked and surrounded Nicias' force, again hurling missiles rather than closing. The Syracusans were now content to wear away at the Athenians, while letting thirst and hunger take their toll. Again, Nicias tried to escape under the cover of night but this time the Syracusans were alert and raised their battle cry. A large number of the Athenians, realizing they were discovered, now laid down their arms and surrendered.

At daybreak the Syracusans renewed their assault. The Athenians tried to escape over the River Assinarus, but as soon as they reached the water their terrible thirst overcame them. They lost all sense of order as everyone tried to be the first to drink, many threw themselves in the river in their desperation. Thucydides describes the final, terrible moments of the Athenian army:

> Forced to huddle together they fell against and trampled one another, some dying immediately upon the javelins, others got entangled together and stumbling over the articles of baggage, without being able to rise again. Meanwhile the opposite bank, which was steep, was lined by the Syracusans, who showered missiles down upon the Athenians, most of whom were drinking greedily and heaped together in disorder in the hollow bed of the river. The Peloponnesians also came down and butchered them, especially those in the water, which was thus spoiled, but which they went on drinking just the same, mud and all, bloody as it was, most even fighting to have it.[4]

Nicias finally asked for terms, reminding Gylippus of all the favours he had done for the Spartans in the past. Gylippus 'thought it would keep his own fame if he should bring home alive the generals who had opposed him'[5] and gave the order to cease the slaughter and take the Athenians prisoner. Nicias surrendered himself to the Spartan, wisely believing that he would be safer in his custody. The Syracusans' blood was up, however, and the killing continued until the dead bodies were lying in heaps before the order was obeyed. Yet the number of official prisoners was small as individual Syracusans now sort to enrich themselves, and many were stolen away to be kept by the victors as spoils of war. Diodorus reports the number of Athenian dead as 18,000.[6] Therefore as many as 15,000 of the Athenians and their allies may have been stolen away by the Syracusans soldiers.

The eight-day retreat from Syracuse was finally over and with it the campaign. For the Athenians it had been a hellish experience of constant fighting, hunger and thirst, culminating in the final massacre at the River Assinarus. By contrast, the Syracusans were jubilant, both in their victory and in the knowledge that the danger of the destruction of their city was finally over. Plutarch describes the extent of their celebrations:

> The fairest and tallest trees along the river bank were hung with the captured suits of armour, and then the victors crowned themselves with wreaths, adorned their own horses splendidly while they sheared and cropped the horses of their conquered foes, and so marched into the city.

They had brought to successful end a struggle which was the most brilliant ever made by Hellenes against Hellenes, and had won the
completest of victories by the most overwhelming and impetuous
display of zeal and valour . . . that the day on which they had taken
Nicias be made a holy day, with sacrifices and abstention from labour,
and that the festival be called Assinaria, from the River Assinarus.[7]

The suffering of the conquered was, however, not yet over. Gylippus wished
to take the captured Athenian generals back to Sparta as he thought that it
would increase his own fame. Demosthenes was the victor over the Spartans
at Pylos and Sphacteria, and Nicias had persuaded the Athenians to make the
peace and free the prisoners taken on the island. The Syracusans denied
Gylippus his request and abused him. Throughout the war his Spartan harsh-
ness and the overbearing way in which he exercised his command had always
been unpopular among many. They also suspected him of having used the
war to his own advantage and of stealing funds, probably with good cause
as he would later be banished from Sparta for just such crimes. Now the war
was over they felt confident enough to give vent to their feelings and
suspicions.

The fate of the generals and the Athenians was debated at length in the
Syracusan assembly. Some were for mercy and argued, as the Plataeans had,
that those who had surrendered should not be murdered by their fellow
Greeks. Further, they claimed that the exercising of mercy would make the
Syracusans better men and bring them even greater renown, much the same
argument that had been used to spare Ducetius. This time, however, most of
the assembly were not in a forgiving mood. Others, those who had been in
communication with Nicias, may have feared that they would be exposed if
he survived. They voted to torture both the Athenian generals to death,
despite any previous assurances that had been given for their safety. Although
most sources state that they were executed, Plutarch recounts a different
version where, warned of the verdict, they committed suicide. The un-
forgiving Syracusans then threw the bodies out into the street where they 'lay
there in plain sight of all who craved the spectacle.'[8]

The prisoners held by the state, at least 7,000, were imprisoned in the
quarries just outside the city. These are now part of a picturesque open air
museum, replete with orange trees, which can be visited today. In ancient
times, however, they were not so pleasant. The Syracusans treated the
prisoners harshly, for the quarries were cramped and had no roof, and their
rations were below starvation level. Thucydides describes their terrible
conditions:

As they had to do everything on the same place for want of room, and
the bodies of those who died of their wounds, or from the variation in

temperature, or from similar causes, were left heaped together one upon another, intolerable stenches arose while hunger and thirst never ceased to afflict them.[9]

To make matters worse, the Syracusans would come out to mock them and the children to bombard them with rocks and other missiles. After about ten weeks most of the surviving allies were sold into slavery. The Athenians themselves, plus any Sicilian or Italian Greeks, no doubt considered to be traitors, remained in the quarries for a further eight months. During this time they were slowly worked and starved to death. A few intrepid or lucky individuals had escaped the retreat and made it to Catane. Others were supposedly spared, or freed, because they could quote Euripides to their poetry-loving captors. Despite this, only a handful of the approximately 50,000 troops who went to Syracuse ever returned to their homes. Death or slavery was the fate of most.

According to Plutarch, the Athenians refused to believe the news of the defeat when it first arrived. A stranger, arriving in the city 'took a seat in a barber's shop, and began to discourse of what had happened as if the Athenians already knew all about it.' The barber ran to give the news to the council and an assembly was called. The stranger could not give a clear source for his information and was accused of being a liar and trying 'to throw the city into an uproar. He was therefore fastened to the wheel and racked a long time, until messengers came with the actual facts of the whole disaster.'[10] The Athenians soon recovered their nerve. They determined 'to resist to the last', began the construction of a new fleet, tightened the budget, and curtailed the power of the assembly by electing a temporary 'board of elders to advise upon the state of affairs' for as is 'the way of a democracy, in the panic of the moment they were ready to be as prudent as possible.'[11]

Throughout the preceding account, the term Syracusans has been used for simplicity's sake, whereas Thucydides usually uses the expression 'Syracusans and their allies'. It is true that the Syracusans over the course of the war did receive aid from a number of allies. From Sicily: Gela, Selinus, Himera and some of the Sicels sent troops. From Greece: Sparta, Corinth, Leucas, Ambracia, Sicyon, Arcadia and Boeotia sent troops and ships, with the latter coming mostly from Corinth. The Athenians, it must be remembered, also brought along a multitude of subjects, allies and mercenaries. The most important assistance Syracuse received was probably at the command level and in training their inexperienced troops – Gylippus on land, and Python and other Corinthians at sea.

Despite the assistance they received, it was a victory primarily of the Syracusans themselves, particularly in the crucial first year, when, despite suffering defeat after defeat, they continued to fight on alone. Even after Gylippus and other allies arrived 'one may say, with all the rest put together, more was provided by the Syracusans themselves, both from the greatness of the city and from the fact they were in the greatest danger.'[12] The Syracusans had defeated the largest expedition ever sent out by the most powerful Greek city and its empire.

The victorious Syracusans shared some of the booty with their allies. The rest they used, as they had after other victories, to beautify the city and its temples, and to reward those how had fought the most bravely.

The capricious Greek gods were, however, jealous of mortal achievements and quick to punish hubris. Despite their disaster in Sicily, the Athenians would recover and continue to fight the Spartans for another nine years. In the end, the Athenians would only be defeated by a combination of oligarchic treachery and the Spartans selling out their professed principles for Persian silver. In contrast, the victorious Syracusans would, only eight years later, find themselves again threatened with destruction by a foreign invader, the Carthaginians. In response to the return of the Phoenician threat, the democracy would be overthrown and 'by using the dread of the Carthaginians' a tyrant would once again seize power in Syracuse.[13]

Chapter 13

The Carthaginians Return

Who are they that constantly broke treaties? The Carthaginians! Who are they that waged war most cruelly? The Carthaginians! Who are they that despoiled Italy? The Carthaginians! Who are they that demand to be forgiven? The Carthaginians! So you see, therefore, how appropriate it is to conquer them.

Cato the Elder[1]

Despite the concentration of the ancient writers on Hermocrates' leadership against the Athenians, politically the big winners after Syracuse's victory were the radical democrats. The reasons for this are unclear but one possibility is that the concentration of the population within the city walls would have tipped the balance of numbers in favour of the democrats. Many of the landless labourers who lived in the countryside would now have been regular attendees at the assemblies.

Although the expression *polis* is usually translated as 'city-state', this gives too much emphasis to the city, which was really the capital of a territory. By far the largest part of the population was the rural poor – landless labourers or small farmers who rented land. Few of the poor could have found work in, or afforded to live in, the city. Their economic existence, particularly for the landless, who would have relied on seasonal work, was often precarious. They would have found it both difficult and expensive to travel to the city to attend the assemblies or the law-courts. The quorum for an Athenian assembly at this time was only 6,000, even though citizen numbers were probably about 50,000. This is the reason why radical democrats favoured payment for such attendances, as it allowed their supporters to be present in numbers.

The rich, the hoplites and cavalry, would normally have houses in the city and manage their farms from there or rent out land for a portion of the harvest. This gave the wealthy both the leisure and resources to indulge in politics and attend the assemblies regularly. The politic leaders of the Greeks always came from the rich for these reasons. The leading politicians, even the radical democrats, were always wealthy men.

During the war, the poor would also have made up most of the rowers of the fleet. Their victories over the hitherto-invincible Athenian navy may also have given them greater confidence. Throughout this period the 'sailor rabble' are always depicted as being the most dedicated and outspoken democrats. The subsequent behaviour of the Syracusan fleet while serving for the Spartans would show that they certainly had democratic leanings and a new-found confidence. The leaders of the radical democrats appear to have been able to use this unusual situation to their political advantage.

Before they began to institute their reforms, however, they set out to remove the leadership of their opponents. First, Gylippus and the Peloponnesians were given a generous slice of the spoils and packed off as soon as possible. Next was the turn of Hermocrates, the leader of the oligarchs. In the initial glow of victory, their hatred towards the Athenians and gratitude for the assistance sent by the Peloponnesians caused the Syracusans to vote to send thirty-five triremes, commanded by Hermocrates, to assist their allies in their ongoing war against Athens. The selection of Hermocrates appears to have been an astute tactic on the part of the democrats. Despite Thucydides' constant, glowing testimonials, it should be remembered that he had not commanded in the fleet against the Athenians and had been sacked as general after a poor showing during the first year of the war. That dismissal may have been politically motivated. His new appointment almost certainly was. It was a position he could not refuse but accepting it removed him from the assembly just as the democrats were about to embark on their program of reform. His absence from the city also allowed his opponents to undermine his authority when the war at sea went against the Spartans.

With their political enemies now weakened, the democrats were able to introduce their reforms. From both Aristotle and Diodorus we learn that the constitution was reformed. Aristotle claims that it was changed from a moderate to a radical democracy. The most important change was the introduction of selecting most of the magistrates by lot rather than by election. As was the case in Athens, generals and a few other important offices were probably excluded. The political theory behind selection by lot was that it would allow able persons to win offices that their lack of wealth would make impossible to win by election.

The leader of these reforms was Diocles, who first come to notice by giving a speech arguing against showing mercy to the Athenian captives. Diodorus describes him glowingly as 'the most influential among the leaders of the populace' and claims that after his death 'they built a temple in his honour'[2] This last claim is generally considered to be spurious as Diodorus appears to have confused this Diocles with an earlier, legendary law-giver of the same name.

Although Syracuse voted to send thirty-five vessels to aid the Spartans, only twenty are recorded as arriving. These, along with two from Selinus, joined the Spartans at Leros, an island just off the southeastern coast of modern Turkey. They distinguished themselves in the capture of the nearby city of Iasus. Although their commander may have been a pro-Spartan oligarch, the crews of the ships soon showed that they shared the democratic leanings of their fellow citizens back in Syracuse. This would soon present problems for their Spartan admiral Astyochus. Later, when their pay fell into arrears, the Syracusans being 'the freest crews in the armament were likewise the boldest in setting upon Astyochus and demanding their pay'. The arrogant Spartan, used to dealing with unfree helots, responded by beating their spokesmen. The Syracusans, 'in sailor fashion rushed in fury to strike Antyochus, forcing him to flee to the shelter of an altar.'[3]

Hermocrates is reported as having supported his countrymen in the pay dispute. He was also accused by the Persian satrap Tissaphernes, who was funding the Spartan fleet, and by Alcibiades, of playing a double game and sabotaging the Spartan cause by withholding the promised pay. Tissaphernes in turn accused him of seeking a bribe and turning against him only when he refused to pay.

Later that year, Alcibiades again changed sides and rejoined the Athenians. The naval war in Ionia quickly swung against the Spartans. At the battle of Cyzicus, a city in the Propontis, probably fought early in 410, Alcibiades and the Athenians decisively defeated the Spartan fleet, capturing all its ships with the exception of those of the Syracusans. The Syracusans burned their own ships before retreating to the coastal city of Antandrus, further south on the western coast of Asia Minor. A new Persian satrap, Pharnabazus, then took over supplying the Spartans. He paid the sailors and put them to work fortifying the city and building new ships to replace those lost at Cyzicus.

Meanwhile, the democracy back at Syracuse used the defeat and the accusations against Hermocrates as an excuse to move against him. They dismissed and exiled both him and the other generals. Upon receiving the news Hermocrates called together an assembly of the Syracusans and claimed that the sentence of exile was 'both unwarranted and unconstitutional'. The men protested loudly and called on the generals to remain in command. They refused, saying that they would not form an opposition party to their own government, but urged the men to speak on their behalf when they returned to Syracuse. Xenophon does make the point that the support for Hermocrates was strongest amongst the captains, marines and steersmen. He later goes on to describe how Hermocrates had always sought favour among this group by continually taking counsel with them during the campaign.[4] These groups are, however, those more likely to have come from the wealthier members of society, unlike the sailors and rowers who would have come from the poorest class. Hermocrates then departed to spend his exile in Sparta.

Back in Sicily, the victory over the Athenians, although overwhelming, had not brought complete peace to the island. About a thousand Athenians had escaped to Catane. From there they joined the Leontines in waging a guerrilla war against the Syracusans. Nor had the original trigger of the war, the ongoing conflict between Selinus and Segesta, been solved. In 410 Selinus again planned to attack Segesta and to seize a large part of its territory.

The victory of the Syracusans over the Athenians had caused great distress in Segesta. They feared that the Syracusans would now assist Selinus in making war on them as punishment for their invitation to the Athenians. The Segestans again looked to an overseas saviour and approached their long-term allies the Carthaginians for assistance. This time they received a much more positive response. After the embassy from Segesta had offered to submit their city to Carthage, there was much debate as to how to respond. According to Diodorus 'the Carthaginians found themselves in no little quandary; for while they were eager to acquire a city so strategically situated, at the same time they stood in fear of the Syracusans, having just witnessed their defeat of the armaments of the Athenians.'[5] At length they voted to support the Segestans. The Carthaginians may have plausibly believed that the total defeat of Segesta would have threatened their hold on the western end of Sicily. They may also have thought that with Syracuse's attention concentrated on the east, now was a good moment to re-assert themselves on the island.

They sent Hannibal, the grandson of the Hamilcar who had died at Himera, to Sicily. If the Carthaginians truly had wanted a negotiated settlement with Selinus and Syracuse then he was a poor choice as an ambassador. Hannibal was reputed to hate the Greeks, much as his more famous namesake two centuries later would hate the Romans. He also had a burning desire to wipe away the stain of defeat at Himera that blemished his family's reputation.

This decision by the Carthaginians reversed a policy they had followed for the seventy years from 480 until 410. During this time the Carthaginians appear to have taken little interest in affairs in Sicily. They had ignored calls for assistance from both Segesta in 416 and Athens in 415. In order to understand why this policy was abruptly reversed in 410 it is necessary to attempt to establish what the Carthaginians were doing during these seven decades. Unfortunately, this period is poorly recorded.[6] There are almost as many theories for this period of Carthaginian history as there are historians. The following attempt to recreate this period should therefore be seen as speculative.

Even the nature of the Carthaginian government is much debated. There are two main schools of thought. One is that the Carthaginian king was really an annually elected magistrate, much like a Roman consul. The other claims that the Magonid dynasty was hereditary and the principal function of the king was to act as a commander in time of war. The testimony of the Greek historians tends to favour the latter view.[7] Aristotle compares the Carthaginian government to that of the Spartans, having kings, a council of elders and an assembly. He further states that 'the Carthaginians choose their magistrates, and particularly the highest of them – their kings and generals – with an eye both to merit and to wealth.'[8] This description is, however, generally taken to refer to the period after the collapse of Magonid power in 396. Prior to this date there is no mention of any assembly of the people. Diodorus (13.43) refers to the Carthaginian Council as a *gerousia,* the word used to describe the Spartan council of elders. This is in keeping with what is known from other Phoenician cities. Serge Lancel claims that 'a Council of Elders must have been in existence from the earliest times in Carthage.'[9] It would appear most likely that until 396 Carthage was ruled by a narrowly-based council and a hereditary king who acted as war-leader. What is certain, however, is that one family, the Magonids, dominated the city for nearly a century.

The details of the history of the city during this period are just as difficult to retrace. Nonetheless, from the few surviving sources and the archaeological evidence it is possible to determine the broad outline. According to Justin, two generations of the descendants of the Hamilcar killed at Himera ruled during this period and 'by these the affairs of the Carthaginians were managed at this period. War was made upon the Moors, a contest was maintained with the Numidians, and the Africans were compelled to remit the tribute paid for the building of the city.'[10] The philosopher and historian, Dion Chrystostom, confirms Justin's claim, stating that, 'the Carthaginians Hanno made Libyans instead of Tyrians, forced them to live in Libya instead of Phoenicia, caused them to possess great wealth, many trading-centres, harbours, and warships, and to rule over a vast land and a vast sea.'[11] This Hanno was the son of Hamilcar. It appears that Carthage spent the greater part of this period conquering the agricultural areas around the city and subjugating the native Libyan population. This was done during the rule of the next two Magonids, Hanno and Hannibal. These campaigns appear to have begun during Hanno's reign and must have commenced as soon as the Carthaginians had recovered from their defeat at Himera.

The area conquered was quite large. The archaeological record shows that the Carthaginians controlled an area that encompassed about half of modern-day Tunisia. The borders would have run in an arc stretching roughly from the modern cities of Tebessa to Le Kef. At some stage the borders were fortified and delineated by a series of trenches. This region included all of the fertile regions of Tunisia. Although writing about the situation two centuries later, the geographer Strabo claims that they: 'gained possession of all that part of Libya which men can live in without living a nomadic life' and 'they had three hundred cities in Libya and seven hundred thousand people in their city'.[12]

The increase in agricultural land does not appear to have led to the creation of a new middle-class of farmers, as would have happened in a Greek city. The Carthaginians subdued the native population and turned them into a subject people. The land was divided up into large estates, farmed by Libyan sharecroppers and by slaves, often Greek prisoners of war. The native population, like the Spartan helots and Sicel *kyllaroi*, was prone to rebellion. The estates of inland Carthage were palatial but heavily fortified.

Since its foundation, the wealth of Carthage had depended on trade. The richest and most powerful men were merchants and the city derived its revenues from customs and harbour duties. The conquest and exploitation of a large and fertile agricultural region must have had an impact on the internal power struggles within the city. Many would now have supplemented, or possibly earned in entirety, their wealth from the exploitation of their estates. It is possible that this group would have different interests, particularly when it came to military security, than the traditional ruling class. This may, at least in part, have played some role in the political conflicts that would erupt during the fourth century.

The conquest of its hinterland won Carthage a huge agricultural territory, larger than that of any Greek city or even Rome at that period. It would have provided Carthage with large amounts of revenue. This, in addition to its vast trade and mining interests, would have made the city immensely wealthy. Wealth and military power were always linked in ancient times, as recognized by Caesar who declared 'that there were two things which created, protected, and increased sovereignties – soldiers and money – and that these two were dependent on each other.'[13] The enormous wealth of Carthage, therefore, ensured that it was also a military power. The Greeks of Sicily would constantly underestimate how rapidly this wealth would enable the Carthaginians to recover from their defeats.

It is sometimes argued by modern commentators that the Carthaginians saw war as an extension of business, running it on a profit-and-loss basis, and were generally not as aggressive as other ancient peoples. This view contradicts the Greek characterization of them as warlike and aggressive. Although this opinion may be dismissed as that of a hostile source, it is not unreasonable to conclude that it may have been shared by the Libyans, the Spanish and the Sardinians. The apparent passivity of Carthage abroad after Himera is more likely as a result of their concentration on their African campaigns rather than any perceived pacifism.

By 410 they appear to have completed their wars to subjugate their hinterland and now controlled not only this region but all the Phoenician cities of North Africa, Spain, and Sardinia. Some historians argue that their empire even spread down the Atlantic coast of Africa, but this is a hotly contested assertion. As Alcibiades claimed was the way of ancient empires, they were now looking to expand further. In Hannibal they also had an ambitious king with a reported hatred of the Greeks. The Greeks of Selinus, formerly friends but now allied to Syracuse, were posing a serious threat to Segesta. Ancient empires were firm believers in the concept of the pre-emptive strike. If another power threatened you, it was best to attack first. If successful you might destroy them, although a more likely result would be to conquer part of their territory. This would both weaken them and strengthen you. It would also ensure that their lands would suffer the inevitable destruction that would accompany any campaign. For all these reasons Sicily would now become the obvious target for Carthaginian conquest.

Diodorus' list of the troops raised for the campaign appears much the same as that for the Himera campaign. Citizen troops from Carthage and the other Phoenician cities of Africa were supplemented by mercenaries raised from Spain, Gaul, Campania and the independent tribes of Africa. The main difference would have been large numbers of troops raised from their Libyan subjects. The few images we have of the Phoenician and Libyan infantry show them as being armed with a long spear and large shield similar to the equipment of Greek hoplites. This, and the references of the Greek historians as fighting in phalanx, indicate that the Carthaginians had now adopted the hoplite style of fighting. Just when this reform took place is unknown but the defeat at Himera would be the obvious catalyst. The Campanians would also have fought as hoplites. The ferocious Spanish and Gaulish infantry would have fought by showering the enemy with thrown spears and then charging fiercely with their swords. Other infantry would have fought mainly as skirmishers armed with javelins or bows. The mercenary infantry from the Balearic Islands were famous slingers. Reportedly, they were trained from boyhood and were not allowed to eat until they could hit their food with their slingshot.

Cavalry was supplied partly by the Carthaginian nobility, with their new landed estates being the source of their mounts. Mercenary cavalry is recorded as being hired from the Campanians. The Gauls, Spanish and Numidian tribes from Africa are all possible sources of further cavalry. The latter were renowned for their light, skirmishing cavalry and were used in large numbers by later Carthaginian armies. The Carthaginians also made use of chariots in war, a weapon abandoned by the Greeks, except for the African cities of Cyrenaica. Later Carthaginian armies were renowned for their large numbers of excellent cavalry.

Hannibal sent a delegation, including representatives of the Segestans, to Syracuse to discuss the territorial dispute between Segesta and Selinus. He believed that the Syracusans would abandon Selinus in the face of Carthaginian support of Segesta. The Syracusans prevaricated, voting to keep their alliance with Segesta and to maintain the peace with Carthage. Most likely they believed that after seventy years of Carthaginian inaction, the same indifference that had forced Segesta to approach Athens, would continue. They cannot realistically have predicted the onslaught that was to come. In hindsight, however, this was a weak position that encouraged Hannibal in his belief that Syracuse would not support Selinus if Carthage actively intervened on the side of Segesta. Perhaps the Syracusans would have been better advised to either force Selinus to make peace or throw their full support behind the city in order to deter Carthage.

The Carthaginians now decided to give military aid to Segesta, sending 5,000 Libyan troops and 800 Campanian mercenaries. The Selinuntians' previous victories had made them overconfident. They again invaded Segestan territory and, despising the enemy, scattered their forces to better ravage the countryside. The Segestans, now reinforced with the Carthaginian troops, attacked, routing the Segestans, killing 1,000 and recapturing the loot.

After this encounter, both sides again sent embassies to seek aid from their more powerful allies. Both promised to assist their allies and as Diodorus declares 'the Carthaginian War thus had its beginning.'[14]

Chapter 14

The First Carthaginian War

At this time Hannibal, the general of the Carthaginians, gathered together both the mercenaries he had collected from Iberia and the soldiers he had enrolled from Libya, manned sixty ships of war, and made ready some fifteen hundred transports. On these he loaded the troops, the siege-engines, missiles, and all the other accessories. After crossing with the fleet the Libyan Sea he came to land in Sicily.

Diodorus 13.54

The Carthaginians, anticipating the magnitude of their task, made their war plans on a grand scale. They appointed Hannibal as commander and put large resources at his disposal. He recruited Punic troops and Libyans from Africa and mercenaries from Spain. In 409 he sailed to Sicily with sixty warships, 1,500 transports and an army reported as being either 100,000 or 204,000 men. As usual, the size of the army is almost certainly exaggerated by the Greek historians Ephorus and Timaeus. It must have numbered in excess of 40,000 troops, however, as this is the figure Diodorus later records for the size of Hannibal's army after the siege of Selinus.

The fleet was spied by some Selinuntian cavalry as it approached. They immediately passed a message to their city, which dispatched letters to Syracuse. Meanwhile, Hannibal had landed at Motya and, after disembarking the army, dragged his fleet up onto land. This gesture was aimed at assuring the Syracusans that he had not come to attack their city but only to assist his allies in Sicily.

Hannibal then marched on Selinus by way of Lilybaeum. Arriving before the city, he immediately invested it and began building siege engines – six towers of great height and six battering rams armoured with iron plates. The people of Selinus were totally unprepared for such an assault. First, they had not considered that they would be attacked by a 'people whom they had befriended.' In addition they 'had for a long time been without experience in sieges.'[1] It was not just their inexperience in sieges that must have surprised them but also the Carthaginians' proficiency in building and using siege engines.

The Greeks were, however, not totally ignorant of siege techniques. Thucydides describes the Spartan siege operations at Plataea. First they enclosed the city with a palisade. Next they attempted to build a ramp leading up to the walls of the city. The Plataeans countered by attempting to dig a tunnel to undermine the ramp. This was only partially successful as eventually the Spartan ramp reached the city walls and they succeeded in knocking down a small section with a ram. The Plataeans had prepared for this by building a counterwork behind the breach. The Spartans now appear to have given up trying to take the city and built a wall of circumvallation to isolate the city and starve it out. What the Greeks of the fifth century appear to have lacked was a professional corps of engineers who could carry out such operations effectively over a long period.

In the above example, both the attackers and the besiegers utilized three of the main methods of siege warfare: ramps, rams and mines. Catapults and other missile-firing engines did not come into use until the next century. The Spartans do not appear to have made any attempt to build towers. Such towers were usually built by attacking forces to be higher than the city's walls. From this vantage point they could rain down missiles onto the defenders and hopefully drive them from their walls, or at least force them to keep their heads down and reduce the effectiveness of their defensive fire. Although these simple, stationary towers were the most common, mobile towers on wheels were also used. These would be pushed up to the city walls and a drawbridge lowered. The attacking troops could then assault the walls from above without the terrible dangers of scaling the walls by ladders.

If these methods proved unsuccessful the Greek besiegers would then be forced to surround the city and starve it into submission or to a point where its weakened defenders could no longer defend against an assault. Neither method was particularly successful if the target was resolute and prepared in their defence. During the Peloponnesian war, the Athenians had besieged the city of Potidea for over two years before accepting its surrender on terms. The Spartans would spend a similar amount of time investing Plataea before it too was forced to surrender.

In this area the Greeks had remained relatively backward compared to the peoples of the Middle East. The oldest depiction of a siege tower comes from reliefs dedicated to the ninth-century Assyrian king Ashurnasirpal II (884–859). The use of towers by the Carthaginians at Selinus is their first recorded employment outside of Asia. The Carthaginians probably learnt of their use and construction from the Phoenician cities of the east. They had been subjects of the Assyrians and had probably experienced their use at first hand during their seventh century revolt.

It was their relative inability to take cities quickly that had caused the Greeks to become reliant on traitors within the walls betraying their city to attackers. This partly explains Nicias' lack of energy in completing the walls around Syracuse. Almost to the end he was pinning his hopes on a fifth column betraying the city to him. The constant class struggles inside the Greek *polis* would continue to make this a successful method by which to capture cities. Even a century later, long after the Greeks had developed up-to-date siege trains, Philip II of Macedonia would boast that he had captured more cities by gold than by soldiers. Pyrrhus of Epirus would make a similar claim, bragging that his chief diplomat Cineas had captured more cities for him with his tongue than his army ever had. The Carthaginians could not expect Selinus to be betrayed to them. Instead, they were about to give the Greeks a brutal lesson in siege warfare.

The Selinuntians did not despair, as they expected that they could hold off the attackers until the Syracusans and their other allies arrived. Selinus is a spectacularly-sited city, perched on cliff tops overlooking the sea. The acropolis, which is closest to the sea, is protected on three sides by steep hill-sides. The residential part of the city then spreads inland to the north, where the slope of the hill declines. The city may also have been protected to the east and west by a river and a harbour. These watercourses are now silted up and may already have been so in 409. The most likely place for the Carthaginians to have launched their assault was against the vulnerable northern walls. Here the hill is at its lowest, with a gentle slope that is no barrier to an attacker.

The Selinuntians prepared for the assault by arming all men of military age, most likely providing the poorest men with state-supplied weapons. The old men were mobilized to provide supplies of food and missiles for the defenders. They were joined by the women and girls, who were unusually allowed to be unescorted in public due to the emergency. Hannibal motivated his troops by promising he would give the city over to them to be pillaged if they took it.

The long period of peace and security had made the Selinuntians com-placent. Their walls were too low and were overlooked by the towers, allowing the Carthaginians archers and slingers to keep the defenders under constant fire. They had also allowed their fortifications to fall into disrepair and a breach was quickly made by the Carthaginian rams. A unit of Campanian mercenaries, eager for loot, forced their way into the city before the breach was fully cleared. This allowed the defenders to rally and to drive them back with heavy losses, as the attackers could not be easily reinforced. At nightfall, the Carthaginians called off the attack. That night, the Selinuntians managed to sneak a number of horsemen out of the city, sending messages to Akragas, Gela and Syracuse, begging them to come with all speed to the relief of their city.

The other Greeks believed that the city would not be stormed but would hold out for a long time under siege and showed no sense of urgency. The Syracusans had made no preparations. They first had to make peace with Catane and recall their troops. Gela and Akragas decided to wait for the

Syracusans so that they could advance as a united force against the enemy.

The next day, Hannibal widened the breach in preparation for an assault while launching diversionary attacks on other parts of the walls. Once the breach was cleared, he assaulted in relays with his best troops. In such instances, the defenders have the advantage of both height and position, being able to fight from three sides of the breach. In addition, as Diodorus claims, they had the courage of desperation: 'it is not possible, however, to overpower by force men fighting for their very existence.'[2] For nine days the Selinuntians held off the Carthaginians with many casualties on both sides. Eventually, the greater numbers of the attackers told, as they were able to relieve their troops with fresh men, while the Selinuntians no longer had any reserves to call on.

On the morning of the tenth day, the Spanish mercenaries of the Carthaginians forced the exhausted defenders back from the breach. The fighting continued within the city as the defenders barricaded the narrow streets, and the women and children threw rocks and tiles down from the surrounding roof tops. The fighting went on into the afternoon with the Carthaginians suffering more losses. Finally, numbers and fresh reserves told and the defenders were broken. Most of the surviving defenders gathered in the *agora*, where they died fighting. Throughout the city the defeated Greeks fell to 'lamentation and weeping. . . . as their eyes looked upon the great disaster that surrounded them, were filled with terror.' Whereas 'among the barbarians there was cheering', as 'elated by their successes' they 'urged on their comrades to slaughter.'[3]

Diodorus then goes on to describe graphically the atrocities that followed after the capture of an ancient city:

> The barbarians, scattering throughout the entire city, plundered what-ever was of value to be found in the dwellings, while the inhabitants they found in them they burned together with their homes and when others struggled into the streets, without distinction of sex or age but whether infant children or women or old men, they put them to the sword, showing no sign of compassion.[4]

By nightfall the city had been sacked, the buildings destroyed and the streets were full of blood and corpses. The Carthaginians had killed 16,000 people and taken 5,000 as prisoners.

Diodorus describes in great detail the fate of the prisoners, their rape by the victors and their subsequent shipment to Libya to be sold into slavery. He adopts a tone of outrage when describing the destruction of Selinus and the fate of the survivors. The Carthaginians 'surpass all men in cruelty [*omotes*] and the unfortunate captives are subjected to their licentiousness [*hubris*].'[5] Yet their treatment was what was to be expected at the time. The fate of Greek cities taken by their fellow Greeks was little different. In the previous decades, massacres at Plataea and Melos had been carried out by the Spartans and Athenians, executing all the men and selling the women and children into slavery, even though the cities had surrendered before being stormed.

These were, however, atrocities committed in cold blood and in an organized manner. A better comparison would be Alexander the Great's storming of the city of Thebes. Both Diodorus and Arrian describe the final fall of Thebes in a similar manner. Alexander's Macedonians and his Greek allies 'in the lust of battle, indiscriminately slaughtered the Thebans, who no longer put up any organized resistance. They burst into houses and killed the occupants; others they cut down as they attempted to show fight; others, again, even as they clung to temple altars, sparing neither women nor children.' Diodorus adds the fate of the women and children 'who having fled into the temples were torn from sanctuary and subjected to outrage without limit.'[6] The Greeks could be just as brutal to their fellow Greeks as any barbarian.

There is, therefore, a certain amount of hypocrisy on Diodorus' part when he describes the Carthaginians as the cruellest of men. His outrage, most likely, stems from the intense dislike, even hatred, which the Greeks displayed towards the Carthaginians. Although they admired their skills as sailors, craftsmen and merchants they generally detested them as being deceitful, greedy, narrow-minded and warlike. Their practice of human sacrifice was also much despised. The expression 'Phoenician story' was used by the ancient Greeks to mean treachery or a lie.

These attitudes appear to have developed early; Homer describes a 'Phoenician, a cunning rascal, who had already committed all sorts of villainy.'[7] This view is perhaps best personified by another Greek historian, Polybius, in his description of the character of the later Carthaginian general Hannibal:

> He even allowed himself to violate the treaties he had made, transferring the inhabitants to other towns and giving up their property to plunder, thereby causing such offence that he was accused both of impiety and cruelty . . . But at any rate among the Carthaginians he was notorious for his love of money and among the Romans for his cruelty.[8]

Our major source for the campaigns of the Carthaginians in Sicily is Diodorus, a Sicilian Greek, who most likely was raised on stories of Carthaginian massacres. These attitudes towards the Carthaginians should be kept in mind while reading Diodorus', or any other Greek historian's, accounts of Carthaginian atrocities.

A small group of 2,600 fugitives escaped from Selinus and found refugee at Akragas, where they were met with kindness and were supported at public expense. Shortly after a contingent of 3,000 picked soldiers from Syracuse arrived at Akragas. The Syracusans sent a delegation to Hannibal offering to ransom the captives and pay an indemnity to prevent the destruction of the temples. They had, however, underestimated the hatred that Hannibal harboured for the Greeks and his desire to punish them for the death of his grandfather.

Hannibal replied dismissively that 'the Selinuntians having proved incapable of defending their freedom, would now undergo the experience of slavery, and that the gods had departed from Selinus, having become offended with its inhabitants.' The survivors then sent Empedion as an ambassador to Hannibal. He is described as having 'favoured the cause of the Carthaginians.'⁹ Probably he acted as their *proxenos* within the city. Hannibal relented to the extent that he released Empedion's relations from the captives, giving permission for the survivors to return to the city provided they pay tribute to the Carthaginians. From this point on Selinus would mostly be a subject city of Carthage. Hannibal reinforced the city's subjugation by destroying the walls of the city. This was one of the main methods conquerors used to compromise a city's freedom and autonomy.

With Selinus now dealt with, Hannibal marched his army north to Himera. He reputedly felt an enormous hatred towards this city, holding it responsible for the defeat and death of his grandfather. Hannibal was determined to mete out a terrible revenge on the city and its inhabitants.

After leaving Selinus, Hannibal marched on Himera with an army of 40,000 troops. Upon arriving, he built a camp on some hills close to the city, quite possibly on the foothills of Mount Calogero, where his grandfather had built his palisade. Here he was joined by another 20,000 troops provided by the Sicanians and Sicels.

Hannibal adopted the same tactics that had been so successful at Selinus. He set up his towers and began battering the walls with his rams. His troops, high in morale after their sack of Selinus, attacked the city in relays, wearing down the defenders.

Hannibal also began undermining the walls. This method involved building a tunnel under the walls of a fortress, shoring up the walls with wooden supports and then increasing the size of the cavity until it was sufficiently large that the ground could no longer support the weight of the walls if the props were removed. The miners would then set on fire the wooden supports, and if they had calculated correctly, the section of the fortifications above would collapse. Defending forces could sometimes detect the construction of mines by observing the vibrations of the diggings. Containers of liquid were often used as otherwise-undetected vibrations would produce ripples on the surface of the liquid. The defenders could respond by building a counter-mine and attacking the enemy sappers, or by building a second wall behind the threatened section.

The Carthaginian tunnel appears to have been undetected and when fired brought down a large section of Himera's walls. The waiting Carthaginian troops immediately assaulted the breach. A bitter fight ensued in the breach, but the desperate Himerians, fearing to share the fate of Selinus, drove out the attackers and repaired the gap. At the same time that the fight was occurring, 4,000 troops from Syracuse and their other allies, under the command of Diocles of Syracuse, arrived to reinforce the defenders.

The Himerians decided not to allow themselves to be completely surrounded by the enemy and planned a counterattack against the Carthaginian lines. The next day they gathered all their hoplites, 10,000 in total, including their allies, and attacked the besiegers. The attack took the Carthaginians by surprise; the Greeks defeated the first troops they met and drove them back in disorder. The Himerians, elated by their success, and under the watchful eyes of the spectators on the city's walls, decided they had won the battle and pursued the routing enemy. They pressed the enemy hard, crying out to give no quarter and killed more than 6,000. In the pursuit, however, the Greeks had over-estimated the scale of their victory. They had only defeated a fraction of the Carthaginian army, which now totalled 80,000 men. Hannibal, seeing that the Greeks had over-committed themselves to the pursuit, led out the troops remaining in the Carthaginian camp. They caught the Greeks as they were tired and disordered from the pursuit. The Carthaginians now routed the Greeks, driving them back into the city and killing 3,000.

After the battle, twenty-five Syracusan triremes sent to reinforce the Himerians pulled into the city. Their arrival caused wild rumours to spread through the ranks of the demoralized Greeks. One claimed that all the Syracusans and their allies were marching to the relief of Himera. Another alleged that Hannibal was preparing his triremes in Motya, manned by his best troops, to sail to Syracuse and seize the city while it was stripped of its defenders, as the Athenians had attempted in 415.

Diocles appears to have taken these rumours seriously and panicked. He decided that Himera was now indefensible and had to be abandoned. The Himerians were disgusted at the decision but, weakened by their losses and abandoned by their allies, had no choice but to agree.

Half the population were ordered to embark on the departing ships, which were instructed to land them in the safety of Messene and then return. The remainder were to stay to defend the city until the fleet returned and could evacuate them in turn. Not all the women and children, however, could fit on the ships and many were forced to march out with their departing allies. Diocles' panic was so great that in his haste he committed the sacrilege of not burying the bodies of the fallen.

Those left behind spent the night under arms guarding the retreat. The next morning the Carthaginians surrounded the city and launched repeated attacks. The defenders fought desperately, no doubt with one eye on the horizon hoping for the return of the fleet. The next day, the ships sailed into sight but it was too late. The rams had breached the walls and the Carthaginians poured into the city. They killed the defenders without quarter until Hannibal ordered a halt. The Carthaginians plundered the city, including the temples. Once the sack was completed they set fire to the city and razed it to the ground. Two hundred and forty years after its foundation, Himera had ceased to exist. Another city of the same name would later be built, but it would occupy a site where there were sacred hot springs, 8km to the west.

Hannibal had not ordered the capture of the survivors because of any feelings of mercy; instead, he had a more gruesome fate planned for them. The few remaining women and children were separated from the men and distributed among the soldiers. The 3,000 surviving defenders were led to the place where his grandfather Hamilcar had been killed by the Greeks and tortured to death. Given the Carthaginians' penchant for human sacrifice, this was most likely a form of religious rite in honour of his ancestor.

After completing his revenge, Hannibal dismissed his native allies. He also sacked his Campanian mercenaries, who were proving to be unruly and demanding a greater share of the loot. Hannibal then embarked the army aboard the fleet and, leaving a garrison to protect his Sicilian allies, returned to Carthage laden with booty. There he was greeted as a conquering hero, and 'the whole city came out to meet him, paying him homage and honour as one who in a brief time had performed greater deeds than any general before him.'[10] Over the course of one campaigning season, Hannibal had skilfully, albeit brutally, completed both his official and personal objectives. The threat to the Carthaginian region of Sicily, known as the Epicraty, had been removed, as had the stain on his family's reputation. In the process two wealthy Greek cities had been destroyed. Both would be refounded but neither would ever fully recover its former splendour.

The disasters at Selinus and Himera, and the poor performance of the Syracusan leadership, caused political dissent at home. Diocles' command had been ineffectual at best and craven at worst. Such disasters often led to democratic assemblies fining, exiling or even executing losing generals. Diocles must have had a strong power base, as he appears to have maintained his position. Nonetheless, the disasters must have weakened his authority and given much ammunition to the enemies of the democracy. It was at this point that Hermocrates, although still exiled from Syracuse, returned to Sicily.

During his time of exile in Sparta, Hermocrates had accompanied a Spartan embassy to Pharnabazus, the Persian satrap of the Hellespont. The Spartans were looking for a Persian sponsor to replace Tissaphernes and provide money for their ongoing war against Athens. Hermocrates had ingratiated himself with Pharnabazus and was given an enormous sum of money. The funds were sufficient to allow him to build five triremes, and to gather a private army of 1,000 mercenary hoplites and another 1,000 from the survivors of Himera. What Pharnabazus hoped to achieve is not recorded. Perhaps he hoped that if Hermocrates was back in power in Syracuse then the city would increase its assistance to the Spartans.

Hermocrates had hoped that his friends within the city, including the returning officers of the fleet, would have been able to facilitate his recall. Late in 409 he returned to Sicily and landed near Syracuse. Yet, despite their setbacks, the democrats were still in control of the assembly and his exile was not overturned. Frustrated in his attempt to enter the city, Hermocrates marched his force across the centre of the island and seized Selinus. He fortified a section of the city and invited the survivors of the city to return. Other volunteers also joined him and soon he had an army of 6,000. Hermocrates now launched a private war against the Carthaginians. He laid waste to the territory of Motya. A force from the city, probably the local citizen levies, bolstered by troops left behind by Hannibal, marched out to meet him. Hermocrates defeated them in battle and drove them back within their walls.

With this success behind him, Hermocrates then marched on Panormus. Again, he ravaged their territory and convinced the local forces to come out and fight him. Once more Hermocrates defeated the enemy in battle, killing 500 and forcing the survivors back within their city. Hermocrates now pillaged the rest of the Carthaginian lands, gathering huge amounts of booty and becoming a hero to the Sicilian Greeks. His campaign was a calculated provocation directed at both the Carthaginians and Syracusans, which he knew must cause a reaction. Perhaps Hermocrates wished to resurrect his policy of Sicilian unity with himself at the head of an anti-Carthaginian alliance.

According to Diodorus, 'the majority of the Syracusans also repented of their treatment of him, realizing that Hermocrates had been banished contrary to the merits of his valour.' The assembly met repeatedly to discuss his recall but, despite their setbacks and his successes, his political opponents were still strong enough to prevent it. Hermocrates in turn, realizing the strength of the opposition 'laid careful plans regarding return from exile.'[11] Despite Diodorus' testimony, it is clear that the majority of his fellow citizens had not repented their treatment of him. They still feared that he was a threat to their democracy, perhaps even more so with a private army at his back.

Hermocrates marched from Selinus to Himera. Here he managed to locate the remains of the fallen Syracusans. He arranged for them to be returned to Syracuse, but as an exile he was stopped at the borders of the *chora*. According to Diodorus, Hermocrates had deliberately acted in this manner in order to undermine Diocles' position:

Now when the bones had been brought into the city, civil discord arose among the masses, Diocles objecting to their burial and the majority favouring it. Finally, the Syracusans not only buried the remains of the dead but also by turning out *en masse* paid honour to the burial procession. Diocles was exiled; but even so they did not receive Hermocrates back, since they were wary of the daring of the man and feared lest, once he had gained a position of leadership, he should proclaim himself tyrant.[12]

Despite his best efforts, the Syracusan people were prepared to sacrifice the incompetent Diocles, but still held fears that Hermocrates harboured ambitions to overthrow the democracy. Hermocrates was not yet prepared for an armed confrontation with his city and returned to Selinus. He continued to plot with his friends in the city and, shortly after, they convinced him that the time was now right for a coup. Early in 408, with 3,000 soldiers, he marched secretly, arriving at the gates of Syracuse during the night. His friends within the city had gathered in the area of Achradine. Under the cover of darkness, Hermocrates and a small number of his troops were allowed into the gates by his followers. The plot was, however, discovered and the Syracusans 'gathered in the market-place under arms, and here, since they appeared accompanied by a great multitude, they slew both Hermocrates and most of his supporters.'[13]

The coup had failed primarily because it was so narrowly based. As a member of the old aristocracy Hermocrates had gained most of his support from his fellow nobles and his private army. The largest group of armed people in any city was, however, the hoplites. Clearly, they were not in favour of returning to an archaic form of government based on the aristocracy and, along with the poor, armed themselves to oppose it. It was Hermocrates' narrow base of support that had doomed him.

Ancient politics were played for high stakes and such class-based power struggles generally brought about the worst in both sides. The victors were inevitably vindictive in their victory, using the opportunity to eliminate their opponents. The Syracusan democrats gave no quarter in the fighting. Those of Hermocrates' supporters who managed to escape were brought to trial and exiled. The relatives of many of the wounded survivors reported them to be dead and spirited them out of the city in order to save their lives. One of these was Dionysius, who would become the next tyrant of Syracuse.

The whole incident demonstrates just how robust the Syracusan democracy was at this time. Hermocrates' exploits had increased the strength of his faction and they had been able to remove his most powerful enemy, Diocles. The latter had, however, probably alienated his own supporters through his incompetence and petty-mindedness. Nonetheless, despite losing their leader, the *demos* was still confident enough to vote down Hermocrates' recall and to defeat his armed rebellion.

Now they had crushed the internal threat to their democracy, the

Syracusans turned their attention back towards their external enemy, the Carthaginians. In 407 they sent an embassy to Carthage to condemn them for the war and demand that they cease from attacking the Greeks of Sicily. In reply the Carthaginians

> gave ambiguous answers and set about assembling great armaments in Libya, since their desire was fixed on enslaving all the cities of the island; but before sending their forces across to Sicily they picked out volunteers from their citizens and the other inhabitants of Libya and founded in Sicily right at the warm [*therma*] springs a city which they named Therma.'[14]

The site of the new city was about eight kilometres to the west of the destroyed Himera but well to the east of previous Phoenician settlements. The easy victories over Selinus and Himera, plus the discord in Syracuse, may have convinced the Carthaginians of their military superiority over the Greeks. They voted to send another large expedition to the island, again placing Hannibal in command. In a manner reminiscent of Nicias, he requested to be excused because of his age but the Carthaginians insisted. They did, however, appoint another general, Himilcon, a member of the same family, to share the burden of command. Their plans were now on a much grander scale as, according to Diodorus, they were now 'elated over their successes in Sicily and eager to become lords of the whole island'.[15]

Chapter 15

The Siege of Akragas

With such a throng of men, women, and children deserting the city, at once endless lamentation and tears pervaded all homes. For while they were panic-stricken from fear of the enemy, at the same time they were also under necessity, because of their haste, of leaving behind as booty for the barbarians the possessions on which they had based their happiness; for when Fortune was robbing them of the comforts they enjoyed in their homes, they thought that they should be content that at least they were preserving their lives. And one could see the abandonment not only of the opulence of so wealthy a city but also of a multitude of human beings.

Diodorus 13.89

Despite their new-found confidence, the Carthaginians made careful preparations for their next campaign. According to the Greek historians, they raised a force of either 120,000 or 300,000 men. Again the latter figure is probably an exaggeration but the lower number is possible if it includes the entire expedition, not just fighting troops. The army was probably in the usual range for such expeditions, 40–60,000 men. It consisted of the customary mixture of nationalities: Phoenicians, Libyans and allied Numidians from Africa, as well as mercenaries from Spain, the Balearic Islands and Campania. The force was to be transported to Sicily by a fleet of reputedly 1,000 ships. The Carthaginians also sent an embassy to Athens seeking an alliance against Syracuse. It is known from a surviving inscription that the Athenians later sent a delegation to Sicily to negotiate with Hannibal but nothing is known of its outcome. There is no record of the Athenians sending any forces, so it must be assumed that they were too much engaged with their war with Sparta in the east to spare any resources.

The invasion began in 406. The Carthaginians despatched forty triremes in advance of the main fleet to prevent any Syracusan interference. This time, however, the Syracusans appear to have been much better prepared. A force roughly equal in size intercepted the Carthaginians off Drepanum (Trapani), the seaport of Eryx. The Syracusans, having learnt the finer points of naval warfare the hard way from the Athenians, now had an experienced navy. They had the better of a long, running battle, destroying fifteen of the enemy vessels and forcing the rest to flee. Hannibal was forced to set out with a further fifty warships in an attempt to drive off the Syracusan fleet and prepare the way for a safe landing of the army.

The news of Hannibal's expedition caused great distress amongst the surviving Greek cities of Sicily. The Syracusans called on the Sicilians to fight for their common freedom. Fearing the demoralization of their Sicilian allies, they also sent emissaries to seek alliances with the Spartans and the Greeks of Italy. The Spartans, heavily engaged against the Athenians, may have sent a military adviser, as they had earlier, but no troops. The Italians sent a large contingent of hoplites.

The city of Akragas feared that it would be the next target of the Carthaginians. It was the second most powerful of the Sicilian cities and much of its prosperity derived from selling its agricultural products to Carthage. Diodorus spends the next four chapters of his history describing both its magnificent temples, and the 'accumulated fortunes of unbelievable size.'[1] The largest of these shrines, an unfinished temple of Zeus, had been begun seventy years earlier with the spoils won at the Battle of Himera. It is perhaps ironic that the people most responsible for Akragas' affluence were now determined to destroy the city.

The people of Akragas prepared for the expected attack by gathering in all their crops and possessions within the city walls. They would need them, as soon most of the population of 200,000 people would be crowded within the walls. Diodorus implies that the great wealth of the city had made its inhabitants soft and unmilitary. He recounts that while the city was under siege they were forced to pass 'a decree about the guards who spent the nights at their posts, that none of them should have more than one mattress, one cover, one sheepskin, and two pillows. When such was their most rigorous kind of bedding, one can get an idea of the luxury which prevailed in their living generally.'[2]

This anecdote is often repeated by modern authors in an attempt to show that affluence had sapped the martial spirit of the Greeks of Sicily. Such accusations ignore the courage that the citizen hoplites of Sicily would demonstrate in the coming campaign and their later wars against the Carthaginians. It is true that the later tyrants would rely heavily on mercenary troops but, if one reads Xenophon's *Hiero*, this was more about their political reliability and willingness to remain under arms for long periods. Soldiering was, of course, their livelihood, whereas the citizen soldier was still keen, just as his forefathers had been, to fight a battle and get home as quickly as possible. As shall be seen in the later campaigns, the Greek generals would sometimes find this aggressive tendency of their citizen troops a liability when attempting to carry out long-term, strategic operations such as sieges or attempts to defeat the enemy by manoeuvre rather than battle.

Hannibal's reinforcing of his fleet appears to have succeeded, as the Carthaginian army was successfully landed. The Syracusan squadron could not expect to defeat the seventy-five triremes the Carthaginians now had at sea. Where they landed is unrecorded but from the previous area of operations Motya or Drepanum are the most likely sites.

In the spring of 406, the Carthaginians marched directly against Akragas. They built two camps. One, atop a hill, contained 40,000 Spanish and Libyan troops. This was probably located on the high ground to the northeast and designed to cut the city off from any help arriving from their fellow Greeks. The other was pitched close to the city and heavily fortified. It probably occupied the lower hills to the southwest and would be the main base for the assault on the city. The Carthaginians dispatched an embassy to the city 'asking them, preferably, to become their allies, but otherwise to stay neutral and be friends with the Carthaginians, thereby remaining in peace; and when the inhabitants of the city would not entertain these terms, the siege was begun at once.'[3]

The Akragantians resolutely rejected these terms, preferring to retain their freedom and autonomy, rather than become the subjects of a foreign power. They armed all those of military age and divided their troops into two contingents, one group to defend the walls and the other to act as a reserve. The defenders were joined by a Spartan soldier of fortune, Dexippus, who had either come to Sicily with Hermocrates or had been sent to Sicily to aid the Sicilians in a like manner to Gylippus. At the request of Akragas he recruited and brought to the city 2,300 mercenaries, including the 800 Campanians who had been dismissed by Hannibal after Himera.

Akragas was strongly fortified and occupied a commanding position. The Carthaginian commanders, having surveyed the walls, believed they had located a weak point. They advanced two mobile towers against the walls, probably at the western Heraclea gate. The attack continued all the first day. That night the defenders launched a counter-attack and succeeded in burning the siege-engines.

Hannibal now determined to stretch the defenders and attack the city in a number of places by building ramps up to the walls. Being short of building supplies, he ordered his troops to tear down the monuments and tombs outside of the walls. One tomb, of the tyrant Theron, was deliberately targeted by Hannibal in revenge for the defeat at Himera. While the tomb was being levelled it was struck by lightning. This was considered to be a terrible omen by the soothsayers and the destruction was halted. Soon after, the Carthaginians were struck by a plague that killed many, including Hannibal. The superstitious soldiers believed this was a punishment for their earlier desecrations. To placate the gods they sacrificed a young boy and drowned a number of cattle in the sea as an offering to Poseidon. Such plagues were common in the ancient world when large numbers of people were forced to remain together for long periods in temporary camps, especially in summer. Sanitation was primitive, even in the best-constructed camps. The Carthaginians were notorious in antiquity for the disorder of the camps, which probably made them even more likely to suffer from diseases.

Despite this setback, Himilcon took command and continued the siege with energy. The Carthaginians built new siege-engines and filled in ditches and creeks that hindered their movement. Towers were once again advanced against the city's walls and assaults launched on a daily basis.

Meanwhile, the Syracusans were keen to come to come to the aid of the besieged, hoping to prevent a repeat of their failures at Selinus and Himera. They gathered a large army, including allies from Messene and Italy, under the command of Daphnaeus. Along the march to Akragas they were joined by troops from Camarina and Gela. The force eventually numbered 30,000 infantry and 5,000 cavalry, and was accompanied by thirty warships.

When Himilcon learned of the approach of the enemy, he dispatched a force of more than 40,000 troops to intercept them. It appears from Diodorus' account that the Carthaginian generals had, following the death of Hannibal, appointed a new deputy commander, Hamilcar, to take charge of the southern camp and siege operations. The Syracusans had already crossed the Himera River and were approaching Akragas when the Carthaginians met them in battle.

The nature of battles between the two peoples had probably changed since Himera in 480. Although the Carthaginian line may have contained some Spanish and Gaulish mercenaries, most of it would have consisted of African troops fighting as hoplites. The battle was therefore most likely a direct clash of two phalanxes of heavy infantry and decided in the Greek manner of fighting. There is no account of the entire battle but Polyaenus records an anecdote that shows Daphnaeus' command in a favourable light:

> The Syracusans and Italians were engaged in a battle against the Carthaginians, with the Syracusans on the right wing, and the Italians on the left. Daphnaeus heard a loud and confused noise on the left, and hurried there; he found the Italians hard pressed, and scarcely able to hold their ground. When he returned to the right wing, he told the Syracusans, that they were victorious on the left; and vigorous effort on their part would make the victory complete. The Syracusans, trusting in the truth of their general's report, boldly attacked the barbarians, and defeated them.[4]

From the account it would appear that both sides, as was the usual practice, had placed their best troops on their right wing. When the Carthaginian left collapsed the Greeks would have hit the exposed flank of the Carthaginian right and broken their entire line. The battle was reputedly long and hard fought but finally the Syracusans were victorious, killing 6,000 of the enemy.

As was usual after defeating the Carthaginians, the Greeks pressed the pursuit far more fiercely than they would have against Greek enemies. The citizen troops of the Syracusan army soon lost order as they pressed the chase. Daphnaeus then ordered his men to cease the pursuit, fearing that Himilcar might lead his forces out and defeat the scattered pursuers, as had happened at the siege of Himera.

The Carthaginian routers passed close to the walls of Akragas as they sought refuge in the camp to the southwest of the city. The fleeing troops would have been within a few hundred metres of the southern wall of Akragas. Seeing their hated enemy in flight, the troops of Akragas implored their generals to lead them out and turn the rout into a massacre. The memory of Himera appears, however, to have left a deep scar on the psyches of the Greek commanders. The generals refused to attack, again fearing that Hamilcar might counterattack with the troops in his camp. The attack might either capture the city while its walls were stripped of defenders or catch the citizen troops of Akragas before they had properly formed their phalanx.

This caution allowed the fleeing Carthaginians to make good their escape. The generals may have had good reason for their concern, as Polyaenus describes a situation, probably earlier in the siege, where Himilcon had ambushed the Akraganians:

> When he saw the enemy march out in great force, he gave secret orders to his officers, at a given signal, to make a hasty retreat. The men of Akragas pressed closely on them in their flight, and they were drawn a considerable distance from their city . . . As soon as they reached the place, where the ambush had been set, Himilcon attacked them vigorously with his forces. He cut many of them to pieces, and the rest were made prisoners.[5]

Daphnaeus soon arrived with the victorious relief army. His troops began to mingle with those of Akragas and all complained bitterly that the enemy had not been destroyed while the opportunity was there. Accusations of treachery soon began to be heard. The men gathered in an impromptu meeting where:

> Great uproar and tumult prevailed in the assembly, Menes of Camarina, who had been put in command, came forward and lodged an accusation against the Akragantine generals and so incited all who were present that, when the accused tried to offer a defence, no one would let them speak and the multitude began to throw stones and killed four of them, but the fifth, Argeius by name, who was very much younger, they spared.[6]

Caven states that the rumours were 'no doubt' false and that this whole procedure was a kangaroo court based on nothing more than class hatred.[7] As with most other cities, the generals of Akragas were elected officials and most would have come from the rich. Akragas' wealth was largely a product of exporting agricultural produce to Carthage. As a result, most of the wealthy in the city would have had extensive contacts with Phoenician traders and would have entertained them in their own homes. With feelings of betrayal running high, such individuals' previous dealings could easily have led to the suspicion that they were still in contact with the enemy. It may be correct to suspect that these particular charges were completely unjust, but over 2,000 years later it is perhaps unwise to state such an opinion so categorically. The evidence of the ancient authors repeatedly emphasizes that such suspicions were often correct. Later events would show that suspicions of treachery were clearly justified.

After the executions the Greeks considered laying siege to the Carthaginian camp but gave up when they saw the strength of its defences. They did, however, send out their cavalry to cut the Carthaginian supply lines and attack their foragers. Presumably the 5,000 cavalry that Daphnaeus had brought gave the Greeks overwhelming cavalry superiority. These operations must have continued for a number of months as the entire siege is recorded as lasting for eight. The besiegers now appear to have become the besieged. Although it is not mentioned, the Syracusan fleet must have been active in these operations otherwise the Carthaginians could have been supplied by sea.

Eventually, the Carthaginians began to die of starvation. The mercenary component of the army, led by the constantly unruly Campanians, confronted Hamilcar and threatened to desert to the Greeks if they did not receive their contracted rations. This strong position of the Greeks was, however, undermined by treachery. Hamilcar learnt of a Syracusan supply convoy coming by sea. It is clear from these events that the Carthaginians must have had agents amongst the Greeks, presumably at a high level, to be given such detailed information. The Carthaginians bribed the mercenaries to wait a few days. Meanwhile, they summoned forty triremes from Motya and planned to attack the convoy.

The inaction of the Carthaginian navy and the lateness of the season, as winter had already set in, had made the Syracusans overconfident. They failed to take adequate measures to guard the supply ships. Hamilcar was able to take them totally by surprise, sinking eight of their warships and driving the rest onto the beach. With the Syracusan warships removed, he was able to capture the entire supply fleet. With one successful action the entire course of the campaign was reversed to such an extent that the Campanians in the service of the Greeks were bought off and deserted to the Carthaginians.

With the fleet lost, the Akragantians began to despair. Despite initially gathering in large amounts of supplies, their initial successes had meant that they had not imposed strict rationing. This, along with the tens of thousands of civilians and soldiers within the city, had meant that the grain was nearly exhausted. Further treachery appears to have occurred as Diodorus relates that:

> Dexippus the Lacedaemonian was corrupted by a bribe of fifteen talents; for without hesitation he replied to a question of the generals of the Italian Greeks, 'Yes, it's better if the war is settled somewhere else, for our provisions have failed.' Consequently, the generals, offering as their excuse that the time agreed upon for the campaign had elapsed, led their troops off to the Strait.[8]

Dexippus appears to have been incredibly venal, even for a Spartan. He would later serve as a mercenary in Asia and would again be accused of treachery by his own troops. Amateurism of command and internal betrayal, the curses of Greek war-making, had turned a potentially winning position into a desperate one.

Following the departure of the Italian troops, the Greek commanders met and decided to make a survey of the supply of food within the city. When they discovered that it was nearly gone, they determined to abandon the city immediately. They issued orders to depart during the next night. For the second time, a significant Greek city was to be abandoned by its inhabitants.

With the decision being taken so quickly, the inhabitants were forced to depart hurriedly, leaving most of their possessions behind. There was no time to make proper preparations for the sick and old and many 'were neglected by their relatives, everyone taking thought for his own safety, and those who were already far advanced in years were abandoned because of the weakness of old age'. Others chose to remain, 'reckoning even separation from their native city to be the equivalent of death, laid hands upon themselves in order that they might breathe their last in the dwellings of their ancestors.'[9] Most, however, chose to leave and departed east. They were given an armed escort by the soldiers as far as Gela. Most continued on to Syracuse. Many were later resettled in Leontini by the Syracusans.

The next day, the Carthaginians took the city, killing all who remained, including those who had fled to the temples for refuge. Akragas had been famously wealthy and had never been taken since its foundation. Himilcon, therefore, collected an enormous amount of booty, including many works of art. The most valuable pieces, including the notorious bull of Phalaris, were sent back to Carthage. This was later captured by the Romans and returned to Akragas, where Diodorus claims that it was still on display during his lifetime. The fall of the city can be dated to December as Diodorus states that it occurred just before the winter solstice.

Unlike Himera and Selinus, the Carthaginians did not destroy the city, but used it as winter quarters for their troops. The further defeat at Akragas caused an understandable loss of morale among the remaining Greeks. Many transferred their families and moveable wealth to the security of the walls of Syracuse or beyond to Italy.

The failure of the Greeks to hold Akragas would not only result in the destruction of the city but also have enormous political ramifications in Syracuse. These, in turn, would result in the overthrow of the democracy and the return of the tyrants.

Chapter 16

The Return of the Tyrants

Now Dionysius, from a scribe and ordinary private citizen, had become tyrant of the largest city of the Greek world; and he maintained his dominance until his death, having ruled as tyrant for thirty-eight years. But we shall give a detailed account of his deeds and of the expansion of his rule in connection with the appropriate periods of time; for it seems that this man, single-handed, established the strongest and longest tyranny of any recorded by history.

Diodorus 13.96

After they arrived in Syracuse, the survivors of Akragas continued to voice their allegations against the commanders. The Akragantians again accused their generals of treachery. All the Greeks condemned the Syracusans for electing incompetent generals and putting them all at risk. The Syracusan assembly met to discuss the situation but nobody was confident enough to put themselves forward and offer suggestions for the continuation of the war. At this point a young soldier named Dionysius rose to speak.

Almost nothing is known of Dionysius' early life, including his date of birth. This was probably around 432, which would have made him too young to fight in the phalanx or with the cavalry against the Athenians. He may have garrisoned the walls or fought as one of the boys who manned the boats in the fighting in the Great Harbour. Unless in a dire emergency, the usual minimum age for fighting in the field army of most Greek cities was one's twentieth year.

There is a tradition among the ancient writers that Dionysius came from a lowly background, 'an obscure and humble position'. This claim that the powerful came from common backgrounds was a common Hellenistic practice that was intended as flattery – making an individual's rise to power a far more impressive feat. The historian Aelian has an extensive list of such individuals, including the Successor king Antigonus. All can be confidently discounted.[1]

Although Dionysius does not appear to have come from one of the traditional aristocratic families of Syracuse, he was certainly from the hoplite class or, given his links to the politician Hermocrates, more likely from the cavalry class, and therefore from a wealthy family. One of his aristocratic opponents sneers at him as being a mere clerk. This is a form of insult often used against non-noble leaders of the assembly. The Athenian demagogue Cleon is accused of being a tanner and the later Syracusan tyrant, Agathocles, a potter. The implication being that one has to work for wages rather than living off one's landed estates. Such accusations are, of course, spurious as all the leaders of the assemblies were wealthy. Cleon would have owned a large tannery and Agathocles a factory. Neither would have got their own hands dirty, the work being done by labourers and slaves.

Dionysius' position was in fact that of secretary to the Syracusan generals. In the courts of Hellenistic kings this was a privileged and profitable position held by the closest companions of the king.[2] Although on a smaller scale, Dionysius' situation shows that he had influential patrons. The position would have been a prestigious stepping-stone to a political career.

As with most powerful men in the ancient world there was also a tradition of prophecy foretelling his later successes. One of Dionysius' powerful backers was Philistus, one of the wealthiest Syracusans. He would later write a history of Sicily in two volumes that has not survived. His work was much admired by both Alexander the Great and Cicero who compared him favourably to Thucydides. Much of the detail of Diodorus' account of Dionysius' reign is believed to derive from Philistus. Cicero records one of these details:

> Now, Philistus, who was a learned and painstaking man and a con-
> temporary of the times of which he writes, gives us the following story
> of the mother of Dionysius, the tyrant of Syracuse: While she was with
> child and was carrying this same Dionysius in her womb, she dreamed
> that she had been delivered of an infant satyr. When she referred this
> dream to the interpreters of portents, who in Sicily were called
> 'Galeotae,' they replied, so Philistus relates, that she should bring forth
> a son who would be very eminent in Greece and would enjoy a long and
> prosperous career.[3]

Such prophecies, along with the tales of Dionysius' humble origin, should be seen as apocryphal. Writers in the Roman period employed such anecdotes to highlight the supposed character of their subject. The assessment of their accuracy and reliability by the authors was often less important than their content.

There are no surviving images of Dionysius but the ancient writers describe him as a big man with fair hair and freckles. At sometime during his life he became blind, or partially blind, in one eye and was insultingly referred to as 'Cyclops' by his enemies. He was strong and enjoyed playing ball games.

Dionysius was intelligent, being interested in music, history, medicine and poetry, including carrying out medical procedures and writing his own plays. Above all of these interests was, however, an overweening desire for power.

Dionysius had been one of those who had survived the aftermath of Hermocrates' failed coup. Presumably, he received some sort of pardon to allow him to return to the city and public life. Dionysius had learnt the lesson of Hermocrates. He would not attempt to come to power in a narrowly-based coup but instead take the route of a leader of the poor, winning over the assembly. Aristotle describes him as one who became a tyrant by being at first a demagogue and 'because he denounced Daphnaeus and the rich; his enmity to the notables won for him the confidence of the people.'[4]

He began his campaign by denouncing the generals for betraying their cause to the Carthaginians and demanded that the assembly exact punishment. Dionysius urged them not to follow the due procedure prescribed by the laws but to condemn them at once. This was an incitement to repeat the sort of show-trial that had occurred at Akragas. The magistrates fined Dionysius for proposing an illegal motion. This was a practice common to Greek assemblies; proposing actions contrary to the laws could result in fines or imprisonment. The power of the assembly was, however, absolute and the people could therefore overturn their own rules at any time.[5]

Philistus came forward to support Dionysius, paying the fine and saying that he would continue to pay fines the entire day if that was necessary to allow Dionysius to speak. Dionysius, now in full flight, 'kept stirring up the multitude, and throwing the assembly into confusion, he accused the generals of taking bribes to put the security of the Akragantians in jeopardy. And he also denounced the rest of the most renowned citizens, presenting them as friends of oligarchy.' He advised the *demos* to choose generals

> not from the most influential citizens, but rather those who were the best disposed and most favourable to the people; for the former, he maintained, ruling the citizens as they do in a despotic manner, hold the many in contempt and consider the misfortunes of their country their own source of income, whereas the more humble will do none of such things, since they fear their own weakness.[6]

Although formerly a follower of Hermocrates and supported by the wealthy, Dionysius was attempting to outflank his opponents from the left by claiming that the democracy was under threat. In doing so he, 'by suiting every word of his harangue to the people to the predilection of his hearers and his own personal design, stirred the anger of the assembly to no small degree'.[7] This was a tactic often used by would-be tyrants, whatever their own politics and background. Alcibiades had done much the same in Athens, but had ultimately failed and ended his life in exile.

The *demos*, infuriated by the repeated failures of their generals, fell prey to Dionysius' rhetoric. They immediately dismissed some of their generals and replaced them with those who had displayed courage during the fighting with the Carthaginians. Dionysius, who was much admired for having fought bravely against the Carthaginians, was one of those elected. In attaining this position, Dionysius had also to overcome the handicap of his age. At no more than twenty-seven, Dionysius was very young to hold such an office in a society where the wisdom of age was revered and the young considered too headstrong to command.

Once he had obtained this position of power, Dionysius immediately began scheming to seize supreme command. He pointedly refused to attend meetings with the other generals, repeating the mantra that they were negotiating with the enemy. Dionysius' intrigues did not go unnoticed and a faction of 'the most respectable citizens' opposed him, 'but the common crowd, being ignorant of his scheme, gave him their approbation and declared that at long last the city had found a steadfast leader.' Dionysius' next tactic was to demand repeatedly that the exiles be recalled. Eventually, he won over the assembly and they voted for his resolution. These were of course his fellow conspirators in Hermocrates' failed coup and could be expected to support him politically. They were just the sort of men Dionysius needed, those 'who wished a change and would be favourably disposed toward the establishment of a tyranny; for they would be happy to witness the murder of their enemies, the confiscation of their property, and the restoration to themselves of their possessions.'[8] In effect, they would be beholden to Dionysius and become part of his faction.

Dionysius then moved to Gela, responding to their request for reinforcements. Here he again stirred up the poor against the rich. The *stasis* within Gela must have been even more acute than in Syracuse as Dionysius persuaded the assembly to condemn many of the richest citizens and confiscate their wealth. With this money he undermined the position of Dexippus, who had earlier been placed in command of the garrison by the Syracusans. He doubled the pay of the mercenaries, winning them to his side. These machinations made him immensely popular among the people of Gela who honoured him with rich gifts. Dionysius tried to win over Dexippus but failed. This setback caused him to return to Syracuse, so perhaps his position was not as strong as Diodorus portrays.

While these intrigues were occurring, the Carthaginians were preparing for the coming year, with Gela as their first objective. The impending attack caused great fear in Gela. They dreaded the thought that they would share the same fate of Selinus, Himera and Akragas. Representations were made to Dionysius, begging him not to desert them. He replied by promising to return with reinforcements as soon as possible.

As soon as Dionysius returned to Syracuse he resumed his usual tricks. He again began accusing the other generals of corruption and dealing with the enemy, claiming they were 'more dangerous enemies than their foreign foes'. The generals were accused of squandering money on festivals but not paying the soldiers. Dionysius also declared that he had received a message from Himilcon who claimed that he 'induced a large number of Dionysius' colleagues not to bother themselves with what was taking place, at least to offer no opposition'. Dionysius then threatened to resign, claiming that he was the only general willing to fight while the others 'were selling out their country'.[9]

It is a sad reflection on ancient Greek politics that these accusations were so often made and so readily believed. The day after he returned to Syracuse an assembly was called. Dionysius repeated his accusations. Some of the assembly cried out that he should be made *strategos autocrator*. There can be little doubt that this proposal was predetermined and made by Dionysius' supporters. They argued that the constant defeats of the Greeks and the present military emergency

> made necessary such a general, through whose leadership their cause could prosper; as for the traitors, their case would be debated in another assembly, since it was foreign to the present situation; indeed at a former time three hundred thousand Carthaginians had been conquered at Himera when Gelon was general with supreme power. . . . And soon the multitude, as is their wont, swung to the worse decision and Dionysius was appointed general with supreme power.'[10]

The use of the term *strategos autocrator* was ominous as it was one of the euphemisms for tyrant. It was the same title that had been held by Gelon during most of his tyranny. The fact that the assembly voted Dionysius these powers displays the state of panic that pervaded throughout Greek Sicily. Dionysius again consolidated his popularity with the mercenaries by doubling their pay.

At this distance in time it sometimes appears astounding that the Syracusans would voluntarily hand over their liberty. This underestimates the emergency that faced the Syracusans and the panic it caused. In two years of fighting the Carthaginians had destroyed three major cities. Syracuse would have been packed with refugees repeating terrible tales of Carthaginian atrocities. The Syracusans would have been brought up on tales of how an earlier tyrant, Gelon, had saved them. More recently was the example of Gylippus, who had overcome the divisions within the Syracusan leadership to defeat the Athenians. Once he had performed his task the Syracusans had rewarded him well but quickly packed him off home. Athens itself, after the disaster in Sicily, had temporarily curtailed their democracy and appointed a narrow council to provide effective leadership. Most of those who voted to appoint a *strategos autocrator* probably believed that it was only a temporary measure. Once the Carthaginian threat had been defeated they supposed that they could give Dionysius a vote of thanks, a big slice of the loot and remove him from his position. Few would have believed that they were voting away the freedom of their city forever.

Some did, however, rightly fear that they had laid the grounds for the democracy to be overthrown and replaced by a dictatorship. In order to protect himself from his opponents, Dionysius would follow the precedent of Phalaris, and many other tyrants, and secure a bodyguard for himself. He used the tried and tested method of falsely claiming that there was a plot against him by enemies of the state. In doing so he was emulating Peisistratus of Athens who had wounded himself and accused his enemies of the crime:

> The Athenians, deceived by his story, appointed him a band of citizens to serve as a guard, who were to carry clubs instead of spears, and to accompany him wherever he went. Thus strengthened, Peisistratus broke into revolt and seized the citadel. In this way he acquired the sovereignty of Athens.[11]

Dionysius called up the army and ordered them to gather at Leontini, expecting most, especially his enemies, would baulk at such a journey. That city was currently full of exiles and refugees, many supporters of Dionysius. While encamped outside the city during the night he had his slaves and supporters raise an outcry. The next morning he gathered those who had made the journey and called an impromptu assembly. He claimed that he had been attacked and, copying Peisistratus, recalled his bravery in the fighting against the Carthaginians. Won over by his tale, those present, mostly his partisans, voted to give him a bodyguard of 600 soldiers. Such an action was possible because the Greeks believed that wherever the people were, was the *demos* and, therefore, an assembly could be held. It would appear that the Syracusans remembered their own history in regards to Gelon's exploits but ignored the fate of the Athenians.

Dionysius, continuing his image of a champion of the poor, recruited 'such citizens as were without property but bold in spirit, more than a thousand in number, provided them with costly arms, and buoyed them up with extravagant promises.' He then set about securing his position by giving all the military commands to his friends and dismissing his enemies. One of the victims of this purge was Dexippus who was promptly shipped off back to Greece. Dionysius recalled the mercenaries from Gela and 'gathered from all quarters the exiles and impious', creating in effect his own personal army. Next he set up his headquarters at the naval base inside the Little Harbour. Now that his position was secure, he 'openly proclaimed himself tyrant.'[12]

Diodorus' description of Dionysius' rise to power reads almost like a textbook on how to become a tyrant. He is credited with nearly every possible subterfuge: demagoguery, military emergency, a false assassination attempt, a bodyguard and a fortified headquarters. Ancient historians often used such devices to highlight the supposed character of their subject. Later authors considered Dionysius to be the archetype of the evil tyrant. This, of course, makes it difficult to discern which of the many stories concerning his life to believe.

Dionysius' rise to power does, nonetheless, resemble that of a number of twentieth-century dictators. He was elected to government by legal, or at least semi-legal, means. Once in a position of authority he used crises, both real and manufactured, to pass emergency measures which overrode the rights of the assembly and placed great power in his hands alone. He was then able to use these powers, and his own private army, to create a dictatorship.[13]

Dionysius took further measures to strengthen his grip on power. He wed the daughter of Hermocrates and married his sister to Polyxenus, Hermocrates' brother-in-law. Most likely this was in an attempt to placate the old aristocracy and reconcile them with the tyranny. Up to this point he had attacked them as he attempted to portray himself as a populist leader. As subsequent events would show, this endeavour to win over the upper classes was not particularly successful. After securing his position, he moved on his political opponents, summoning an assembly and having them condemn to death Daphnaeus and another leading politician, while others were banished. The charges are not recorded but were most likely to have been treason. The fact that Dionysius felt, at this stage, the need to call an assembly does, however, imply that his grip on power was not yet total and he felt the need for his assassinations to at least appear legal. Traditionally, the place for such trials was the assembly, but Dionysius' later career shows that he was not above taking such decisions unilaterally.

Diodorus now states that Dionysius' rule was secure and would continue until his death. Those that did oppose him were either cowed into submission by the executions of his opponents or by the threat of his bodyguard. Others were willing to acquiesce to his rule out of fear of the Carthaginian threat. They hoped that he would put an end to the military incompetence that was seen as the result of electing multiple generals largely for political reasons. Diodorus' own account shows that his position was not totally secure, however, as he records a number of later revolts against the tyranny.

Exactly how Dionysius exercised his power is not certain. Caven believes that after the first revolt against the tyrant in 403 he came to a formal agreement with the Syracusans. They would allow him to maintain his private fortress and conduct military affairs unmolested, while in return he 'recognized the autonomy of the city; that is to say he guaranteed the right of the citizens to live their lives and to administer the domestic affairs of the city in accordance with the laws.'[14] Although this separation of powers is probably correct, it is unlikely that it was a formal agreement. The relationship would have varied over its course with the shifting balance of power between Dionysius and the people of Syracuse. Tyranny by its very definition is unconstitutional and based on force. In the end, Dionysius' political power would have relied on his ability to intimidate and terrorize his subjects through his mercenaries and informers.

Although Caven argues convincingly that the Syracusans retained a large decree of autonomy in their domestic affairs, this is only half of the equation. The Greeks always linked autonomy with freedom. One of the recorded definitions of freedom was to be 'governed according to the constitution of its choice, and free from the imposition of tribute or of a foreign governor or garrison.'[15] Although this definition derives from an agreement between the Athenians and their subject allies, it is a useful yardstick by which to measure the relationship between a tyrant and his subjects.

The expression 'tribute' does not apply in this circumstance, but if Dionysius unilaterally controlled the revenues of Syracuse this would certainly be seen as a limitation on, or destruction of, the people's freedom. As was outlined earlier, an ancient state derived its revenue mostly by a tithe on agricultural produce and land taxes. Syracuse certainly imposed a tithe, as the size of it was renowned throughout the Greek world. The city would also have imposed harbour, customs and market levies. In addition, Syracuse received tribute from the Sicels whenever it was able to impose its dominance over them. These revenues would have been spent on public works, wages for public officials and ongoing costs for the military – paying garrisons and exercising the fleet. As commander of the armed forces, Dionysius would have been responsible for expenditure on the military.

Apart from their campaigns, tyrants did, however, have a constant need for money to pay their foreign mercenaries in order to control the civilian population. This was recognized by Aristotle, who claimed that unlike legitimate kings: 'the tyrant is desirous of riches, the king, of what brings honour. And the guards of a king are citizens, but of a tyrant mercenaries.'[16]

In addition, he would have needed revenue for the upkeep of his later fortress of Ortygia. His private entourage of advisers and visiting philosophers would also have expected payment. Just how avaricious such sycophants could be is demonstrated by one of the courtiers of the Hellenistic king Lysimachus. He reputedly demanded a talent in compensation for being the butt of a practical joke involving a wooden snake. Just who controlled these revenues, the tyrant or the assembly, is not recorded.

The finances of ancient states were, however, run on a very hand-to-mouth basis. Although normal revenues should cover the day-to-day running of the state there was little surplus for extraordinary demands. The most common of these was military campaigns. Making war was incredibly expensive. The army of 35,000 men that the Syracusans sent to Akragas would have cost about six to seven talents per day in wages. The thirty warships that accompanied it, assuming they were all triremes, would have added nearly a talent to the daily cost. A reasonable approximation for the wages bill of the entire force is then around seven talents per day. This would have given a total cost of over 1,500 talents for the eight months of the campaign.[17] This is an enormous amount, even for a city as wealthy as Syracuse. To place this amount in perspective, the wealthy Ionian cities of Asia, along with a number of native peoples, paid only 400 talents in annual tribute to the Persians. The Athenians originally collected 460 talents of tribute per year from their empire.[18]

A successful campaign could offset these costs, or even run at a profit, through the pillaging of enemy territory and cities. Nicias had raised 150 talents from the sack of one small Sicanian town. A better idea of the enormous amounts that could be collected is the 40,000 talents of booty that Ptolemy III won during the Third Syrian War of 246/5 – a figure to be compared to the annual revenue of Ptolemy II of 14,800 talents.[19] The possibility of winning large amounts of booty was a considerable motivation for governments, generals and common troops. An unsuccessful campaign such as that of Akragas could be financially disastrous, forcing governments to resort to a number of emergency measures to raise the necessary money.

Caven has plausibly suggested that 'as part of their compact with Dionysius, the Syracusans undertook to pay him a regular subsidy.'[20] This payment would have come out of the regular revenues of the state. Dionysius' constant campaigning and mercenary bodyguard would have meant that Syracuse's revenues were not always sufficient to meet his needs. During these periods, he would have resorted to emergency levies to raise funds. Aristotle and Polyaenus both list a number of scurrilous methods of extorting money attributed to Dionysius. One of his levies was specifically linked to military matters:

> Intending to build a fleet of triremes, Dionysius knew that he should require funds for the purpose. He therefore called an assembly and declared that a certain city was offered to him by traitors, and he needed money to pay them. The citizens therefore must contribute two staters apiece. The money was paid; but after two or three days, Dionysius, pretending that the plot had failed, thanked the citizens and returned to each his contribution. In this way he won the confidence of the citizens; so that when he again asked for money, they contributed in the expectation that they would receive it back. But this time he kept it for building the fleet.[21]

Such taxes could be high, although the twenty percent property tax recorded in one source would appear to be improbably excessive. On some occasions the hard-pressed Syracusans simply refused to pay. 'When his treasury was low, Dionysius imposed a tax on the people. They were unwilling to pay, saying that they had often been forced to make contributions, and Dionysius did not think it wise to compel the payment of it.' Another time, 'being in need of funds, he requested the citizens to contribute. On their declaring that they had not the wherewithal' he tricked them out of their money anyway.[22] These examples are sometimes used to argue that Dionysius could only raise such revenues if the assembly voted for them. In both these instances, however, the opposition appears to have been in the form of a refusal to pay rather than the voting down of the measure by the assembly. Aristotle, in his examples, consistently refers to Dionysius announcing or decreeing a proclamation (*kerukeuma*) to the assembly. On balance, it would appear more likely that Dionysius had assumed the power to issue unilateral edicts to the Syracusans to demand money in order to fund his military operations. This would have been seen as a form of tribute by the Syracusan citizens and a clear violation of their freedom.

Dionysius also earned a reputation for impiety by stealing 'objects from all the temples in Syracuse. From the cult statue of Zeus he removed the clothing and other ornaments, which amounted it is said, to eighty-five talents of gold.' In ancient times this was the equivalent of about a thousand talents of silver, enough to pay the force sent to Akragas for about six months. The borrowing of money from temples was not unusual by ancient cities in times of emergency, but here Aelian states that Dionysius repeatedly robbed the temples and despoiled (*sulao*) the statues of the gods. Such acts were considered sacrilege, but throughout his career this does not appear to have bothered Dionysius, who 'when the workmen hesitated to touch the statue, he dealt the first blow.'[23]

Aristotle, and other ancient sources, claim that Dionysius' heavy taxation was a deliberate plot in order that: 'he should impoverish his subjects; he thus provides against the maintenance of a guard by the citizen and the people, having to keep hard at work, are prevented from conspiring.'[24] This is perhaps too cynical. Dionysius' heavy taxation was most likely the result of military need rather than a calculated plot against the people.

One of the most cherished freedoms of a Greek *polis* was the ability to control its foreign policy and power to make war or peace. As *strategos autocrator*, Dionysius would most likely have annexed these powers to himself. A later treaty between himself and the Athenians is signed in his name, not on behalf of the Syracusans. Although ostensibly free and autonomous, under the tyranny the Syracusan assembly had ceased to be a national government but instead had become little more than a town council. The Syracusans no doubt viewed this in the same way as Plutarch, himself a magistrate of Chaeronea under Roman rule. He lamented that: 'Nowadays, when the affairs of the cities do not include leadership in war, or the overthrow of tyrannies, or the making of alliances . . . you who rule are a subject, and the state you rule is dominated by proconsuls.'[25]

The presence of a foreign garrison was always particularly hated and seen as a limitation on freedom, as it was a permanent threat. Although Dionysius was not a foreign governor, his garrison of foreign mercenaries was certainly resented by the Syracusans. One opponent of the tyrant claimed that 'the acropolis, which is guarded by the weapons of slaves, is a hostile redoubt in our city; the multitude of mercenaries has been gathered to hold the Syracusans in slavery'. By the constant presence of his mercenary garrison, the tyrant could always influence the decisions of the assembly through sheer intimidation. On at least one occasion Dionysius was saved from the wrath of the assembly by the presence of a Spartan emissary and because his 'mercenaries flocked about Dionysius, and the Syracusans in dismay made no move, although they called down many curses on the Spartans.'[26] Again, the Syracusans would have seen such actions as a gross violation of both their freedom and autonomy.

The overwhelming image of Dionysius in the ancient world was that he was ruthless in his desire for power. Unlike many other tyrants, he 'was far from being sensual, or luxurious, or avaricious, and was covetous indeed of nothing but absolute and firmly-established sovereignty.'[27] In his obsessive desire for power, not only did he intimidate the assembly with his mercenaries, but was also condemned in antiquity for terrorizing and murdering his political opponents.

Dionysius was supposed to have been incredibly suspicious of assassination attempts and conspiracies. He used both informers and stratagems to unmask his opponents. On at least one occasion he supposedly pretended to be dead. The result was that 'those who were hostile to the tyranny joyfully met together, and congratulated each other on the happy event. As soon as he was informed of their names, Dionysius ordered them to be seized, and put them to death.' His informers included prostitutes who as slaves could only give evidence under torture; such torture being applied, they revealed 'the opinions which they had heard their lovers express about the tyranny.' Syracuse was reputedly rife with informers, who were naturally despised.[28]

In order to hold onto power, Dionysius 'was cruel; for in his eagerness to secure it he spared the life of no one that he thought to be plotting against it.' Plutarch claims that he killed 10,000 or more citizens. Justin reports that there were 3,000 prisoners in his jails at the time of his death.[29] Although one must keep in mind the earlier caution regarding such anecdotes relating to Dionysius' rule, the accusations of terror and injustice are so universal among the ancient writers that they must have some basis in fact.

At some stage during his rule, Dionysius decided that the position of general was insufficient and by 393, at the latest, he had adopted the trappings of monarchy, a purple cloak and a four-horse chariot drawn by grey horses. He most likely also adopted at some time the title *basileus* (king), emulating Gelon. Some historians argue, however, that the later tyrant Agathocles was the first after Gelon to take the title king and Dionysius was known as *archon* (chief magistrate). The Athenians refer to him by this title in one surviving inscription. He did not adopt the action of later tyrants of minting coins in his own name, but up to this time nor had any other Greek ruler.

On balance, however, the numerous citations to both Dionysius and his heir Dionysius the Younger being known as king would tend to favour this title. Dionysius was certainly intent on creating a hereditary dynasty, as one treaty with the Athenians was made in his own name and those of his descendants. Whether Dionysius seized greater political power when he adopted his new title cannot be determined. It is known that the assembly was still meeting at the time of his death. There is also some, albeit slim, evidence that Dionysius may have attempted to create a hero-cult, a semi-divine status, for himself and his family.[30]

The ancient Greeks believed that under a tyranny the people ceased to be citizens but became instead subjects. If the earlier definition of freedom is used it can be seen that Dionysius did destroy the freedom, and seriously erode the autonomy, of the Syracusan people. Although perhaps exaggerated, Cicero's description of the condition of the Syracusans would therefore appear to be largely correct: 'while Dionysus its tyrant reigned there, nothing of all its wealth belonged to the people, and the people were nothing better than the slaves of an impious despot.'[31]

In the spring of 405 all this was in the future. Dionysius had been appointed *strategos autocrator* not to make himself tyrant but on a platform to more effectively fight the Carthaginians. He would soon get his opportunity to make good his promises.

Chapter 17

The Battle of Gela

For the fate that had befallen Selinus and Himera and Akragas as well terrified the populace.

Diodorus 13.111

At the beginning of the summer of 405, Himilcon burnt the city of Akragas. His hatred for the Greeks was emphasized by his treatment of their temples. He mutilated the statues and vandalized those that had not been sufficiently destroyed by the fire. One temple in particular was singled out for destruction: the temple to Zeus. Construction of this had begun after the Battle of Himera, funded by pillage from the battle and constructed by Carthaginian prisoners of war. When completed it would have been the largest Doric temple ever built but was still under construction. In one of the ironies of history it was torn down and destroyed by another group of Carthaginian soldiers.

Himilcon then led his army to Gela, pillaging the countryside as he advanced. After arriving at the city, he pitched his camp on the plain to the west of the city, fortifying it with a trench and a wooden palisade. He did not, however, bring up his fleet as the coast near Gela is very exposed.

Despite his earlier promise, Dionysius had been too involved in the politics of Syracuse to return speedily to Gela. Fearing the worst, the Geloans voted to evacuate their women and children to Syracuse, before the city was fully surrounded. The women refused to leave; they occupied the temples around the *agora*, pleading to remain in their city and share its fate. The men reversed their decision and allowed them to stay. Gela was strong in cavalry and sent out large detachments, supported by infantry, to harass the enemy foragers. Their knowledge of the terrain gave them the advantage and they repeatedly ambushed the enemy, killing many and bringing back prisoners for questioning.

The Carthaginians repeated their previously successful siege tactics, advancing their rams against the walls and attacking in relays to exhaust the enemy. The Geloans resisted bravely, successfully driving off the assaults. Each night, with the aid of the women and children, they repaired their walls.

Diodorus claims that the city lacked natural defences but this is not quite true. Gela is built on a long ridge that has steep slopes on three of its sides, particularly that facing the sea. The western end, against which the Carthaginians launched their assault, has a more gradual gradient. As I discovered from walking the area, the ground here is mostly soft sand and, if it had been in 405, would have been an obstacle for an attacking army's siege engines. The Carthaginian engineers probably reinforced the ground on the approach to the city.

Dionysius eventually gathered an army consisting of Syracusans, Greek allies from Sicily and Italy, and mercenaries. Infantry numbers are given as either 30,000 or 50,000. The discrepancy may be a result of the lower number referring only to hoplites, whereas the higher number might include light infantry. In addition, there were 1,000 cavalry and fifty triremes. Dionysius made camp on the shoreline, most likely at the eastern end of the city. He sent his light infantry and cavalry to join the Geloans in harassing the Carthaginian foragers and supply lines. This was a repeat of Daphnaeus' strategy at Akragas, where he had almost succeeded in starving the enemy into retreat. The skirmishing went on for twenty days, but then Dionysius decided to attack the Carthaginian position. Dionysius may well have been under intense pressure from his Greek citizen troops, who always preferred a decisive engagement to a long campaign. He may also have felt a need to prove himself and justify his command.

He devised an ambitious plan whereby he would fix the Carthaginian camp with a frontal assault while outflanking their position by ships on the seaward side. He divided his infantry into three divisions. The first, made up of his Italian allies, was to attack the camp by moving south of the city along the shoreline. He would occupy the centre, advancing with his mercenaries through the city and attacking out from the western gate. The Sicilian infantry would advance on the right, to the north of the city. The cavalry were stationed to protect the exposed right flank. The fleet was to attack as soon the allied infantry made their assault.

The attack began well on the left. The fleet made their assault as the Carthaginians were distracted by the advance of the Italians. This was made easier as the enemy had neglected to fortify their camp along the shoreline. The Carthaginians rushed to defend the beach, weakening their defence of the palisade. This allowed the allied Italian infantry to force their way into the Carthaginian camp.

Things were not, however, going so well for Dionysius in the centre. His mercenaries made slow going through the tangle of streets in the city and failed to get into action. The Sicilians on the right were also slow to advance. This allowed the Carthaginians to withdraw troops from other parts of their line and counterattack the now exposed flanks of the Italians. The Geloans were the only ones to give assistance to the Italians. Their attack, however, was too late and too limited to be of much help, as they were reluctant to abandon their walls in the face of the enemy.

The Spanish and Campanian infantry led the attack on the Italians, driving them out of the fortifications and killing more than a thousand of them. Their pursuit was hampered, however, by crews of the ships who showered them with arrows. This allowed most of the Italians to retire to safety.

Meanwhile, on the right, the Sicilian infantry had finally pressed home their attack, routing the Libyans opposed to them and breaking through the palisade. The Carthaginians were now able to make use of their interior lines. They rallied their Spanish and Campanians, who, supported by the Carthaginian infantry, launched another counterattack. They caught the Sicilian infantry disorganized and drove them back, killing 600. The supporting Greek cavalry also withdrew. Dionysius, having finally marched through the city, found that his army had been defeated and he too retired back into the city.

Dionysius' first engagement with the Carthaginians had ended in defeat. The plan was innovative but too complicated for his mostly-citizen troops. It required three divisions plus the fleet to coordinate their attacks while they were invisible to one another due to the hill of Gela. It should be noted, nonetheless, that it was the citizen levies who successfully pressed home their attacks. They were ultimately defeated by the failure of Dionysius and his mercenaries to support their flanks. This point was not lost on Dionysius' enemies.

Dionysius, after taking counsel with his advisors, decided that the city was now indefensible. He ordered the citizens to abandon their city during the night. Meanwhile, he covered the retreat by sending a herald to the enemy to concede the defeat and, as was customary, to arrange for the burying of the dead the next day. Two thousand light troops were left behind to light fires and make noise during the night. By these ruses the Carthaginians were tricked into believing that the city was still defended. Later that night, Dionysius and the army withdrew. The next day the Carthaginians entered the city and plundered it. The Greek retreat, however, was not yet over. Dionysius decided he could not hold Camarina and ordered the population to abandon their city and retreat to Syracuse. The piteous scenes of the retreat from Akragas were now repeated as all were terrified of 'the savagery of the Carthaginians', who 'were without compassion for the victims of Fortune of whom they would crucify some and upon others inflict unbearable outrages.' The roads to the east now 'teemed with women and children and the rabble in general.'[1]

The Syracusans had allowed Dionysius to come to power largely on the promise that he would be a more effective commander and turn the course of the war around. Yet in his first campaign as general he had been a dismal failure, despite his promises. His plan of attack had been overly-complicated, allowing his troops to be isolated and defeated in detail. Even more telling, it had been the citizen troops who had fought bravely, in stark contrast to the failure of both himself and his mercenaries to engage. In fact Dionysius' command had been even less successful than that of Daphnaeus, who had at least defeated the Carthaginians in battle, defended Akragas for an entire summer and come close to winning the campaign. In a matter of a few weeks Dionysius had lost a battle, ordered the abandonment of two more Greek cities, and, like the unfortunate Diocles, abandoned the dead without burial.

The sight of so many refugees filled the soldiers with pity for them and anger against Dionysius. They began to suspect that he had deliberately betrayed Gela and Camarina. They recalled his failure to attack at Gela, 'the fact that none of his mercenaries had fallen; that he had retreated without reason, since he had suffered no serious reverse; and, most important of all, that not a single one of the Carthaginians had pursued them.' As well as the usual suspicions of treachery, they also accused him of deliberately 'using the dread of the Carthaginians to be lord of the remaining cities of Sicily without risk.'[2]

The Italian Greeks simply deserted and returned home. Many of his domestic enemies now believed that his failures and subsequent loss of support among the troops gave them the opportunity to revolt and overthrow the tyranny. The Syracusan cavalry, those who had suffered most from his populist policies, planned to assassinate him on the retreat. This plot was abandoned when they saw that his mercenaries remained loyal to him. They were on double pay and had nothing to gain, and everything to lose, from his overthrow. The cavalry changed their plans and resolved to carry out a coup within the city, which was largely devoid of troops. Returning quickly, they arrived at the gates before news of the defeat and entered the tyrant's stronghold in the dockyards without opposition. They plundered his house, seizing all the valuables. When his wife tried to intervene they raped her in turn and killed her, believing that this shared crime would ensure that they remained loyal to one another in the face of Dionysius' outrage.

Dionysius, learning of the coup, picked out his most trustworthy troops and raced to the city. He hoped to surprise the rebels before they could gain support from the rest of the mutinous army. The rebels, believing their coup to be successful, were taken completely unawares. Dionysius arrived at the city during the night with 100 cavalry and 600 infantry. Finding the city closed, he piled reeds against the gates and set them alight. Once the gates were down Dionysius entered the city. The bravest of the rebels, alerted by the fire, rushed to oppose him without waiting for the bulk of the force to gather. Outnumbered, they were overwhelmed by Dionysius' mercenaries and slaughtered to a man. The main body of the cavalry now panicked and fled to the city of Aetna. Dionysius took a terrible revenge on his opponents, 'ranging through the city, slew any who came out here and there to resist him, and entering the houses of those who were hostile toward him, some of them he killed and others he banished from the city.'[3] When the remainder of the army arrived the next day his opponents found him in complete control of the city. The Syracusans accepted the situation but the survivors of Gela and Camarina, who felt betrayed by Dionysius, departed to Leontini.

With his army now scattered, Dionysius must have feared an immediate Carthaginian advance on Syracuse. Fate, however, came to his aid. Plague had once again broken out in the Carthaginian army and more than half had reportedly died. The Greeks would have seen this as further divine retribution on the enemy for their destruction of temples and their murder of supplicants. Himilcon sent an embassy to Syracuse to negotiate a peace. Dionysius was, given his own circumstances, more than willing to come to an agreement. Peace was made on the following terms:

> To the Carthaginians shall belong, together with their original colonists, the Elymi and Sicani; the inhabitants of Selinus, Akragas, and Himera as well as those of Gela and Camarina may dwell in their cities, which shall be unfortified, but shall pay tribute to the Carthaginians; the inhabitants of Leontini and Messene and the Siceli shall all live under laws of their own making, and the Syracusans shall be subject to Dionysius; and whatever captives and ships are held shall be returned to those who lost them.[4]

Once the peace had been made, the Carthaginians broke up their army and the African portion sailed home, leaving their Campanian mercenaries to garrison the island. The Africans, however, took the plague with them and it soon began to ravage Carthage and its subject cities.

Despite their weakness the Carthaginians had imposed severe terms on Dionysius. In return for them accepting his rule over Syracuse, he had to cede hegemony over the captured Greek cities. The surviving Greek inhabitants would be allowed to return home but they would not be allowed to rebuild their walls and must pay tribute to their Phoenician overlords. Both these conditions would have been seen as violations of their freedom and autonomy. All the other Greek cities and the Sicels were to become independent of Syracuse. The loss of control over both the Sicels and Leontini must have been a bitter pill for the Syracusans to swallow. Syracuse's empire had now shrunk to the city itself and its *chora*.

Chapter 18

Dionysius' Conquest of Eastern Sicily

In Sicily, Dionysius, the tyrant of the Sicilians, after concluding peace with the Carthaginians, planned to busy himself more with the strengthening of his tyranny; for he assumed that the Syracusans, now that they were relieved of the war, would have plenty of time to seek after the recovery of their liberty.

Diodorus 14.7

Now that the external threat of the Carthaginians had been removed for the moment, Dionysius set about consolidating his rule. This was necessary, as the whole justification for his position as *strategos autocrator* was at an end now that the war against the Carthaginians was over. Dionysius, however, had no intention of relinquishing his command or abiding by the treaty. His former stronghold in the naval arsenal had not proved strong enough, so he now embarked on a plan to fortify the island of Ortygia.

First, he built a wall to separate the island and the naval dockyards from the rest of the city. He further strengthened this position by fortifying the acropolis of the island as a place of final refuge. Once the island was cut off from the rest of the town, he built a city within a city, complete with the places of government business. He expelled the original inhabitants of the island and gave their homes to his closest friends and a garrison of mercenaries. Just how Dionysius paid for all this, as he had just lost a costly war, is not recorded. It is possibly from this period that he first gained his reputation for stealing money from temples and repressive taxation.

While Dionysius was ensuring his physical safety, he did not neglect to continue his campaign of building political support among both his closest supporters and the lower classes. He redistributed the lands of those that he had forced into exile, giving the best estates to his friends. The remainder he divided up among the poorest citizens, dispossessed refugees and freed slaves, who he called 'New Citizens'. These people would, of course, become loyal partisans of the tyrant and bitter opponents of the exiles, in order to protect their new property.

In the summer of 404, once his political position appeared to be secure,

Dionysius set out to re-establish control of the Sicels and punish them for allying themselves with the Carthaginians. He had, however, miscalculated his support among the hoplites. Now that they were armed and gathered together, they began to discuss the situation and regretted that they had not joined the cavalry in overthrowing the tyranny. Their commander, one of Dionysius' appointees, threatened 'one of those who were freespoken' and when the man retorted he struck him. The soldiers were outraged, as had been the sailors fighting for Sparta. Sixty years of democracy had left its mark. They rose in revolt, killing their commander 'and, crying to the citizens to strike for their freedom, sent for the cavalry from Aetna' to join their rebellion.[1]

Dionysius, surprised and 'terror-stricken at the revolt,' fled back to his fortress in the city.[2] The rebels now elected their own generals and, joined by the cavalry, made their base on the Epipolae. They sent embassies to Messene and Rhegium requesting naval support, as the tyrant controlled the dock-yards. These cities sent eighty triremes to assist the rebels. The rebels put a bounty on the tyrant's head, promising a huge reward to anyone who killed him. They also promised citizenship to any mercenaries who would desert to them. While all this was going on, they began their military campaign, constructing siege engines and launching daily assaults upon the island. Prior to this, they must have captured the remainder of the city outside of the tyrant's base on Ortygia.

Under siege in his private fortress, Dionysius despaired of holding on to the tyranny. He was in such anguish that he was planning to seek death in battle rather than be captured. Dionysius called a meeting of his closest advisers; some supported his death-wish, and others proposed that he flee. Finally, Philistus advised him to stay and fight or be dragged out dead. Dionysius took Philistus' advice and decided to defend his tyranny. To buy time, he made an agreement with the rebels that they allow him to leave the city by ship. Meanwhile, he sent a message to Campanian mercenaries of the Carthaginian garrisons promising them huge rewards if they supported him.

The rebels were lulled into a false sense of security. They released the cavalry and with the coming of spring in 403, many of the hoplites, thinking the tyranny was already defeated, dismissed themselves and dispersed to their homes. The Campanians sent 1,200 cavalry who surprised the scattered rebels and forced their way through to Ortygia. Another 300 mercenaries arrived by sea.

The dumbfounded rebels now began bickering among themselves. Some wished to renew the siege while others wished to flee the city. Dionysius, learning of the dissension, led his army out and routed the disorganized insurgents. He did, however, prevent his mercenaries from pursuing and slaughtering the fleeing hoplites, hoping to reconcile with them at a later date.

More than 7,000 refugees fled to join the cavalry at Aetna. Dionysius, continuing his policy of reconciliation, offered an amnesty to those who would return to the city. Most, having left their families behind, accepted his offer. The die-hard opponents of the tyranny, no doubt including all of those who had murdered his wife, remained at Aetna.

It is interesting to compare these events in Syracuse with those in Athens. Following their defeat by the Spartans in 404 a narrow oligarchy called 'The Thirty' seized power in Athens. In 403, the same year as the revolt against Dionysius, they were driven out by an armed revolt of Athenian exiles and the democracy returned. What The Thirty appear to have lacked was a stronghold like Ortygia and the means to hire a large, standing force of mercenaries. Dionysius' foresight in the preceding year had served him well.

The Campanians were well paid, then dismissed as soon as possible due to their history of faithlessness. They made their way to the Elymian city of Entella, where they persuaded the citizens to let them settle. They then treacherously murdered the men and seized the city and its women for themselves. This vicious act created a precedent that their countrymen would follow whenever any city was foolish enough to allow them within its walls in large numbers. Messene and Rhegium would both suffer the same fate a century or so later.

Once the reconciled rebels had returned to the city, Dionysius took steps to ensure that they would be unable to successfully rebel again 'since he had learned by experience that the Syracusans would endure anything to escape slavery.'[3] The revolt against Dionysius had come close to success due to the hoplites deciding to join the exiled cavalry in opposing the tyranny. It was only their fear for the safety of their families that had brought an end to their revolt. Later, when the hoplites had left the city to bring the harvest from their farms, Dionysius sent his mercenaries into their homes to seize their arms. From this time on he would

> march a hundred stades from the city, whenever he had occasion to fight against an army, and then he handed every man his weapons. When the war was finished, before they re-entered the city, and the gates were thrown open, the men were ordered to ground their weapons, which were carried away and kept under guard.[4]

Dionysius also received aid from the Spartans who sent Aristus to Syracuse

> ostensibly pretending that they would overthrow the government, but in truth with intent to increase the power of the tyranny; for they hoped that by helping to establish the rule of Dionysius they would obtain his ready service because of their benefactions to him . . . and by such conduct brought disgrace both upon himself and upon his native land.[5]

Now that his hold on the city was finally secured, Dionysius turned his attention to the Ionian Greek cities of Naxos, Catane and Leontini. This decision was no doubt influenced by the surrender of Athens to Sparta the year before. This time there would be no chance of an appeal from the cities to their Ionian kinsmen to send them assistance. For some reason, he felt confident enough to embark on this campaign despite the fact that the independence of the cities of the Sicels and Leontini had been guaranteed in the peace treaty with the Carthaginians.

First of all, Dionysius stormed Aetna and crushed the Syracusan rebels, removing any threat to his rear. The surviving exiles fled to Rhegium. Next he marched on Leontini, but when they refused to surrender he was forced to withdraw as he had no siege train with him. As a diversion, he then attacked the Sicel city of Enna. Here he showed the Machiavellian side of his character, first supporting the local would-be tyrant to seize power, but then falling out with him and assisting the people to overthrow him. Diodorus claims that Dionysius left the city ungarrisoned and in the hands of its people, hoping that this would win him support among the other Sicel towns. Plutarch suggests, however, that this benign view of Dionysius' campaigns against the Sicels may be propaganda, as Diodorus' possible source for these events, Philistus, 'passed over all those outrages committed by Dionysius on the barbarians which had no connection with the Grecian affairs.'[6]

After failing to take the Sicel city of Herbita, he finally marched on Catane. Here he was admitted to the city by the treachery of one of its generals. The city was occupied by a Syracusan garrison and the population sold into slavery. Diodorus claims that Naxos was also taken by treachery but Polyaenus has a slightly more detailed account:

> Dionysius, having persuaded some men in Naxos to betray the city to him, advanced to the walls late in the evening, attended by seven soldiers. The conspirators on the towers suggested to him that he should attack the city with all his force. But he wished to make himself master of it without any loss, and demanded the surrender of the garrison on the walls. If they refused, he threatened to put every man to the sword. At the same time, on his orders one of his ships entered the port of Naxos, with trumpets on board, and boatswains, who informed the Naxians, that they all belonged to separate ships, which they would soon see in their harbour. The terror of so great a naval force, and the threats of Dionysius, prevailed upon the Naxians to surrender their city, without a blow being struck.[7]

Despite their surrender, the city was razed and its inhabitants were enslaved. In both Catane and Naxos, Dionysius kept his word to the traitors, giving them rewards and including them in his entourage. The territory of Naxos was given to the Sicels in a further attempt to win their goodwill. Catane was later handed over to another group of Campanian mercenaries.

Finally, Dionysius advanced on Leontini and laid siege to the city. Leontini had long been both a thorn in the side of Syracuse and the object of its ambitions. He sent an embassy to offer the inhabitants citizenship of Syracuse if they surrendered the town. Isolated and fearing the fate of the Naxians and Catanians, they surrendered and were removed to Syracuse. Some may have been settled in a new city, Adranum, which Dionysius had founded just south of Mount Aetna. The incongruous result of this campaign was that Dionysius, emulating Gelon, had destroyed almost as many Greek cities as had the Carthaginians. These campaigns probably occupied the years from 403 until 401.

Dionysius had achieved what Syracusan governments of all political forms had desired for over a century. The Ionian-speaking cities were captured and their populations enslaved. There appears to have been a hatred of the Ionian Greeks of Sicily by their Dorian neighbours that was no longer as pronounced in relations between the Greeks further east. There, if we accept the testimony of the poets and historians, it was more of a disdain for their perceived characters.

This deep-seated detestation might have had purely ethnic roots. This would explain the more lenient treatment meted out to Leontini, whose population included large numbers of Dorian refugees from Akragas, Gela and Camarina. More likely, however, it would have also included political and strategic considerations. The Ionian cities were blamed for inviting the Athenians to twice invade Sicily. They had enthusiastically allied themselves with the invaders and allowed their cities to be used as bases for making war on their Dorian neighbours. This was, not unnaturally, deeply resented by the Syracusans. It was also in direct opposition to the ideological basis of their hegemony, as spelt out by Hermocrates at the conference in Camarina, that of Sicily for the Sicilians.

Another obvious cause was sheer avarice. The Syracusans had long coveted the rich farmlands of the Laistrygonian Plain. The two cities that had controlled the plain, Leontini and Catane, were now occupied by mercenary garrisons loyal to the tyrant. The whole southeastern corner of Sicily was now firmly under the control of Dionysius. The annexation of further agricultural land would enhance Syracuse's revenues and allow Dionysius to pursue his ambitions to increase Syracuse's military power.

Dionysius appears to have spent the next few years consolidating his political control and his territorial gains. He was, however, at heart a war leader, and the military struggle against the Carthaginians was the justification for his tyranny. According to Diodorus: 'Dionysius, the tyrant of Siceli, since his government was making satisfactory progress, determined to make war upon the Carthaginians; but being not yet sufficiently prepared, he concealed this purpose of his while making the necessary preparations for the coming encounters.'[8] First on Dionysius' agenda was to make Syracuse impregnable. The Athenian invasion had shown that the key to the city was the heights of Epipolae. In 401, he decided to fortify the entire area so that the city should never be cut off by land from the rest of Sicily. He planned to build a five-kilometre-long wall along the northern edge of the heights.

This was an immense project requiring huge resources. Dionysius conscripted 60,000 labourers from the countryside. Such large-scale public works were mostly worked by free citizens rather than slaves. Rather than being resented, they were a popular method for the poor to earn good wages. A mason and a gang of 200 labourers were assigned to each section of about twenty-five metres. Dionysius wanted the work completed quickly, so he turned the building into a competition with prizes for the quickest to complete their sections. He and his friends joined in the work. Dionysius reportedly:

> laid aside the dignity of his office and reduced himself to the ranks. Putting his hands to the hardest tasks, he endured the same toil as the other workers, so that great rivalry was engendered and some added even a part of the night to the day's labour, such eagerness had infected the multitude for the task.[9]

This account brings to mind, at least to the more cynical modern reader, the image of modern politicians and dictators, in their brightly-coloured hard hats, turning over a few spades of earth for the television cameras. Ancient Greek politics was, however, much more personal, and the tyrant may well have had to put in a few days hard labour. Dionysius' careful preparations and incentives had succeeded; to everyone's astonishment, the work was finished within twenty days. This first project was only the beginning. Over the next four years, the walls were extended to enclose the entire Epipolae and the city, a total length of twenty-seven kilometres, longer than those of any other Greek city. The city, provided the walls were sufficiently defended, was now impregnable from the landward side. Sections of the walls can still be viewed in the outer suburbs of modern Syracuse.

Dionysius' recruitment of 60,000 men gives us a fascinating glimpse into the demographics of Sicilian Greek society and the influence this may have had on the politics of its cities. Accurate numbers of citizens of Greek cities are few, and making any conclusions based on such figures therefore has its dangers. Nonetheless, such an attempt does shed some light onto the politics of Syracuse. Diodorus tells us that these labourers were only a select group. Therefore, the total number was considerably higher. The only figures we have for the numbers of those belonging to the wealthy hoplite class are that there were somewhat more than 7,000. At the Battle of the Anopus River the Syracusans fielded 1,500 cavalry, who would have come from the wealthiest class. Comparable figures for Athens at the outbreak of the Peloponnesian War are 29,000 hoplites, some of whom were resident non-citizens, and 1,000 cavalry. No figures are given for the poorest class of citizen, but from hints elsewhere they probably numbered not many above 30,000, more numerous than the upper classes but less than double. Later figures confirm this low ratio.

In contrast, it can be seen that the poorest classes in Syracuse made up a considerably larger proportion of the population. Perhaps they outnumbered the wealthier classes by a ratio of four to one or even greater. In addition, the account of Diodorus (13.82–4) demonstrates that the rich of Sicily were profligately rich by Greek standards and willing to publicly demonstrate their wealth on a grand scale. This vast difference in both the numbers of the rich and poor, and the enormous gap in their levels of wealth, may have been one of the causes of the intense class struggle on the island, which was extreme even by Greek standards.

For sixty years the democracy had managed to keep a lid on these conflicting forces, but the renewed Carthaginian threat had destroyed the equilibrium. The failure of the elected generals had caused both fear and the suspicion that the wealthy were siding with the hated Carthaginians. First, Hermocrates had tried to overthrow the democracy and set up either a tyranny or a narrow oligarchy based on the aristocratic cavalry. This had failed because the both the poor and the hoplites were opposed to the introduction of such an exclusive regime.

Dionysius, who had been a supporter of Hermocrates, appears to have learned the lessons of his failure. The justification for his tyranny was to make the military more efficient and take the war to the Carthaginians. Like many a dictator, he was originally voted emergency powers by a democratic assembly. Despite the fact that most of his inner-circle of supporters was either family or extremely wealthy, such as the historian Philistus, he consolidated his coup by turning demagogue and successfully won over the poor. He was able to implement, to a limited extent, that most popular of measures, a redistribution of land. Initially, this was done at the expense of the exiled cavalry and later with the conquered lands of the Ionian Greeks. In addition to this measure, Dionysius' policies of public building and re-armament would have created many well-paid jobs for the poorest citizens. In a manner similar to earlier tyrants, Dionysius also gave citizenship and land to both freed slaves and mercenaries. These new citizens would of necessity have been extremely loyal to the tyrant, fearing that a return to democracy may have taken away their citizenship, as it had after the earlier overthrow of Thrasybulus.

Dionysius' destruction of the Ionian cities had caused fear in the kindred city of Rhegium that they too would share the same fate. Their disquiet was no doubt encouraged by the Syracusan exiles who had settled there after the destruction of Aetna. They decided to make war on Syracuse before the regime became too strong.

In 399, they crossed the straits with a force of 6,000 infantry, 600 cavalry and fifty triremes. They had obviously come to an arrangement with the generals of Messene, arguing 'that it would be a terrible thing for them to stand idly by when Greek cities, and their neighbours, had been totally destroyed by the tyrant.'[10] The Messenians called up an army of 4,000 infantry, 400 cavalry and thirty triremes to join the allied force. The generals, however, had not obtained a vote from the Messenian assembly before raising the army. Once they had reached the borders of their own state, dissension broke out in the ranks. It was argued that they should not go to war with Syracuse because Dionysius had done them no wrong. The soldiers argued that they had been illegally conscripted. They refused to cross the border and deserted en masse. The Rhegians were not strong enough to confront the Syracusans on their own and were forced to return home. The two cities sent an embassy to Syracuse and peace was concluded. The whole episode had been a fiasco. Dionysius was willing to make peace as he had already determined to make a new war against the Carthaginians.

Chapter 19

The Destruction of Motya

For the Sicilian Greeks, eager to return cruelty for cruelty, slew everyone they encountered, sparing without distinction not a child, not a woman, not an elder.

Diodorus 14.53

During the years of peace, many of the remaining independent Greek cities had allied themselves with Carthaginians, perhaps uneasy that they too might share the fate of Naxos. Dionysius decided that 'so long as he was at peace with the Carthaginians many of his subjects would be wanting to join their defection, whereas, if there were war, all who had been enslaved by the Carthaginians would revolt to him.'[1] Like many an ancient ruler, Dionysius believed that his subjects would be less likely to rebel if they were kept busy fighting someone else.

There was another reason why the timing was right for an attack. The plague that had been taken back to Africa had continued to ravage the Phoenician cities. Dionysius planned for a long and difficult campaign, recruiting many military engineers from both the Greeks and Phoenicians. The arsenals of Syracuse not only produced the latest siege-engines but also produced new weapons for the first time. Warships larger than the trireme were now built. These were quadriremes (fours) and quinqueremes (fives). The names of these warships refer to the number of oarsmen in each file of rowers. A trireme had three banks of oars, one above the other, with each man seated on a bench. There is no evidence that the ancients increased the number banks of oars beyond three. Instead, they increased the number of rowers per bank by placing two men to an oar. This could be done and still allow the rowers to sit at their bench. This allows the size of the ship to be increased to a hexere (six) without fundamentally altering the design of the ship. Later, bigger ships, sevens or above, did require new designs as once three men were placed on an oar they needed to stand to row efficiently. A quadrireme either had two banks of oars with two men to each bench or three banks with two men to the upper bench. A quinquereme had two men on the upper two benches. Quadriremes had already been introduced by the

Carthaginians, but are never mentioned in their fleets during the coming war. In an effort to win the naval arms race, Dionysius not only emulated them, but also surpassed them by building fives. His building program included constructing 200 new ships and refitting the 110 already in service. If completed, this program would have meant a fourfold increase in the size of Syracuse's fleet compared to that used against the Athenians fifteen years earlier. There is, however, no record of this number of ships ever serving under Dionysisus' command.

The Syracusans were also credited with the invention of the catapult. Dionysius' catapult probably derives from an earlier weapon, a hand-held crossbow known as the *gastraphetes* (belly-shooter). The innovations his engineers made were to mechanize the draw and release of the missiles, eventually incorporating a winch. These early catapults were probably still flexible bows, relying on the power stored in the bow-arm itself. Later, during the reign of Philip II of Macedon, this method was replaced by the torsion catapult using springs of tightly bundled hair or animal sinew, which produced even greater power. The other innovation was to place the bow on a pedestal, allowing it to become larger. These early catapults fired arrows about the size of a javelin or rocks about the size of a fist. Their main advantages were that they outranged human-held bows, had considerably more penetrative power and were remarkably accurate. This last attribute made them particularly effective in sieges. Their fire could easily be concentrated on a single spot, which with repeated hits could destroy the battlements on top of a city wall or remove the armour of a siege tower. Their accuracy was such that Julius Caesar was impressed when, at the siege of Avaricum, a single catapult shot down four successive Gauls who occupied the same position on the walls.

In addition, a number of personal armaments were produced. It is recorded that 140,000 shields and 14,000 suits of armour were made. These numbers seem extravagant and are possibly exaggerated, but it is generally believed that Diodorus sourced them from the contemporary historian Philistus. According to Diodorus, 'the Syracusans enthusiastically supported the policy of Dionysius.'[2] This popular support was probably a combination of a desire to take the war to the Carthaginians and because it would have provided further work for the poorer citizens of Syracuse. Only after he had completed this re-armament did Dionysius begin to recruit further mercenaries, in order to save the cost of their wages.

This passage in Diodorus raises the question of how Dionysius paid for his policy of re-armament. Although Dionysius is portrayed in the sources as often introducing heavy and unpopular taxes, this does not appear to be the case in this instance. The obvious source of finance was the pillaging of Naxos and Catane, which would have brought in large amounts of cash.

Once the ships were built, however, Dionysius could use the system known as *trierarchies*, in which wealthy individuals financed the costs of operating a trireme for one year. From Lysias (32.24) we know that this could amount to almost a talent per year. The figure for the new larger vessels would have been higher. Although a form of taxation on the rich it was, unless repeated too frequently, not too onerous. It was often seen as an opportunity for self-promotion and the *trierarchs* would compete with one another to lavishly decorate their vessels.

By the end of 398, Dionysius' preparations were complete. He now began gathering his army. Soldiers were conscripted from both Syracuse and the allied Greek cities. He also recruited many additional mercenaries, mostly from the Spartan-controlled Pelopponesus.

Despite his previous treaty with Messene and Rhegium, Dionysius feared that once the war had begun they would ally themselves with the Carthaginians. He therefore set out to bribe them onto his side, ceding a large section of land to the Messenians. He also promised that he would win a similar territory for the Rhegians and approached them for a wife. Since the death of his first wife, Dionysius had not remarried. He now desired to marry, have legitimate children and create a dynasty, 'in the belief that the loyalty of his offspring would be the strongest safeguard of his tyrannical power.'[3]

The assembly of the Rhegians, no doubt influenced by the exiled Syracusans resident in the city, refused his approach. In fact, they insulted Dionysius, saying that they would rather see one of their women married to the public executioner. Such people were usually considered polluted and not allowed within a city's walls. Instead, Dionysius obtained a wife, Doris, from the leading family of Syracuse's traditional ally, Locri. In order not to upset the Syracusans, he also married a local woman, Aristomache, at the same time. Such polygamy was usually frowned upon in Greek society, outside of royal families, but Dionysius was already adopting the trappings of royalty. His four-horsed chariot was used to bring Aristomache to the wedding.

The marriages were celebrated with lavish festivities. On his wedding night, Dionysius took great care to ensure nobody, except the three involved, knew which marriage was consummated first. Doris would be the first wife to give him a child, his first son and heir, Dionysius, usually referred to as 'The Younger'. She would have two further children. For several years, Aristomache had trouble conceiving but eventually would give birth to four children, two boys and two girls. As was usual among dynasties, multiple households led to conspiracies over favouritism. Doris' mother was accused of using potions to prevent Aristomache from conceiving. As a result, Dionysius had her poisoned.

According to Diodorus, Dionysius used the occasion of his marriages to renounce 'the oppressive aspect of his tyranny, and changing to a course of equitable dealing, he ruled over his subjects in more humane fashion, no more putting them to death or banishing them, as had been his practice.'[4] Clearly, he had begun his infamous policy of eliminating his enemies early in his a reign.

Once he had completed his marriages, Dionysius called together the assembly of the Syracusans and announced his decision to go to war. The citizens eagerly supported his proclamation as they were

> no less eager than he for war, first of all because of their hatred of the Carthaginians who were the cause of their being compelled to take orders from the tyrant; secondly, because they hoped that Dionysius would treat them in more humane fashion because of his fear of the enemy and of an attack upon him by the citizens he had enslaved; but most of all, because they hoped that once they had got weapons in their hand, they could strike for their liberty, let Fortune but give them the opportunity.[5]

The first act of the war was to seize the goods of the Phoenician merchants and to expel any resident Phoenicians from Syracuse and the allied cities. In some cities hatred of the Phoenicians was so strong that they tortured many before evicting them. Diodorus, in his usual partial manner, blames these outrages on the Carthaginians themselves as retribution for their previous sins. In reality these were war crimes against innocent civilians who were clearly living and doing business peacefully among the Greeks. It is also very possible that these outrages were deliberately encouraged by the tyrant in order to make sure that there could be no future compromise between the allies and the Carthaginians. Three centuries later, Mithridates of Pontus would use a similar stratagem of collective guilt when he ordered his allied Greek cities of Asia Minor to massacre their Roman populations.

Now that he was ready for war, Dionysius sent a messenger with a letter to the Carthaginian council, declaring war upon them unless they restored freedom to the Greek cities they had occupied. The Carthaginians were reportedly unready for war due to their losses from the plague and their lack of preparation. This last reason is difficult to understand. As has been seen, Dionysius had been openly preparing for war for at least two years, during which time Syracuse's harbours had been visited by many Carthaginian traders. Perhaps they believed that Dionysius had been planning to attack Messene and Rhegium. If so, this was an amazing feat of self-deception. Nonetheless, now war had been forced upon them, they immediately sent agents to Europe to recruit mercenaries.

The beginnings of Dionysius' campaign were a procession. The Greek cities flocked to him. Contingents soon joined him from Camarina, Gela, Akragas, Himera and Selinus. Dionysius now commanded an immense army by Greek standards, possibly the largest until the later years of Alexander the Great's campaigns, a century and a half later. If the figures are accurate, the force totalled 80,000 infantry, 5,000 cavalry, nearly 200 warships and 500 merchant vessels carrying the siege-train and supplies.

Dionysius' first objective was the Elymian city of Eryx. The city occupied both a spectacular and strong position, situated on a mountain 750 metres high, situated just inland and about 30 kilometres north of the main Carthaginian city of Motya. Diodorus asserts that the 'the people of Eryx were awed by the magnitude of the force and, hating the Carthaginians as they did, came over to Dionysius.'[6] The second part of this claim is perhaps a little disingenuous on Diodorus' part, as the people of Eryx had long been loyal allies of the Phoenicians against the Greeks and would later continue to be so. The first part of the passage is more likely to be accurate.

The citizens of Motya, expecting to receive aid from Carthage, were prepared to resist. The city occupies an island roughly circular in shape, about 2km in diameter, in a shallow harbour. It is well protected from the weather by the mainland to the north and east and a long island to the west. There is a very narrow opening to the sea to the north, between a headland and the western island, about a kilometre wide and a broader mouth to the south. It was joined to the mainland, to the northeast, by a causeway roughly 2km long. At low tide the remains of this causeway can still be seen and until recent times it could be crossed by vehicles. The local museum contains photographs of donkey-carts using the causeway. In preparation for the siege, the Motyans destroyed a large section of the causeway.

After observing the area, Dionysius set up camp to the north of the city and ordered the construction of moles along the route of the causeway. The warships were hauled out onto the shore, just below the promontory at the northern end of the harbour, where there was a small Phoenician settlement and cemetery. The ships were protected by a palisade of wooden stakes. This was done to both dry out the hulls and to use the crews, more than 40,000 men, for the construction of the moles, allowing the rest of his army to campaign elsewhere. The merchant vessels were moored along the shore outside of the harbour. Dionysius left the siege-works under the command of his admiral and brother Leptines, while he attempted to isolate the city by attacking the allies of the Carthaginians. Leptines was a more popular and charismatic figure than his brother. He was courageous in battle, but an incautious commander and prone to ignoring his brother's orders.

All the Sicanian towns came over to Dionysius except one, Halicyae. Elymian Segesta remained loyal, as did Entella, which had recently been occupied by Campanian mercenaries. Phoenician Panormus and Soluntum also held out. Dionysius ravaged their territories and then laid siege to Segesta and Entella, launching continuous assaults against both.

Meanwhile, the Carthaginian commander, Himilcon, was still gathering his forces. As a diversion he sent ten triremes on a raid against Syracuse. In

an impressive feat of seamanship, they managed to enter the harbour undetected and sank nearly all the ships that had been left behind. If Dionysius
had completed his building program this may have been in excess of a
hundred vessels.

In the west, Dionysius had abandoned his interior campaign, apparently
without capturing any of the besieged towns, possibly because his siege
train had remained at Motya, and returned to the coast. Perhaps the
Carthaginian raid had influenced him to complete his attack before further
reinforcements could be sent from Africa. He had also determined that if
Motya fell then all the others would surrender. Later events would show
this belief to be false.

With the army now returned, work on the moles accelerated. Himilcon,
learning that Dionysius had beached his warships, continued to show daring
at sea. He took a fleet of 100 triremes to Motya to attack the Syracusan fleet.
Arriving to the south of the city, he used the cover of night and the island to
the west of the harbour to again take the Syracusans by surprise. Himilcon
succeeded in destroying a number of the merchant vessels moored along the
beach and then entered the harbour to attack the fleet.

Diodorus' account is confused here as he first describes the Carthaginian
triremes as entering the harbour, but then states that the Greeks would have
to attack at a disadvantage due to the narrow entrance to the harbour.

Polyaenus states more plausibly that 'Himilcon blocked up the harbour of
Motya'.[7] It would therefore appear that the Carthaginians occupied the
narrow straits, where the confined waters would prevent the Syracusans from
using the advantage of their numbers. Perhaps they made a brief demonstra-
tion within the harbour before taking up position in the straits.

Dionysius then used a brilliant stratagem to solve this problem. Employing
the great numbers of his army, he hauled his triremes over the headland and
launched them into the open waters of the sea. Himilcon was now 'afraid that
Dionysius, after securing his own ships, would take an opportunity of
attacking the Carthaginians in the rear, and shutting them up in the harbour.'[8]
He turned to attack the first vessels as they were launched but was held back
by the firepower of the Greeks, as Dionysius had packed his ships with extra
archers and slingers. Their fire was supported by Dionysius' new catapults
firing from the land. The bombardment by the catapults killed many and
'created great dismay, because it was a new invention at this time.'[9] Himilcon
used the favourable wind to make good his escape. Ancient warships never
raised their sails in battle, as they were too much of an encumbrance. It was,
however, common for losing fleets to set sail in order to escape quickly.
Outnumbered and outmanoeuvred, Himilcon now retreated all the way back
to Carthage, leaving the people of Motya to their fate.

With the threat of the Carthaginian fleet removed, the Greeks completed
their moles. Dionysius 'advanced war engines of every kind against the walls

and kept hammering the towers with his battering rams, while with the catapults he kept down the fighters on the battlements; and he also advanced against the walls his wheeled towers, six stories high, which he had built to equal the height of the houses.'[10] The defenders responded by raising men above the engines on cranes, hurling incendiaries onto the Greek's siege-engines. The Greeks were able to put out the fires and continued to batter the walls. Eventually, the walls were breached and the climax of the assault had come. As Diodorus describes:

> Since now both sides rushed with one accord to the place, the battle that ensued grew furious. For the Sicilian Greeks, believing that the city was already in their hands, spared no effort in retaliating upon the Phoenicians for former injuries they had suffered at their hands, while the people of the city, envisioning the terrible fate of a life of captivity and seeing no possibility of flight either by land or by sea, faced death stoutly. And finding themselves shorn of the defence of the walls, they barricaded the narrow lanes and made the last houses provide a lavishly constructed wall.[11]

The Carthaginians now fought with desperation, for if they could not drive the Greeks out of the city the enemy's superior numbers would result in its capture. They built barricades between the houses and showered the attackers with missiles from above. The remains of dozens of these arrowheads are on display in the island's museum.

To finally overcome the defences, Dionysius brought up his mobile towers, reputedly six stories high, equal to the height of the houses within the city. They dropped their gangways onto the rooves of the houses and the attackers were now able to fight the defenders in hand-to-hand combat. The Phoenicians fought with great desperation as flight from the surrounded city was impossible. They were fighting not only for their own survival but that of their families who 'stood by entreating them not to let them be surrendered to the lawless will of victors . . . others, as they heard the laments of their wives and helpless children, sought to die like men rather than to see their children led into captivity.'[12] With the strength borne of desperation, the Motyans fought back fiercely and the fighting lasted for days.

The Greeks had made it their habit to break off the fighting at nightfall. Dionysius, noticing that the Motyans had become used to this practice, resolved on a night attack to break the deadlock. Once darkness had fallen, he sent a group of elite troops to mount the houses by scaling-ladders. They gained a foothold inside the barricades and broke down a section, allowing reinforcements into the bridgehead. Eventually, the superior numbers of the attackers overcame the exhausted defenders. The massacre then began, as the Greeks, remembering the atrocities at Selinus and Himera, slaughtered everyone without distinction of age or sex.

Dionysius attempted to end the slaughter, not out of mercy, but because he wished to raise revenue by selling as many survivors as possible into slavery. The vengeful Greeks refused to be reined in. Dionysius then sent heralds throughout the city advising the survivors to seek refuge in the temples. On this occasion the Greeks, unlike the Carthaginians, respected convention and ceased their killing. They then turned to the more profitable exercise of plundering the city. Dionysius allowed this as he hoped that pillage would increase their appetite for further fighting.

His mercy did not, however, extend to the Greek residents of Motya who had fought to defend their new home. They were crucified as an example to other Greeks who might consider fighting for the Carthaginians. This example does not appear to have been particularly successful, as Greeks continued to fight on the side of Carthage. Sometime later, Dionysius decided that it was more useful to reverse the policy. After another victory, Polyaenus claims that he

> obliged the Carthaginians to pay a very high ransom for their prisoners; but he released the Greeks, who had been captured while in the service of Carthage, without any ransom at all. The partiality shown by the tyrant caused the Carthaginians to become suspicious of the Greeks, and they discharged all the Greek mercenaries from their service. Thus Dionysius rid himself of these Greeks, who were a formidable foe.[13]

As the summer had come to an end, Dionysius decided to return to Syracuse with the bulk of his army. He left Biton in the ruins of Motya with a garrison consisting mostly of mercenaries. Leptines also remained with a fleet of 120 ships, with orders to oppose any further attempt by the Carthaginians to cross to Sicily, and to renew the attacks on Segesta and Entella.

Dionysius' capture of the main Carthaginian city of Motya was seen as an outstanding victory at the time. It was the greatest victory of the Greeks over the Carthaginians since long ago Himera. The Sicilian Greeks must have rejoiced, expecting that Carthaginian power on the island had been destroyed. Future events would show, however, that it was largely a hollow victory. Stunned by their defeat and 'the magnitude of the armament of Dionysius' the Carthaginians 'resolved far to surpass him in their preparations.'[14] They now turned their immense wealth towards raising a new force and conquering the entire island, hoping to end the Greek threat for once and for all.

Chapter 20

The Second Carthaginian War

Now that the Carthaginians have suffered defeat on land as well as on sea they entered into negotiations with Dionysius without the knowledge of the Syracusans.

Diodorus 14.75

With their cities and allies now faced with destruction in Sicily, the Carthaginians decided to throw the full force of their power into a campaign to restore their position on the island. Himilcon, as king, was once again to command the expedition. They recruited their forces, citizens, allies and mercenaries from Africa and Spain. Ephorus claims that the force totalled 300,000 infantry, 4,000 cavalry, 400 chariots and 400 warships. Timaeus, always ready to contradict Ephorus, states that slightly less than 100,000 troops were transported from Africa and 30,000 recruited in Sicily. Timaeus' lower figure is probably still an exaggeration or includes non-combatants.

With the coming of the campaign season in 396, Dionysius once again led his army west and ravaged the territory of his remaining enemies. Halicyaea finally came over and concluded an alliance. Segesta, however, continued to resist. The Segestans launched a surprise attack against the invading army and succeeded in setting their camp ablaze. Most of the tents and horses were lost in the inferno. Despite this setback, Dionysius continued the campaign, moving on to pillage the countryside of Panormus and Soluntum without meeting any opposition.

In the late summer, the Carthaginian expedition finally sailed. Himilcon, fearing his plans for the invasion would be betrayed to the Greeks, gave sealed orders to his captains. They were only to open them if they became separated from the main fleet. The destination was Panormus, the largest surviving Phoenician city in Sicily. The fleet was observed as soon as it came within sight of the western coast of Sicily. Leptines sailed out of Motya to attack the enemy. He succeeded in sinking fifty ships, mostly transports, but a favourable wind allowed most of the Carthaginian vessels to escape under sail to the safety of Panormus. Being heavily outnumbered, Leptines could not have hoped to stop the Carthaginian fleet. He probably concentrated on harassing the enemy and destroying any Carthaginian stragglers.

Once he had disembarked his army, Himilcon advanced directly against Eryx. The large pro-Carthaginian faction within the city opened its gates to him. Presumably, Drepanum also fell. With his rear now secure, he marched to Motya and quickly captured the remains of the city from Biton's garrison of mercenaries. Dionysius had now lost both his naval bases on the west coast and therefore command of the sea. Despite this he remained besieging Segesta. His troops were, as usual, eager to give battle against the hated enemy. The tyrant believed, however, that it would be too dangerous to fight so far from home, particularly as he was experiencing supply problems, perhaps as a result of the earlier destruction of his camp.

Dionysius decided to lift the siege and retreat to the east. Before leaving, he attempted to get his new Sicanian allies to abandon their homes in exchange for better territories to the east. Centuries of conflict with the Greeks had, not surprisingly, made them wary of ever trusting their promises. Most refused, and once the threat of the Greek army was removed they reverted to their traditional alliance with the Carthaginians. The year's campaign had been a costly failure for the Greeks. The Carthaginians had recaptured Motya and their allies had quickly rejoined them. Himilcon decided against rebuilding Motya. Instead, he founded a new city, Lilybaeum, on the peninsular to the south of the lagoon. This city would soon become the best fortified and most important Carthaginian city in Sicily. Polybius later described it as, 'excellently defended both by walls and by a deep moat all round, and on the side facing the sea by shoaly water, the passage through which into the harbour requires great skill and practice.'[1] It would successfully resist sieges by both Pyrrhus of Epirus and the Romans.

Himilcon had, in the previous year, shown himself to be a cautious commander and perhaps this had caused Dionysius to underestimate his abilities. His campaign of 396 was similarly cautious but well planned. He had successfully driven Dionysius out of the Epicraty, with little fighting and few losses.

After laying the foundations for the new city of Lilybaeum, Himilcon continued his offensive. He determined to attack Syracuse from the north rather from the west. This route had two advantages. First, he would avoid having to take the now re-occupied cities of the southern coast. Second, if he captured Messene, with its fine harbour, he could control the straits and prevent the Syracusans from receiving reinforcements from Italy and Greece.

Although Messene's independence had been guaranteed by the treaty of 405, it had forfeited its neutrality by later allying with Syracuse. Himilcon now sailed along the northern coast with a fleet of 600 vessels. Without the protection of Dionysius' army, Himera and Cephaloedium (Cefalu) were easily overawed and went over to the Carthaginians. Himilcon next seized the island of Lipari, an ally of Syracuse. The island would become an important Carthaginian naval base and remain so until it fell to the Romans in 252. With the entire northern coast under his control, Himilcon then sailed against Messene. He disembarked his army at Cape Pelorus, 20 kilometres north of the city.

Perhaps believing themselves to be secure under the treaty, the Messenians had allowed their walls to fall into disrepair. There was great debate in the city. Some, due to the state of their walls, wished to march out and fight the Carthaginians at a distance from the city. They were encouraged by an ancient prophecy that stated that 'the Carthaginians must be bearers of water in Messene,'[2] interpreting this to mean that they would defeat and enslave the enemy. Others despaired at the size of the force that had come to attack them, especially as their own cavalry was absent, serving with Dionysius. They evacuated their families and possessions from the city to the fortresses in the surrounding hills. Nonetheless, the decision was taken to fight and the Messenians sent their best troops to defend the coastal pass to the north of the city.

Four years earlier, Messene had possessed a fleet of thirty ships but there is no record of it taking part in the defence of the city. Perhaps, as with the walls, it too had fallen into disrepair or it was deemed too small to achieve anything against the enormous Carthaginian fleet. Himilcon, learning of the Greek advance, decided to use his naval superiority to outflank the enemy and seize the unprotected city. He sent 200 triremes to attack the town. The Messenian advance force observed the movement of the fleet and rushed back to the city. The ships, however, made use of a strong northerly wind and arrived before the defenders could return. The Carthaginian sailors and marines quickly forced their way through the dilapidated walls. Some of the garrison fought but most escaped to join their families in the safety of the forts. Two hundred defenders were cut off in the harbour and in desperation they attempted to swim across the straits. Most were overcome by the strong current but fifty survived.

Himilcon now moved his entire force to the city. He attempted to reduce the remaining forts but found it too time consuming. It was delaying him from the more important march south. Instead, he recalled his army for a brief rest before they marched against the main objective of his campaign, Syracuse. Himilcon had decided that Messene was too distant from the rest of the cities allied to Carthage and therefore too difficult to maintain. He did not wish, however, to leave it to be re-occupied by the Greeks due to its strategic position. Therefore, he razed the city so thoroughly that 'no one would have known that the site had been occupied.'[3]

Despite Dionysius' earlier attempts to win them over, the Carthaginian success convinced the Sicels to once again rebel against their hated Syracusan overlords. Himilcon persuaded them to build the city of Tauromenium

(Taormina) on a steep hill, near the coast, about 30km south of Messene.

Dionysius had returned to Syracuse, having dismissed most of his allies. Two years of campaigning had obviously caused manpower problems within the city, as he was forced to free slaves, perhaps 10,000 in total, in order to man another 60 warships. In preparation for the coming invasion, he made great efforts to provision and strengthen his outlying fortifications. Leotini's citadels were of particular importance as the harvest was stored there. The Campanian mercenaries settled in Catane were forced to resettle inland at Aetne, a more defensible position. Once these preparations were completed, he led his force of 30,000 infantry, 3,000 cavalry and 180 warships, many of them the new 'fours' and 'fives', to camp at a sheltered anchorage about 30km north of Syracuse.

Himilcon led his army down the coast and joined with his fleet, at the site of Tauromenium. A recent eruption of the nearby volcano of Mount Aetna had blocked the coastal road. Himilcon was therefore forced to march his army by the much longer inland route around the mountain. The fleet, under its commander Magon, was ordered south to occupy the now-abandoned Catane.

Dionysius, learning of the separation of the enemy's forces, decided to occupy Catane first and attack the Carthaginian fleet while it had no support from the land. Magon had over 500 ships. Although many of these would have been merchant vessels, the Carthaginians had brought 400 warships to Sicily, and after Leptines' initial attack no further losses are recorded. Magon's warships would therefore have heavily outnumbered Leptine's 180. Dionysius therefore ordered Leptines to maintain close order while he attacked the enemy fleet. These tactics would nullify the Carthaginians' superiority in numbers, preventing them from breaking the Syracusan line and make better use of his larger warships in close combat. The Syracusan control of the shoreline would also provide a refuge for any of their damaged vessels.

When Magon saw the Greeks advancing upon him his first thought was to seek the safety of the land, but when he realized that this was occupied by the Syracusan army he reversed his decision and decided to fight. He drew up his fleet away from the shoreline and awaited the enemy attack. This would both rest his crews and make it easier to maintain his line, whereas advancing on the enemy at sea always risked the possibility of losing formation. This danger particularly applied to newly-raised crews, such as the Syracusans' ex-slaves.

Upon sighting the enemy, Leptines, who was always an aggressive commander, ignored his brother's orders. He advanced with his best thirty vessels, probably quinquiremes, far ahead of the rest of his fleet. At first his more powerful ships sunk a number of the enemy triremes but soon the greater Carthaginian numbers began to tell. They did not bother to ram but locked their vessels alongside the enemy's and turned the fight into a series of boarding actions. In danger of being overwhelmed, Leptines was able to use the superior size of his ships to break off and flee to the open sea. The remainder of the fleet, attacking in disorder and without its commander, was overcome by the superior numbers of the Carthaginians. As the battle had been fought away from the coast, the Carthaginians sent lighter vessels along the shore and killed many of the survivors attempting to swim to safety, without the army being able to intervene. The Greeks lost a hundred ships and over 20,000 men. Carthaginian losses are not recorded but were considerably less than those of the Greeks.

The battle had been a disaster for the Greeks, potentially exposing Syracuse to an attack from the sea while the army was absent. Fate intervened, saving the Greeks and giving Dionysius a second chance to defeat the Carthaginian fleet. After the battle a storm hit the exposed Carthaginian fleet and forced it to seek refuge on the shore. The Carthaginian army had not yet arrived and the fleet was open to an attack from the Syracusan army. For some reason Dionysius failed to launch the attack. His nerve appears to have failed, for the defeat at sea had 'raised the spirits of the Phoenicians and markedly discouraged the Sicilian Greeks.'[4] Dionysius was also a cautious commander. Rather than risk attacking the Carthaginians and exposing the city to an attack by sea, he was determined to retreat to the security of the walls of Syracuse.

Nonetheless, the naval defeat was a calamity for the Greeks, as the Carthaginians now gained complete control of the sea. They sailed unopposed into Catane, towing their captured vessels behind them. These were later repaired and added to the Carthaginian fleet. Dionysius now ordered the army to retreat back to Syracuse. The troops, however, condemned him for his lack of nerve. The citizen hoplites, true to their perception of war, did not want to stand another long siege, but to fight and defeat the enemy in an open battle. They argued that 'their unexpected appearance would strike terror into the barbarians and they could repair their late reverse.'[5] At first Dionysius supported this argument but later succumbed to his advisers who reminded him of the fate of Messene, taken by the Carthaginian fleet while its army was absent. He again decided to retire to the city. This decision alienated what was left of his Sicilian allies, who deserted him and returned to their homes.

The year since Himilcon had landed in Sicily had been a disaster for the Greeks. Motya had been retaken, Himera won over, Messene destroyed, Catane captured and over 100 warships lost. Dionysius' justification for his rule had always been that it had been necessary in order to effectively fight the Carthaginians. Yet, despite his sack of Motya, he had achieved little and the Greeks were in a worse position than they had been before he had seized power. His lack of success since Motya was recognized by his political enemies. In a forthcoming meeting of the Syracusan assembly they would denounce his failures:

First of all at Panormus, when the enemy were disembarking and were in bad physical condition after the stormy passage, he could have offered battle, but did not choose to do so. After that he stood idly by and sent no help to Messene, a city strategically situated and of great size, but allowed it to be razed, not only in order that the greatest possible number of Sicilian Greeks should perish, but also that the Carthaginians might intercept the reinforcements from Italy and the fleets from the Peloponnesus. Last of all, he joined battle offshore at Catane, careless of the advantage of pitching battle near the city, where the vanquished could find safety in their own harbours.[6]

Himilcon again rested his army at Catane. While there, he approached the Campanian garrison of Aetne, promising them a large amount of land if they deserted the Greeks and telling them how content their compatriots in Entella were in their alliance with the Carthaginians. The Campanians were tempted, but unwilling to change sides as Dionysius had taken a number of hostages to ensure their loyalty. Carthaginian rule generally appears to have been more popular than that of the Greeks to the other peoples of Sicily. This is even admitted by the Syracusans themselves. As one speaker claimed, if defeated

we shall have to obey the commands of the Carthaginians, and if conquerors, to have in Dionysius a harsher master than they would be. For even should the Carthaginians defeat us in war, they would only impose a fixed tribute and would not prevent us from governing the city in accordance with our ancient laws.[7]

The Sicels, Sicanians and Elymians would surely have agreed with these sentiments, but would have named the Syracusans as a whole, not just Dionysius.

With the war going so badly, the Syracusans again sent to the Italian Greeks and the Peloponnesians for help. Himilcon decided to demonstrate his power to the citizens of Syracuse. He sent 250 warships and hundreds of merchant ships unopposed into the Great harbour of the city. The triremes were decked out with the spoils of war from his victory over Leptines in order to demonstrate the size of the victory and to dismay the onlookers.

In conjunction with the naval display, Himilcon brought up his army to the walls of the city and formed them for battle. The army was reputedly 300,000 strong. Again, this number must be rejected as the usual Greek propaganda figure, or guess, for the size of any large Carthaginian army.

Dionysius' walls now proved their true value. The Syracusans remained steadfastly within their fortifications, so Himilcon was forced to begin the serious work of laying siege to the city. For a month the Carthaginians pillaged the countryside to gather materials for the siege, to keep the soldiers happy and to demoralize the Syracusans. This included the plundering of a number of temples 'for which acts of impiety against the divinity he quickly suffered a fitting penalty.'[8] Unlike the Athenians before him, Himilcon wisely occupied the Temple of Zeus. Less prudently, he built his main camp on the same swampy plain 2km to the south of the city. Dionysius conducted an active defence, constantly raiding the Carthaginian lines.

In order to fortify his camp, Himilcon destroyed all the tombs in the area, including that of Gelon. Believing that the siege would be a long one, he also built three forts around the harbour: one at Plemmyrium, another along the southern shore, and the last at Dascon. Meanwhile, Dionysius' brother-in-law, Polyxenus, returned from the Peloponnesus with thirty warships and the Spartan admiral Pharacidas. Himilcon may have been better advised to have followed his original plan and occupy Messene, in order to prevent such reinforcements, rather than destroying the city. Although the Carthaginian fleet had occupied and fortified the Great Harbour, it was still possible for the reinforcements to evade the Carthaginians and enter the naval base in the Little Harbour.

Soon after, Dionysius left the city with a naval force in order to escort a supply fleet into the city. While he was absent, the Syracusans took the opportunity to launch five ships and capture a Phoenician supply vessel. The Carthaginians sent out forty ships to prevent them. The Syrascusans retaliated by manning all their available vessels and sailed out to meet them. The outnumbered Carthaginian squadron was heavily defeated, losing twenty-four ships, including their flagship. The Greeks chased the survivors back to their anchorage before retiring in triumph with their captured vessels, including the enemy flagship. From the description of the battle, the Carthaginians squadron was probably based at Plemmyrium, their nearest base to the Little Harbour. This would have allowed the Syracusans to defeat this isolated contingent before the rest of the fleet in the Great Harbour could intervene.

The Syracusans, winning the victory without Dionysius, 'were now puffed up with pride'. With Dionysius away, the elated Syracusans now began to openly speak of how 'to end their slavery to Dionysius, even though they had an opportunity to depose him; for up until then they had been without arms, but now because of the war they had weapons at their command.'[9]

With his rule once again under threat, Dionysius returned to the city. With so many armed citizens about the place, he was unable to use his mercenaries to terrorize the population into subservience. Instead, he summoned an assembly and praised them for their victory, promising a quick end to the war. Just as he was about to dismiss the meeting, one of his opponents Theodorus, a cavalryman noted for his courage, rose to denounce the tyranny and Dionysius' leadership:

Although Dionysius has introduced some falsehoods, the last statement he made was true: that he would speedily put an end to the war. He could accomplish this if he were no longer our commander – for he has often been defeated – but had returned to the citizens the freedom their fathers enjoyed . . . it behoves us, fellow citizens, to put an end not only to the Phoenician war but to the tyrant within our walls . . . he lords it over the city, not like a magistrate dispensing justice on equal terms, but like a dictator who by policy makes all decisions for his own advantage. For the time being the enemy possess a small portion of our territory, but Dionysius has devastated it all and given it to those who join in increasing his tyranny.[10]

Theodorus asked how men who were brave in the face of the Carthaginians were cowards when it came to confronting the enemy at home. He went on to compare Dionysius unfavourably with Gelon, who had ensured that the Greek cities had never even caught sight of the enemy, whereas Dionysius had lost most of Sicily. Theodorus then denounced the tyrant for his destruction of Naxos and Catane, failing to mention that Gelon had been guilty of similar crimes. He then denounced Dionysius' domestic crimes, robbing 'them of their freedom, slaying those who spoke openly on behalf of the laws and exiling the more wealthy; he gave the wives of the banished in marriage to slaves and to a motley throng; he put the weapons of citizens in the hands of barbarians and foreigners.' Not only did he compare Dionysius' poor military record with that of Gelon but also with the democracy that had destroyed the Athenian invasion. He asked why when 'our fathers left not a man free to carry back word of the disaster . . . shall we, who have such great examples of our fathers' valour, take orders from Dionysius, especially when we have weapons in our hands?'[11] All of which appear to have been legitimate criticisms.

Theodorus finished his speech with a call to overthrow the tyranny while they were gathered together, armed and had allies with them from Italy and the Peloponnesus. If Dionysius surrendered, he should be allowed to depart into exile with his possessions, otherwise he should be overthrown by force and brought to justice.

After the speech the Syracusans were keen to overthrow the tyranny but they made the error of looking to their allies for assistance. Once again, they where betrayed by the Spartans, the self-proclaimed bringers of freedom to the Greeks. Pharacidas, a friend of the tyrant, climbed up to the speaker's platform and declared that they had come to assist the Syracusans to fight the Carthaginians, not to overthrow Dionysius. With the Spartans supporting the tyrant, the people lost their nerve and the wavering mercenaries flocked back to Dionysius. Once again, the tyrant had survived a revolution.[12]

This failure of the assembly is the last time we hear of a mass revolt against the tyranny. From this point on, any opposition appears to go underground and rely on conspiracies.

By camping in the marshy area to the south of the city, the Carthaginians had suffered the same fate as the Athenians. The summer had been particularly hot and a plague broke out within their army. The Greeks claimed that this was divine retribution as a result of the Carthaginians' desecration of the temples and tombs. The symptoms 'began with a catarrh; then came a swelling in the throat; gradually burning sensations ensued, pains in the sinews of the back, and a heavy feeling in the limbs; then dysentery supervened and pustules upon the whole surface of the body.' Some also became disorientated and most died after five or six days. The disease was extremely virulent and those most likely to catch it were those tending the sick or dead. This increased both the death rate and the spread of the disease, as soon the men refused to tend the sick or bury the bodies. 'For not only did any not akin abandon one another, but even brothers were forced to desert brothers, friends to sacrifice friends out of fear for their own lives.' [13] Tens of thousands are reported to have died. As with many diseases described by the ancient writers, it is impossible to determine exactly what this disease was due to the large number of symptoms. There was, probably, more than one epidemic sweeping the camp.

As soon as news of the plague reached the Greeks, Dionysius decided on immediate action. With revolt simmering in the city, he would have felt compelled to justify his command and to keep his soldiers occupied. He ordered Leptines with eighty ships to attack the Carthaginian fleet at daybreak, while he, emulating Gylippus, made a night march against the enemy camp. Dionysius used the opportunity to rid himself of a particularly fractious group of a thousand mercenaries. He ordered them and the cavalry to attack one of the outlaying Carthaginian strongholds. The cavalry were given secret orders to abandon the mercenaries during the attack. The ruse succeeded and the mercenaries were wiped out.

Dionysius laid siege to the main camp and stormed the fort on the southern shore of the harbour. The Carthaginians were taken completely unprepared by the night march, as were the Athenians before them. At the same time, the fleet and the cavalry attacked the fort at Dascon. The Carthaginians at first attacked the cavalry, but then they saw the fleet also closing on the fort, and rushed back to protect their warships. They were too late, and the Greek vessels were able to repeatedly ram the enemy vessels; some were shattered while others were boarded and taken. Dionysius brought up reserves of infantry to reinforce the attack on Dascon. He found a number of Carthaginian penteconters and merchant vessels drawn up on the shore and set them ablaze. The youths and old men joined in the fun, manning light vessels and pillaging the ruined Carthaginian fleet. Once again, the population of the city gathered on the walls to watch and to celebrate the victory:

Some raised their hands to heaven and returned thanks to the gods, and others declared that the barbarians had suffered the punishment of heaven for their plundering of the temples. For from a distance the sight resembled a battle with the gods, such a number of ships going up in fire, the flames leaping aloft among the sails, the Greeks applauding every success with great shouting, and the barbarians in their consternation at the disaster keeping up a great uproar and confused crying.[14]

The fighting ended at nightfall, but Dionysius kept the Greeks in the field, pitching camp near the Temple of Zeus.

Having been defeated on land and sea, and besieged within the main camp, Himilcon entered into secret negotiations with Dionysius. He offered to withdraw back to Africa and pay 300 talents in reparations. Dionysius refused to allow the entire army to escape, but offered a secret deal allowing the Carthaginian citizen troops to escape. Showing a complete disregard for the lives of his mercenaries, Himilcon agreed. Dionysius kept the negotiations secret from the people of Syracuse because 'he knew that the Syracusans and their allies would never allow him to make any such terms with the enemy.' Diodorus claims that Dionysius struck this disreputable deal as he did not want to completely destroy the Carthaginian threat 'in order that the Syracusans, by reason of their fear of the Carthaginians, should never find a time of ease to assert their freedom.'[15] Although resentful of not being allowed to destroy their hated enemy, the Syracusans would have seen the victory as an escape from disaster and a triumph. The city had survived a siege and emerged victorious for the second time in less than two decades.

On the appointed day, Himilcon sailed away in forty triremes. The Corinthians, obviously not privy to Dionysius' schemes, chased them and sank one vessel. The Sicel allies of the Carthaginians also made good their escape to their homes. The remainder of the army, abandoned by its commanders, either fled in disorder or surrendered. Those that fled were soon captured. One group of Spanish troops massed together and threatened to resist. Dionysius, rather than risk a fight, enrolled them into his own mercenaries. The enemy camp was given over to his troops to plunder and the captives were sold into slavery.

News of the defeat and the betrayal of their soldiers caused the native population of Africa to rebel, having long hated the oppressive rule of the Carthaginians'.[16] The revolt was also joined by the slaves working the Carthaginian estates. Many of these were possibly Greek prisoners of war. They gathered together an army reputedly 200,000 strong and lay siege to Carthage. The rebels, however, were totally disorganized and soon began to quarrel over the leadership. They also began to run out of supplies due to their large numbers. The Carthaginians were able to bring in supplies by sea from Sardinia. They were also able to buy off sections of the insurgent army. It is probably during this siege that one of the stratagems that Polyaenus attributes to Himilcon occurred.[17] He laced wine with opium and left it in the suburbs for the Africans to find. Once they had drunk it they lapsed into a stupor and were massacred by the Carthaginian defenders. Their disunity, lack of provisions and treachery soon demoralized the rebels and they broke off the siege, scattering back to their homes.

It is likely, however, that the defeat at Syracuse and the revolt ended the Magonid dynasty. Himilcon blamed the defeat on his sacrileges and committed suicide by starving himself to death. Although little in Carthaginian history is certain, it is probably from this point that the dynasty was overthrown and replaced by two elected magistrates, called *suffetes*. At some later date, an assembly of the people was also created.

Despite the plunder won in his victory, the long period of campaigning appears to have left Dionysius short of funds with which to pay his troops. His mercenaries in particular were on the verge of rebellion. Fearing that they might join forces with the citizens and overthrow him, he arrested their leader. Another 10,000 he bought off by handing over the city of Leontini and distributing its land to them. Any of the earlier refugees still remaining agreed, or were forced, to return to their home cities. Others were sent to help repopulate Messene and found the new city of Tyndaris on the northern coast. Dionysius' inability to pay his troops may even have spread to his citizen levies. Polyaenus describes unrest among the Syracusans when he refused to pay the older hoplites.[18] He then assuaged the assembly by promising to use them to garrison his forts on full pay. Once they were dispersed in this manner, he reneged on his promise. Dionysius quickly rebuilt his force of mercenaries to ensure his continued security.

The Carthaginians' defeat before Syracuse and the rebellion at home had severely compromised the Carthaginian position in Sicily. They withdrew their garrisons and abandoned all but their traditional areas to the west. Notwithstanding his lack of funds, Dionysius was able to go over to the offensive. He campaigned against the Sicels, forcing most back into their alliances with Syracuse. The outlying Phoenician towns of Cephaloedium and Soluntum were surrendered to Dionysius through treachery. Dionysius relocated Soluntum from the coastal plain to the mountain overlooking the bay. Both cities retained Phoenician populations, as can be seen in the ruins of their temples at Soluntum. The results of the Carthaginian victories of a decade earlier had been completely reversed.

Dionysius was poised to invade the Carthaginian territory to the west but was distracted by events back in the east. His colonization of Messene with mercenaries loyal to him did not go unnoticed in Rhegium. The people of Rhegium, including the large numbers of Syracusan exiles, feared correctly that he had ambitions to take their city and thereby control both sides of the straits. They settled the survivors of Naxos and Catane in Mylae. In 394, they crossed the straits and laid siege to Messene. The Messenians, including the former mercenaries, marched out and defeated the Rhegians in battle. They followed up their victory by immediately marching on Mylae and capturing the city, but allowed the refugees to depart peacefully.

Dionysius, with the situation so favourable, decided that the time had come to attack Rhegium. Before he could begin this campaign, however, he came into conflict with the Sicels of Tauromenium. He marched on the city and laid siege to it. The Sicels defended their new city stubbornly, believing that it was liberated territory previously stolen from their ancestors by the Greeks. The siege dragged on into the winter. As the acropolis of the city was both high and well fortified the Sicel guards became complacent. In December, the Greeks used the cover of a moonless night and snowstorm to scale one of the undefended peaks of the acropolis. From here they broke through the defences and entered the city, but the slippery conditions hindered the attackers and the Sicels were able to counterattack and drive them out, killing more than 600. Dionysius barely escaped and most of those who did had to abandon their armour in their flight.

The power of an unpopular tyrant such as Dionysius depended on force and military success. Defeats like that at Tauromenium always encouraged revolt. In this instance, both Akragas and Messene used the opportunity to banish Dionysius' supporters and renounce their alliance with him, asserting their freedom and autonomy.

The winter of 394/3 saw Dionysius distracted by approaches from the east. In 394, the Spartans had suffered a terrible naval defeat at the hands of a Persian fleet, commanded by an Athenian admiral. As a result, Sparta had lost the Asian empire it had acquired after the defeat of Athens in the Peloponnesian War. Sparta approached Dionysius for help. At first, he was inclined to give aid to his most powerful backer and prepared thirty ships. Approaches from Athens, plus the renewal of the Carthaginian threat, caused him to change his mind and the squadron was never sent.

Dionysius' distractions in the east had given the Carthaginians a breathing space with which to recover their position. Their new commander, Magon, gave sanctuary to the refugees from Dionysius' wars and once more found willing allies among the Sicels. The Carthaginians again opened their coffers and used their wealth to rebuild their forces. In 393, they launched another attack on Messene, ravaging the countryside but withdrawing when the Syracusans approached.

On this occasion, Dionysius marched out to confront the Carthaginians who had retreated from Messene and made camp at the allied city of Abacaene. The two sides fought a battle and the Greeks were victorious. Dionysius did not, however, follow up his victory. Once more he allowed himself to be diverted by the prospect of capturing Rhegium. He returned to Syracuse and sent an expedition of 100 triremes against the city. As this was done only a few days after his return, the campaign must have been already planned.

The Syracusan fleet launched a night attack against Rhegium, setting fire to the gates. At first, the Rhegians tried to extinguish the flames, but their commander, Heloris, a Syracusan exile, ordered them to halt and instead to feed the fire. This tactic succeeded, as the conflagration delayed the Syracusan assault and allowed the Rhegians to gather their forces. Failing in his surprise attack, Dionysius ravaged their countryside, but was unable to draw them into battle and concluded a one-year truce.

The attack on Messene demonstrates the predicament that the Greek cities of Sicily faced. If they allied themselves with Dionysius their freedom and autonomy was compromised. On the other hand, if they remained independent they were not powerful enough to resist the attacks of the Carthaginians. This was a dilemma common to many less powerful Greek cities, but the presence of a foreign enemy on their island made the situation all the more desperate for the Sicilians. Rhegium and the other Italian cities faced a similar threat from the native Italian tribes.

As the fourth century continued, the smaller Greek states would find their freedom and autonomy coming under increasing threat from the growing power of Carthage, Syracuse, Rome and Macedonia. One method of protecting one's freedom was to ally with one of the larger powers. The smaller city would cede control of foreign policy and questions of war and peace to the hegemonic power. It would also agree to provide the larger state with fixed contributions of money and soldiers. In return, it would attempt to negotiate a treaty that would include clauses protecting their autonomy. The most important of these would be that the more powerful state would not place a garrison within their city nor unilaterally increase the rates of the contributions.

Some states would attempt to defend their autonomy by forming military alliances with other smaller cities. In these, the city would maintain its own internal laws but foreign policy and questions of war and peace would be voted on in a federal council. This method would leave the city with greater freedom, and a say in military decision-making, but at an increased threat of conquest by the larger empires.

Dionysius' obvious designs on Italy convinced the Italian Greek cities to form such an alliance, known as the Italian League. This was aimed not only at defending themselves against the Syracusans, but also against the growing threat of the indigenous tribes of southern Italy: the Lucanians, Bruttians and Apulians.

Dionysius' Italian ambitions had allowed the Carthaginians to once again recover from a difficult position. Magon was reinforced with, reputedly, another 80,000 troops from Africa, Sardinia and Italy. He marched west through central Sicily in an attempt to win over the Sicels. Learning of the Carthaginian advance, Dionysius marched out with an army of 20,000 troops to confront them near the Sicel city of Agyrium. The local tyrant, Agyris, supposedly the most powerful of the local Sicel leaders, had defied the Carthaginians. Dionysius now won him over to the Greek cause with the promise of annexing to him the lands of those who had allied themselves with Magon.

As usual, the Syracusan citizen hoplites demanded that Dionysius lead them into battle immediately and decide the campaign. He was unwilling to do this for a number of reasons. The Carthaginian army was much larger, it was running out of supplies and suffering badly from the guerilla attacks of Agyris' troops. Dionysius believed that he simply had to wait and the Carthaginian army would be forced to retreat. The Syracusans had no patience with this strategy and marched off home. This appears to have been simply a military rebellion, and there is no record of any subsequent attempt to overthrow the tyranny. In revenge, Dionysius proclaimed a decree, freeing the slaves of the deserters but later changed his mind.

Magon's supply difficulties must have been extreme, as he approached Dionysius with the offer of a new treaty. The two leaders concluded a peace on similar terms to that of 405, except that the Sicels were to be subject to Dionysius and that he was to receive Tauromenium. After the conclusion of the treaty, Magon returned to Carthage. Dionysius, after taking possession of Tauromenium, banished most of the Sicel population and settled the city with his own mercenary troops. The war had ended in a stalemate, with neither side having the strength to conquer the entire island. Both Diodorus and Justin accuse the tyrant of deliberately allowing the Carthaginians to survive so that their threat would force the Syracusans to continue to submit to their rule.[19] Whether or not this is correct, Dionysius' Italian ambitions had become an obsession and would continue to distract him from the task of driving the Carthaginians from the island.

Chapter 21

Italian and other Diversions

*Dionysius . . . thinking that peace might be dangerous to his power,
and idleness in so great an army fatal to it, transported his forces into
Italy; with a wish, at the same time, that the strength of his soldiers
might be invigorated by constant employment, and his dominions
enlarged. His first contest was with the Greeks, who occupied the
nearest parts of the coast on the Italian sea; and, having conquered
them, he attacked their neighbours, looking upon all of Grecian
origin who were inhabitants of Italy, as his enemies.*

Justin 20.1

Now that peace had been made with the Carthaginians, Dionysius was
determined to expand his empire into southern Italy. The main target of
this campaign would be Rhegium, possession of which would give him
control of the straits. In 390, he crossed into Italy with 20,000 infantry,
1,000 cavalry and 120 warships, landing at Locri. Advancing into
Rhegium's territory, he used the normal strategy of pillaging the countryside in order to persuade the enemy to come out and give battle. Rhegium's
Italian allies responded quickly, sending sixty triremes to reinforce the
Rhegians. Most of Dionysius' fleet and army were away on pillaging raids
but he attacked this force with his fifty available ships. At first, his bigger
ships gave him the advantage, but the Rhegians sallied out and supported
the fleet with missile fire from the land, allowing their allies to escape by
clinging to the shore. The battle was ended when a gale struck. The Italians
were able to escape to the friendly coast, but Dionysius' fleet lost seven
ships to the storm, with all their crews being captured as they swam ashore.
Dionysius and the rest of the fleet escaped to Messene. With winter
approaching, he withdrew his forces back to Syracuse. Over the winter, he
made an alliance with the Lucanians to conduct a joint attack against the
Greeks of Italy the next year.

The Lucanians were a federation of eleven Italian tribes who occupied a
territory stretching north from the Gulf of Tarentum to the western coast,
cutting off the 'toe' which was inhabited by the Bruttians. The northern

boundary with Campania was the River Silarus. Strabo describes the Lucanians as 'Samnite in race' and says that 'their government was democratic, but in times of war they were wont to choose a king from those who held magisterial offices.'[1] The evidence suggests that the Lucanians fought in a similar way to other Italian hill tribes, skirmishing from afar with javelins and preferring not to close in hand-to-hand combat until the enemy was demoralized. Justin claims that 'the Lucanians were accustomed to breed up their children with the same kind of education as the Spartans . . . thus were they prepared for the toils of war.' Livy, in contrast, describes them as 'fickle and reckless'.[2] During the fourth century they began to exert increasing military pressure on the Greek cities of southern Italy.

At the beginning of the campaigning season, Dionysius returned to Messene and sent his brother Leptines, with the fleet, ahead to support the Lucanians. They began their offensive by attacking the city of Thurii. The Thuriians called on their allies to send assistance. On this occasion, the pillaging of the countryside had its desired effect. The Thuriians did not wait for their allies, but marched out with an army 15,000 strong to confront the enemy.[3] The Lucanians withdrew, but this was a plan to lure the Thuriians away from their city and into difficult territory where their more lightly-armed troops would have a tactical advantage. They lured the Greeks into a valley surrounded on three sides by hills and cliffs and then sprang their ambush.

Such tactics seem to have been popular among the Italian hill tribes. Fifty years later, the Samnites would draw a Roman army into a similar ambush. Although Diodorus does not describe how the Greeks were trapped, it was no doubt analogous to Livy's description of the later ambush:

> The Roman column descended into this plain from the first defile with its overhanging cliffs, and marched straight through to the other pass. They found it blocked by a huge barricade of felled trees with great masses of rock piled against them. No sooner did they become aware of the enemy's stratagem than his outposts showed themselves on the heights above the pass. A hasty retreat was made, and they proceeded to retrace their steps by the way they had come when they discovered that this pass also had its own barricade and armed men on the heights above.[4]

The Lucianians had surrounded the Greeks with an army of 30,000 infantry and 4,000 cavalry. They attacked and easily overwhelmed the Greeks. The Lucanians had a long-standing enmity with the Thuriians and took few prisoners, killing 10,000. The survivors fled to a hill by the sea where they saw an approaching fleet. Believing it to be that of their allies, they swam out to the ships. The ships were, however, those of the Syracusans, sent to assist the Lucanians. The fleet was under the command of Leptines, who does not appear to have shared his brother's ruthlessness and was appalled at the massacre of his fellow Greeks by barbarians. He gave refuge to the Thuriians and ransomed the 1,000 prisoners the Lucianians had taken at a *mina* each, about 430 kilograms of silver in total, or nearly seventeen talents. Leptines went surety for this amount with his own money. He then brokered a peace deal between the two sides.

Leptines' generosity and intervention made him extremely popular but infuriated his brother. Dionysius' whole plan had been to use his alliance with the Lucanians to conquer the Greeks of Italy, but Leptines' treaty had ruined this strategy. Leptines was stripped of his command. Another of Dionysius' brothers, Thearides, was appointed to command the fleet.

Despite Leptines' disloyalty, Dionysius was determined to continue his Italian campaign, even without his allies. In 389, he crossed into Italy with an army of 23,000 men and laid siege to the city of Caulonia, which lay on the coast about seventy kilometres east of Rhegium. Thearides was sent to Lipari, where he captured a squadron of ten Rhegian ships. Their presence would imply that despite their treaty with Dionysius, the Carthaginians were lending at least moral support to his enemies. The Italian League now mustered its troops at Croton. The command was given to Heloris, as it was believed that 'he could be best trusted, because of his hatred, to lead a war against the tyrant.'⁵ The allies now advanced along the coastal road to relieve Caulonia with an army of 27,000 men.

As they approached the city, Dionysius abandoned the siege and advanced to meet the relieving army. The two sides met at the Eleporus River, about 20km east of Caulonia, with the Italians camped alongside the river and the Syracusans about seven kilometres away. Heloris appears to have neglected to send out patrols and remained ignorant of the presence of the enemy. At dawn, he advanced to meet the enemy with himself and 500 elite troops, probably other Syracusan exiles, and therefore cavalry, in the vanguard. Dionysius formed up his troops into a battle-line and also advanced. With his army already arrayed for battle, Dionysius immediately attacked and took the Italians by surprise while they were still strung out in a marching column; some had still not even left the camp. Heloris and his bodyguard withstood the initial attack briefly, but were soon overwhelmed and wiped out. The other Italians attempted to rush to the rescue but entered the fight in scattered groups and were easily defeated by the formed phalanx of the Syracusans.

The Italians broke and fled. Many sought refuge on a nearby hill, where they were surrounded by the victorious Syracusans. The hill was poorly chosen as it had no supply of water. Dionysius invested the hill and made certain that it was closely watched both night and day. The Italians asked for terms but were offered only unconditional surrender. At first they refused, fearing Dionysius' reputation for brutality, but eventually thirst forced them to surrender. Over 10,000 prisoners were taken. Dionysius surprised them by releasing them without ransom. He also concluded peace with the cities, leaving them all independent. In gratitude, the Italians awarded him gold crowns and believed that this was probably 'the finest act of his life.'[6]

Now he had broken the Italian alliance, Dionysius turned on Rhegium. If Diodorus is to be believed, the tyrant desired to capture the city not only for its strategic position but in revenge for their insult over his request for a bride. The Rhegians, knowing that if the city were taken Dionysius would take terrible revenge, asked for terms. Dionysius demanded payment of 300 talents, all seventy of their warships surrendered and 100 hostages. The relieved Rhegians agreed. Dionysius then returned to Caulonia, making another agreement with its citizens. They were allowed to live on the condition that they migrate to Syracuse where they would be given citizenship and be exempt from taxation for five years. The city was then levelled and the territory given to those faithful allies of Syracuse, the Locrians. The same treatment was meted out to the city of Hipponium, on the western coast of the toe of Italy.

Rhegium was now completely without allies and totally isolated by land. The peace Dionysius had concluded was simply a ruse designed to strip the city of its navy. Now the city was also cut off from the sea and would have little chance of receiving supplies or assistance if it were besieged. The following year, Dionysius again prepared to cross into Italy. He developed an elaborate ruse by which he could break the peace 'without prejudice to his own standing.'[7] First, he requested that the Rhegians supply him with provisions, promising to later replace them. They complied, but Dionysius found constant excuses to extend the army's stay, intending to drain the city's supplies. Eventually, the Rhegians began to suspect his motives and refused to supply any more food. Dionysius had now established his excuse and began his siege of the city.

The Syracusans launched daily assaults on the walls but the Rhegians, under the command of their general Phyton, sallied out and burnt many of his engines. Dionysius was wounded in the groin by a spear during one assault. The siege continued for eleven months until the population was starving. In desperation, they began to eat the grass growing outside the city's walls, but Dionysius sent in cattle to strip the vegetation. Starvation forced the Rhegians to finally surrender unconditionally. Upon entering the city, the Syracusans found piles of the dead and took not many more than 6,000 prisoners. The death toll within the city must have been horrendous. Those survivors who could not pay a ransom were sold into slavery.

Dionysius lived up to his reputation for brutality and vented his anger on Phyton for his defiance. First, he drowned his son and then tied him to one of his siege-towers and tortured him. When Phyton was told of his son's death he retorted: 'He has been more fortunate than his father by one day.' This defiance enraged Dionysius even further and he had him dragged around the city and flogged. Phyton continued to defy the tyrant 'and cried out that he was punished because he would not betray the city to Dionysius, and that heaven would soon visit such punishment upon Dionysius himself.'[8] Dionysius' cruelty and Phyton's courage soon began to arouse sympathy among even the most hard-bitten of the soldiers. The tyrant then put an end to the spectacle and drowned him. Dionysius then razed the city. He later built a palace on the site and the territory was annexed to Syracuse.

At some stage during the siege, there must have been a truce for the Olympic games. A truce was always announced before each of the Olympic festivals. Wars were forbidden, as were legal prosecutions, which carried the death penalty. This truce was taken very seriously by the Greeks, and the Spartans were once heavily fined for breaching it.

Dionysius entered teams in the four-horse chariot race. This was the most prestigious and expensive of the events as only the wealthiest could afford to enter a team. The prize and the fame belonged to the owner of the team, not to the driver. Surviving odes to the winners only ever mention the owners, unless they were also the drivers. As with the modern Olympics, the honour of winning not only accrued to the individual but also to the state. Alcibiades, whose horses won the race in 416, claimed that by entering seven teams and by winning earned not only fame for himself but also displayed the power of Athens: 'custom regards such displays as honourable, and they cannot be made without leaving the impression of power.'[9]

By entering multiple teams, Dionysius was trying not only to increase his own fame but also that of Syracuse. Dionysius was also 'madly addicted to poetry' and wrote his own works. He also sent a team of actors to recite his poems to the crowd. Diodorus describes the reaction of the audience: 'when they observed how poor his verses were, they laughed Dionysius to scorn and went so far in their rejection that some of them even ventured to rifle the tents.'[10] The situation was made worse when his chariot teams all crashed during the race. As well as the ridicule, the opponents of Dionysius insinu- ated that representatives of an impious tyrant should not be able to compete at sacred games. The Athenian orator Lysias claimed that the two great oppressors of the Greeks were the Persian King and Dionysius. He urged that they

> ought therefore to relinquish our mutual warfare, and with a single purpose in our hearts to secure our salvation; to feel shame for past events and fear for those that lie in the future, and to compete with our ancestors, by whom the foreigner, in grasping at the land of others, was deprived of his own, and who expelled the despots and established freedom for all in common.[11]

Rather than bring glory to Syracuse, the whole affair made the tyrant a laughing stock. When news of the derision displayed toward his poems reached Dionysius, he is supposed to have fallen into fits of depression and threatened to give up writing. Eventually, his flunkies convinced him that the criticism was the result of jealousy and to continue writing. Dionysius is recorded as producing a number of plays and a history. He even purchased the writing desk of the famous Athenian tragedian Aeschylus in order to gain inspiration.

After the fall of Rhegium, Syracuse was finally able to enjoy a period of peace. Dionysius used this period of leisure to further indulge his cultural aspirations. His court was filled with poets and philosophers. He used the presence of the former to attempt to improve his own writing. Most of his courtiers praised his work and Dionysius 'boasted far more of his poems than of his successes in war.' One, however, the famous poet Philoxenus, refused to play the game. He was rewarded by being imprisoned in the quarries. Later, after being pardoned, he was again asked his opinion of Dionysius' work. He did not reply directly 'but called Dionysius' servants and ordered them to take him away to the quarries.'[12] This time he was forgiven for his wit, but soon learnt to be less candid. Philoxenus later fled from Syracuse and wrote a poem entitled 'Cyclops' which satirized the tyrant and his court. In it, he claimed to have cuckolded Dionysius by seducing his mistress Galatea.

Around this time, the Athenian philosopher Plato also visited Dionysius' court. Plato had first-hand experience of both the murderous oligarchy of The Thirty and the restored democracy that followed it. He disapproved of both; the former for its injustice and avarice, and the latter for its execution of his teacher Socrates. Plato became obsessed with the concept of justice. As an aristocratic intellectual, he believed that only those schooled in philosophy could fully understand the notion, and therefore should rule over the un-informed. Plato argued that 'there will be no cessation of evils for the sons of men, till either those who are pursuing a right and true philosophy receive sovereign power in the States, or those in power in the States by some dis-pensation of providence become true philosophers.'

Plato despised all the major existing forms of government among the Greeks. He believed that oligarchy was flawed because the mere possession of wealth did not equate to wisdom and differences in prosperity between the classes would lead inevitably to conflict between the rich and the poor. He despised democracy as giving too much freedom to the uneducated, making them drunk on freedom. This would cause them to fall under the sway of a demagogue, leading inevitably to tyranny. As he has his hero Socrates say: 'I was going to observe, that the insatiable desire of this and the neglect of other things introduces the change in democracy, which occasions a demand for tyranny . . . Thus liberty, getting out of all order and reason, passes into the harshest and bitterest form of slavery.'[13] Plato believed, however, that tyranny, the inescapable result of democracy, was the worst form of government. In a tyranny, the capricious desires of the ruler became law and there was no check upon his absolute control over his people. Neither this, nor his proposal to ban poetry in his ideal society, would have endeared him to Dionysius.

The above is only a brief overview of his beliefs, as at the time of his first visit to Sicily, Plato was still developing his ideas. Twenty years later he would publish them in completed form in *The Republic*. The theories of Plato and his followers would play an influential role in the politics of Syracuse following the death of Dionysius.

Plato strongly disapproved of the opulence enjoyed by the rulers of the cities of Italy and Sicily, claiming that:

> The kind of life which was there called the life of happiness, stuffed full as it was with the banquets of the Italian Greeks and Syracusans, who ate to repletion twice every day, and were never without a partner for the night . . . For with these habits formed early in life, no man under heaven could possibly attain to wisdom – human nature is not capable of such an extraordinary combination. Temperance also is out of the question for such a man; and the same applies to virtue generally. No city could remain in a state of tranquillity under any laws whatsoever, when men think it right to squander all their property in extravagance, and consider it a duty to be idle in everything else except eating and drinking and the laborious prosecution of debauchery. It follows necessarily that the constitutions of such cities must be constantly changing, tyrannies, oligarchies and democracies succeeding one another, while those who hold the power cannot so much as endure the name of any form of government which maintains justice and equality of rights.[14]

Prior, to his visit to Syracuse, Plato had become friendly with, and teacher of, Dion, brother-in-law of Dionysius, who had convinced the tyrant to invite him. Plutarch describes Dion's deeds in flattering terms: 'that wisdom and justice must be united with power and good fortune if public careers are to take on beauty as well as grandeur.'[15] Despite this glowing reference, Dion would later show himself to be just as ambitious as his master. Naturally, Plato disapproved of the life-style and policies of the tyrant and gave voice to his objections. As has been noted, Dionysius did not take kindly to criticism. The sources record several rancorous exchanges between the two. In one, Plato 'maintained that the interest of the ruler alone was not the best end, unless he were also pre-eminent in virtue.' To this Dionysius angrily retorted 'you talk like an old dotard. And you like a tyrant, rejoined Plato.'[16]

Hardly brilliant repartee, but the Greeks usually discussed such things at dinner parties, known as *symposia*. A rich man would invite a number of men (respectable women never attended) to his house where they would drink, eat and be entertained by musicians, dancers and prostitutes. The evening would usually begin with discussion of the arts and politics, but as the evening progressed, and the participants became drunker, the conversation would degenerate and the more physical entertainments commence. This exchange probably took part later in the evening. In a normal symposium, the exchange of views would be fairly robust. At the court of a tyrant, or king, it would often degenerate into a competition as to who could lavish the most praise on the host. As can be seen from the example of Philoxenus, criticism was rarely appreciated.

In another angry exchange, Dionysius asked the philosopher why he had come to Syracuse. When Plato said 'that he was come to seek a virtuous man, the tyrant answered and said: "Well, by the gods, it appears that you have not yet found such a one."'[17] According to some later stories, Dionysius arrested Plato and sent him to the island of Aegina to be sold in the slave market. Plato's friends rallied round and bought his freedom. They quickly returned him to Athens with the good advice that 'a wise man should associate with tyrants either as little as possible or with the best grace possible.'[18]

The two protagonists would also insult each other in writing. Dionysius would produce a comedy satirising Plato. He, in turn would clearly use Dionysius as his model for the abuses of the tyrant in *The Republic*, which among other things include:

> The famous request for a bodyguard, which is the device of all those who have got thus far in their tyrannical career . . . And if any of them are suspected by him of having notions of freedom, and of resistance to his authority, he will have a good pretext for destroying them by placing them at the mercy of the enemy; and for all these reasons the tyrant must be always getting up a war.[19]

This period of peace, rather than make Dionysius happy and secure, appears to have had the reverse effect. The ridicule of his poetry and criticisms of some of his philosopher hangers-on reputedly drove Dionysius into a fit of depression and paranoia. Diodorus claims that:

> His condition grew constantly worse and a madness seized his mind, so that he kept saying that he was the victim of jealousy and suspected all his friends of plotting against him. At last his frenzy and madness went so far that he slew many of his friends on false charges, and he drove not a few into exile, among whom were Philistus and his own brother Leptines, men of outstanding courage who had rendered him many important services in his wars.[20]

Caven argues convincingly that there was in fact a genuine plot at this time, by his closest supporters, against the tyrant.[21] The plot was centred on his brother Leptines and Philistus. Their motive may have been a result of their opposition to Dionysius' Italian ambitions. Being close to the tyrant, these two were spared and sent into exile, Leptines at Thurii, where he was honoured due to the mercy he had shown after the defeat by the Lucanians. He was later recalled. Philistus went to Adria in Italy, where he began writing his history and did not return until after the death of Dionysius. Others, including his guard commander Marsyas, were executed. It may be during this period that the more extreme stories of Dionysius' paranoia arise, such as not allowing a barber to shave him, strip searching all visitors and forcing his wives, against all concepts of modesty, to come to bed naked, in case they were concealing a weapon.

Although Dionysius' security measures were satirized by the ancient comics they may have been quite reasonable. Two near contemporary Thessalian tyrants, Jason and Alexander of Pherae, were both assassinated by relatives, and several of Dionysius' successors were murdered by their own followers. To paraphrase the old joke: it is not paranoia if people really are trying to kill you. Dionysius' security measures may well have been one of the main reasons for the extraordinary length of his tyranny. Tyrannicides were generally honoured heroes in ancient Greek cities.

During this period of peace, Dionysius finally threw his lot in with Sparta, sending twenty ships to assist the Spartans against Athens. He also embarked on a building program that included a gymnasium outside of the city on the Anapus River and numerous 'temples to the gods and whatever else would contribute to the growth and renown of the city.'[22]

Dionysius' next war of conquest was against the kingdom of Epirus in northwestern Greece. He planned to expand his empire into the Adriatic Sea, thereby securing the sea route from Sicily to Greece. A few years earlier, the Syracusans had founded a colony at Lissus (Lezhe, in Albania). Dionysius had also assisted in the foundation of another Greek colony in the Adriatic, Pharos (Hvar in Croatia), by the people of the island of Paros. His pretext was to assist Alcetas, an exiled claimant to the throne of Epirus. He made an alliance with the Illyrians, a non-Greek people living on the eastern shores of the Adriatic, against the Epirots, sending 2,000 soldiers as well as equipment. His allies were too successful; the Illyrians won a major victory over the Epirots, killing 15,000. They then attacked Pharos. Dionysius turned on his new allies, sending his forces from Lissus to defeat the Illyrians and save Pharos.

Poetry, philosophy, conspiracies and Adriatic conquests may have kept Dionysius distracted for a while, but they were not the main purpose of his rule. The driving out of Sicily of the Carthaginians was, and it was here that Dionysius again directed his ambitions. The waging of a major military campaign required money. This is recorded as being in short supply; perhaps this was one of those occasions when the Syracusans refused to pay the extra levy. Dionysius was forced to resort to other methods to raise funds: a short, easy campaign that was little more than piracy. On the excuse of suppressing pirates, he attacked the Etruscan city of Caere, just north of Rome. He plundered the nearby temple of the sea-goddess Leucothea and defeated the local army in a battle. From this freebooting expedition, Dionysius raised at least 500 talents. Polyaenus records an anecdote that having learned that his troops had stolen over 1,000 talents, he offered to let them keep half provided they handed over the other half. He then forced them to give up the remaining half.[23] Dionysius then used the proceeds of his raid to fund the hiring of mercenaries in preparation for a new war against the Carthaginians. The raid itself may have been a deliberate provocation against the Carthaginians, as Caere was an old ally and had a large Carthaginian population.

Dionysius was determined on a new war with the Carthaginians, but first he needed to find an excuse for breaking the peace. In 383, Dionysius, in gross violation of the existing treaty, made a military alliance with the Greek cities of Sicily that had been ceded to Carthaginian control. Reputedly, they were eager to revolt against their foreign overlords. The Carthaginians sent an embassy to Dionysius demanding an end to the alliances and the recognition of their control over the Greek cities. When Dionysius refused their claims, a new war was inevitable.

Chapter 22

Dionysius' Final Campaigns

Well, Jupiter on Olympus did not strike him with a thunder-bolt, nor was he worn away by painful and lingering disease, and despatched by Aesculapius, but he died in his own bed, and that the drama of tyranny might have a splendid end, was carried to the pyre of Typanis, and as though the power which he had himself acquired by crime were just and lawful, he handed it on as an inheritance to his son. My discourse deals with this subject unwillingly, for it has the appearance of authorising wrong-doing.

Cicero, *On the Nature of the Gods* 3.35[1]

In preparation for the coming conflict, known as the Third Carthaginian War, the Carthaginians formed an alliance with the Greeks of Italy. Most likely this was with a reformed Italian League. Although the League may have been broken up after Dionysius' victory at the Eloporus River, and votes of thanks given to the tyrant, the Italians must have resented his destruction of Rhegium, Caulonia and Hipponium, and his expansion into the Adriatic. Even Syracuse's old ally Locri had changed sides. So great was their fear of Dionysius that the Italians were willing to emulate the tyrant and ally themselves with barbarians against their fellow Greeks. The Carthaginians sent large forces, citizen and mercenary, to both Sicily and Italy, forcing Dionysius to divide his forces and fight on two fronts. Unfortunately for us in attempting to follow the course of this war, our major source, Diodorus, appears to have lost interest in the deeds of Dionysius. His account of the war occupies only three chapters and it appears to occur over only one campaigning season. This time-scale is overwhelmingly rejected by historians. Other evidence shows that the war lasted much longer, most likely until 378, or possibly 374.[2]

Details of the first years of the war are few, with Diodorus recording only that fighting was continuous on both fronts. This makes any account of events for these years speculative at best. The war commenced in 383, and Dionysius appears to have commanded the campaign in Italy, so this is probably where the main clash initially took place. Presumably, the Syracusans stood on the defensive in Sicily and the fighting was inconclusive. In Italy, the Syracusans appear to have been largely successful.

From the sources, we can get some details of the conflict. The exact order of events is unknown, but the following account would appear to be the most likely. Locri would have been Dionysius' first objective and this was soon taken. It must have been during this campaign that Dionysius committed the impiety of plundering the temple of Persephone at Locri. After which, he is supposed to have gloated: 'Do you perceive, friends, how prosperous a voyage the immortal gods give to the sacrilegious?'[3] This crime was later emulated by Pyrrhus of Epirus, but unlike Dionysius, he was reputedly punished by the gods. It was claimed that Pyrrhus' attempt to conquer Italy was ruined by 'the wrath of the goddess whose sanctity had been violated, a wrath of which not even Pyrrhus himself was unaware.'[4]

Perhaps the goddess did punish Dionysius for his hubris, as in his next campaign he sent a fleet to take Thurii but this was destroyed, as was Pyrrhus', by a storm. Dionysius' brother Thearides was killed in this attack. It was probably his death that led to the recall of Leptines. Dionysius was possibly running out of people he could trust. The attack on Thurii may have been an attempt to bypass and isolate Croton, forcing it to surrender without a fight.

The failure at Thurii meant that Croton had to be attacked directly. Dionysius took it 'by stratagem, scaling it on the side away from the sea,'[5] most likely in 379. If Justin can be believed, Dionysius also made an alliance with the Gauls who had sacked Rome in 387 'and being reinforced with assistance from Gaul, renewed the war as it were afresh.'[6] A formal alliance with such a distant people would appear unlikely, but it is possible that he may have negotiated successfully for large numbers of Gaulish mercenaries.

After taking Croton, Dionysius returned to Sicily, probably in 378. The Carthaginians took advantage of his absence by sending a fleet to Italy and returning the exiles of Hipponium to their city. The Syracusans confronted the Carthaginians at the otherwise unknown city of Cabala. This is usually assumed to have been located in eastern or central Sicily. This encounter would be one of two pitched battles that Diodorus claimed settled the war. At the Battle of Cabala the Greeks were victorious, killing 10,000 and capturing 5,000 of the enemy. Many of the surviving Carthaginians fled to the shelter of a hill but were attacked again, with their commander Magon being killed in the combat. Diodorus then has the two enemies fighting another battle a few days later but he appears to have overly abbreviated his narrative. Most likely, the second battle took place sometime later in the same year. Polyaenus' description of what happened after the Battle of Cabala is preferable to Diodorus' condensed account:

> When the Carthaginians were blocked up by Dionysius in a spot, where they had no supply of water, they dispatched an embassy to him with

proposals for peace. He agreed to this, on condition that they should evacuate Sicily, and reimburse him for the expenses of the recent war. The Carthaginian deputies agreed to the terms, but as they were not empowered to conclude the treaty without the authority of the admiral, they asked for leave to shift their camp to the place where the admiral lay; then the treaty, cleared of all obstacles, could be ratified. Dionysius, against the advice of Leptines, agreed to their request. As soon as they had changed the site of their camp, the Carthaginians sent back the ambassadors of Dionysius, and refused to conclude the treaty.[7]

Dionysius, after his victory, was elated by his success and was in no mood to compromise. The last two decades of constant warfare had hardened Greek attitudes. Dionysius demanded that they abandon all of Sicily to Greek control and pay the costs of the war. The Carthaginians were not willing to accept such terms, but by pretending to consider them they had 'with their accustomed knavery'[8] tricked Dionysius and made good their escape.

The Carthaginians chose Himilco, son of Magon, as their new commander, and he led the army west to the town of Cronium, near Panormus. Himilco, having reached the safety of the Epicraty, reorganized the Carthaginian army: 'with laborious exercise, hortatory speeches, and training in arms, he rendered the army obedient and competent.'[9] Although not mentioned by the sources, he must have reinforced his force with the garrisons of western Sicily and possibly any Sicanian or Elymian allies.

Despite the Carthaginian escape, Dionysius was still determined to destroy them. Marching west in pursuit of the enemy, he made an alliance with Himera, presumably it had earlier returned to Carthaginian control when confronted by Magon's army. The people of Himera agreed to supply him while he campaigned, without much success, against the surrounding Sicanian towns. Dionysius' prolonged presence soon made the people of Himera suspicious of his intentions:

and they refused to supply him in the same generous manner that they had done before. Dionysius therefore made his lack of provisions a pretext for breaking with the men of Himera; he advanced against their city with all his forces, and took it by storm.[10]

It was probably this delay that allowed Himilco to rebuild the Carthaginians' forces. Dionysius, after leaving Himera, advanced on Cronium. Himilco was absent from the town, most likely gathering reinforcements. The Greek advance had put him in danger of being cut off from the rest of his forces. Once again, he was able to outmanoeuvre the Syracusans: 'taking advantage of a wind that blew directly towards them, he set the wood on fire; and while the enemy were surrounded by a cloud of smoke, he slipped past them, and reached the walls.'[11]

Confident that his army could again face the Greeks, Himilco marched out and gave battle. The Greek army fought in two wings, one commanded by Dionysius and the other by Leptines. Dionysius led the best troops and most likely had command of the traditionally stronger right wing. Leptines led his contingent into the fray, and although he 'excelled in courage, ended his life in a blaze of glory, fighting heroically.'[12] The Carthaginians, emboldened by their success, broke his command. The battle was then most likely a repeat of the fight outside of Akragas, but in reverse. The victorious Carthaginian right would have swung into the exposed flank and rear of Dionysius' command, which up to that point had been pushing the Carthaginians back. This assault shattered the Greek phalanx and the entire army was routed. As was all too common in battles between the two foes, the Carthaginians eagerly pressed the pursuit, calling out 'to one another to take no one captive; and so all who were caught were put to death . . . So great was the slaughter, as the Phoenicians recalled past injuries, that the slain among the Sicilian Greeks were found to number more than fourteen thousand.'[13]

The surviving Greeks were able to make good their escape to their camp with the coming of night. The victorious Carthaginians withdrew to Panormus and did not follow up their victory. Most likely, the battle was fought late in the year. The Carthaginians may also have received news of the renewed outbreak of plague and rebellion at home. Nonetheless, the defeat at Cronium was decisive and Dionysius was forced to make peace on the Carthaginians' terms. These are recorded by Diodorus:

> That both parties should hold what they previously possessed, the only exception being that the Carthaginians received both the city of the Selinuntians and its territory and that of Akragas as far as the river called Halycus. And Dionysius paid the Carthaginians one thousand talents.[14]

This is the first time that the Halycus River would be named as the boundary of Carthaginian control in Sicily. Just where the northern border was situated is not recorded, but presumably it was somewhere to the west of the city of Himera. The Halycus would become the traditional border between the two peoples and be named in a number of later treaties. It is sometimes argued that this treaty was the first to acknowledge Syracusan hegemony over the cities to the east of the river[15], but this is not what Diodorus records. The previous treaties had declared that the Greek cities were to be free and autonomous, but paying tribute to, and recognizing the authority of, Carthage. It was Dionysius' violation of these terms that had led to the Third Carthaginian War. After such a clear victory, it is unlikely that the

Carthaginians would forsake their reasons for going to war. The treaty had also acknowledged direct Carthaginian control of Selinus. The reality of this can be seen in the large number of Carthaginian buildings that occupy the ruins of the acropolis of Selinus.

The fate of the Greeks of Italy is not recorded, but presumably they were abandoned by their Carthaginian allies, to be preyed upon by both Dionysius and the Italian tribes over the next decade. Dionysius of Halicarnassus records that Dionysius continued

> To lord it over those cities for twelve years. Then some, who stood in dread of the tyrant, entrusted themselves to the barbarians, while others, who were being warred upon by the barbarians, handed over their cities to the tyrant; and no matter at whose hands they were suffering, they were always wretched and discontented.[16]

The passage implies that Dionysius still controlled the Italian part of his empire until his death in 367, about twelve years after the capture of Croton. His successor, Dionysius the Younger, continued to control much of Southern Italy until his overthrow. At some stage during this conflict, Dionysius was at war with the Lucanians and attempted to protect his Italian conquests by building a wall across the 'toe' from the site of Caulonia to Hipponium. Strabo claims, however, that the real reason for the wall was 'to break the alliance which the Greeks had with one another, and thus command with impunity the people inside; but the people outside came in and prevented the undertaking.'[17]

This constant campaigning in Italy had a terrible effect on the Greek cities whose territories had been repeatedly pillaged. They were weakened to the extent that they were no longer able to adequately defend themselves against the incursions of the southern Italian tribes. Over the remainder of the fourth century they would suffer a number of defeats at the hands of the Lucanians and Apulians. The Italian League, now led by its largest and richest city, Tarentum, would be reduced to begging for military aid from a series of adventurers from Sparta and Epirus. All would ultimately be defeated. Some cities would, in desperation, later place themselves under the protection of Rome. This was always a fatal decision for any city's freedom, as the Romans never voluntarily released an ally from its obligations. These alliances gave Rome the justification for its later conquest of the region.

The most likely reason for the Carthaginians not making better use of their victory at Cronium was a renewed outbreak of plague in Carthage at this time. This seriously weakened them and both the Libyans and Sardinians took the opportunity to rebel. Diodorus states that the plague only ended once the appropriate sacrifices, presumably children, had been made. Once the plague was over, however, the Carthaginians easily defeated the rebels and regained control of their empire.

By 373, Dionysius' position in Italy appears to have become secure enough for him to again send aid to his ally Sparta in its ongoing war against Athens. In 376, Athens had won a decisive victory at the Battle of Naxos and re-covered control of the Aegean. The scene of the fighting now shifted to the Ionian Sea, to the west of Greece. Dionysius would have seen an Athenian presence here as a threat both to his sea lanes and his Adriatic possessions. He sent ten ships to assist the Spartans at Corcyra. The squadron was ambushed and captured by the Athenians. The crews were ransomed but its commander Crinippus committed suicide. The ships were also transporting two statues of gold and ivory destined for the sanctuaries of Delphi and Olympia. The cash-strapped Athenians sold the statues in order to pay their crews, despite this being an act of sacrilege. Dionysius wrote a letter of protest to the Athenian assembly but it appears to have been ignored.

Sparta's control of the Pelopponesus was finally shattered in 371, when it was defeated by the Thebans at the Battle of Leuctra. In the three-way struggle for control of Greece it was usual for the two lesser powers to unite against the most powerful. In 369, Sparta and Athens forgot their past differences and united against Thebes. Dionysius joined the new alliance and sent a force of twenty ships and 2,000 mercenaries; expendable Gauls and Spaniards, to assist their allies. These acquitted themselves well and the Athenians, in an attempt to ingratiate themselves with their erstwhile enemy, voted a decree of thanks to Dionysius, awarding him honorary citizenship and a gold crown. Dionysius had, however, apart from sending a similar contingent of merce-naries in 368, lost interest in events in Greece and was once again determined to make war against the Carthaginians.

Diodorus records that in 368, Dionysius decided to renew the conflict against the Carthaginians as he believed that they 'were in no condition for war because of the plague which had raged in their midst and the defection of the Libyans.'[18] This campaign is usually referred to as the Fourth Carthaginian War. Diodorus' passage presents problems, as earlier he had placed the outbreak of the plague and rebellion at 378. After the human sacri-fices had been made, the plague subsided and the Carthaginians quickly subdued the revolt. Now either there were two outbreaks of both plague and rebellion, or these disasters took the Carthaginians ten years to overcome. Justin reports that 'an invasion of Sicily by the Carthaginians obliged Dionysius to return thither; for that people, having recruited their army, had resumed the war, which they had broken off in consequence of the plague.'[19] As he names the commander of this expedition as Hanno, Carthage's newly-appointed commander, he is probably referring to the Fourth rather than the Third War. Both historians are guilty of overly-abridging their accounts in this instance. The most likely scenario was that the plague and revolt continued, at least intermittently, to trouble the Carthaginians until 368, and that Diodorus has again abridged his narrative and, as he sometimes does, is looking forward to later events.

From the earlier passage of Dionysius of Halicarnassus, it appears that the tyrant spent much of this decade campaigning in southern Italy. Hence there may be some truth in Justin's claim that he returned from Italy to Sicily for this war. Diodorus states that Dionysius alleged that the Carthaginians had violated his territory as a justification for renewing the conflict. Perhaps he exaggerated some petty border incident, accounting for Justin's claim that he was responding to a Carthaginian invasion.

Although the events leading up to Dionysius' declaration of war cannot be recreated with certainty, the most likely scenario is that Dionysius spent many of the years from 378–368 campaigning in Italy, while the Carthaginians were weakened by the plague and rebellion. By 368, the Carthaginians had overcome these adversities but were still recovering. Their government also appears to have been seriously divided, as a personal enemy of the commander Hanno, one Juniatus, described as 'the most powerful of the Carthaginians at that time,' was passing on information to Dionysius.[20] Dionysius, 'having large armies' at his command, decided to strike before the Carthaginians had fully regained their strength.[21] He then brought back the bulk of his forces from Italy to Sicily in preparation for an attack on Carthaginian territory. The tyrant was now over sixty years of age and may have felt this was his last chance to fulfil his life-long ambition of driving the Carthaginians completely from Sicily.

Dionysius gathered a force of 30,000 infantry, 3,000 cavalry and 300 triremes. The Carthaginians appear to have been caught largely unprepared. Dionysius crossed the Halycus River into Carthaginian territory. Selinus and Entella both went over to him. Next, he took Eryx and its port Drepanum, ravaging enemy territory as he advanced. Finally, he advanced on his most important objective, the new Carthaginian base at Lilybaeum. Here he finally encountered stiff resistance from a strong Carthaginian garrison and abandoned the attack after a short siege. Lilybaeum was already a strong fortress, and presumably Dionysius did not want to continue the siege over winter.

After receiving information that dockyards in Carthage had caught fire, and that their entire fleet had been destroyed, Dionysius sent most of his fleet back to Syracuse for the winter. This was probably done to save money. He stationed the remaining 130 ships, reportedly his best, in winter quarters at Drepanum. The report of Carthaginian losses was false. Once the bulk of the Greek fleet had departed, the Carthaginians launched 200 ships and attacked the unsuspecting Syracusan fleet at Drepanum while it lay at anchor. Surprise was complete and they captured most of the Syracusan ships. It is very possible that the false intelligence was deliberately produced by the Carthaginians, who had uncovered the treachery of Juniatus. According to

Justin, this betrayal caused the Carthaginian government to pass a decree 'that no Carthaginian should thenceforward study the Greek literature or language, so that no one might be able to speak with the enemy, or write to him, without an interpreter.'[22]

The defeat of his fleet undid much of Dionysius' gains and appears to have disheartened him, perhaps as he was already ill. Over the winter, 'the two states agreed to an armistice and separated, each going to its own cities.'[23] From the terms, Dionysius must have abandoned his gains, handing Eryx, Entella and Selinus back to the Carthaginians.

The successes of Dionysius earlier in the year had produced another round of compliments from the Athenians. The political pamphleteer Isocrates made him the hero of his new treatise. Isocrates was in his late sixties, and, having lost his inheritance, had spent much of his life as a teacher. He lectured on the value of self-control, the seductive nature of power and the destructiveness of unnecessary war. Above all, Isocrates believed that the Greeks should unite in order to destroy their barbarian enemies, particularly Persia. Later in life, he lost faith in Athens and its democracy, and sought a saviour from among the powerful individuals who began to proliferate during the later fourth century. In the 380s, he had condemned Dionysius, but in 367 he pinned his hopes on him, despite his earlier teachings. He wrote him a letter which asked him to unite with Athens in the common cause. Just what this cause was is not known as only fragments of the letter survive, but judging from Isocrates' later writings, it was most likely a war of conquest against the Persians. Isocrates would later put his faith in Philip of Macedonia.

The praise of Dionysius was not limited to Isocrates. At the Lenaean festival, held during the winter of 368/7, the Athenians voted Dionysius' tragedy, *The Ransom of Hector*, first prize. To have done otherwise would have been diplomatically imprudent. This benign attitude towards Dionysius did not last beyond his death. It is often argued that many of the negative anecdotes that have survived concerning the tyrant are the product of Plato and his followers.

After the failure of his campaign, Dionysius returned to Syracuse. Here he received a report of his first prize at the festival. The news was rushed to Syracuse by one of the players, hoping to obtain a reward. Dionysius was overjoyed that finally his literary skills had been recognized. Against his usual nature he embarked on a lavish round of sacrifices, feasts and drinking. During one of the drinking bouts, he over-indulged and fell violently ill. Diodorus now records an anecdote that Dionysius had received an oracle that he would die when he had conquered his 'betters'. Assuming that his 'betters' were the Carthaginians, he had always refrained from achieving a total victory over them in order to outwit Fate. The god, however, could not be denied and Dionysius, 'though a wretched poet' had defeated his 'betters' at the festival.[24] Dionysius soon died of his illness, thereby fulfilling the prophecy. Diodorus' account should be seen as part of the tradition of ridiculing Dionysius' pretensions as a playwright. At this time Athens was allied to Syracuse, and the widespread belief was that the Athenians had rigged the vote to honour their new benefactor regardless of the merits of his work.

Justin claims that Dionysius 'being reduced and weakened by continual wars, was at last killed by a conspiracy among his own subjects.' There is, however, no evidence to support Justin's claim. Cicero laments that he was not punished by the gods for his crimes but died peacefully in his bed.

Other accounts do record a court conspiracy during the tyrants' last days, but this was to ensure the succession of his eldest son, Dionysius the Younger, against any claims of the sons of his Syracusan wife, Aristomache, put forward by her brother Dion. Such conflicts over succession were endemic when the dynast had more than one family. The obvious heir was the oldest son, Dionysius, who was about thirty years old. According to Plutarch, his father was so mistrustful that 'fearing that if he should get wisdom and associate with men of sense, he would plot against him and rob him of his power, used to keep him closely shut up at home, where, through lack of association with others and in ignorance of affairs, as we are told, he made little wagons and lampstands and wooden chairs and tables.'[25] Dion was supposed to have considered him unfit to rule as he was 'dwarfed and deformed in character from his lack of education.'[26] Dion would later show himself to be a ruthless politician and would seize the tyranny for himself. It is more likely that his plotting on behalf of his nephew was an attempt to improve his own position.

Despite his supposed lack of education, Dionysius the Younger proved himself the master of the situation. To prevent Dion conferring with the tyrant: 'Dionysius the Younger, who, taking alarm at it, compelled the physicians to give his father a sleeping potion, that Dion might have no opportunity of addressing him. The sick man, having taken the draught, ended his life like one buried in deep sleep.'[27] The plot was only an attempt to silence Dionysius. His death was the result of his illness, not foul play.

If any of the Syracusans believed that Dionysius' death would lead to the downfall of the tyranny they were sadly mistaken. His eldest son would quickly appropriate his powers. He immediately appeared before an assembly, cowed by thirty-eight years of tyranny, and demanded that they 'maintain toward him the loyalty that passed to him with the heritage that he had received from his father; then, having buried his father with magnificent obsequies in the citadel by the gates called royal, he made secure for himself the administration of the government.'[28] The era of the democracy was well and truly over. The age of the tyrants of Syracuse would continue.

Chapter 23

Conclusions

Dionysius rose to power on the promise that he would deal effectively with the Carthaginian threat. When he took command, the Greeks had seen the cities of Selinus, Himera and Akragas lost to the Carthaginians, who at the time seemed all-conquering. Dionysius' command did not get off to a promising start, as Gela and Camarina were soon lost. By the end of his reign, however, all of these cities, except Selinus, had been recovered and re-populated by the Greeks. As a result, Dionysius was recognized as having saved Sicily from Carthaginian subjugation. Syracuse had grown in strength to become the most powerful of Greek cities, whose alliance was sought by both Athens and Sparta.

All this had come, however, at a terrible cost to other Greek cities of Sicily and Italy. Dionysius had destroyed almost as many Greek cities as had the Carthaginians. Rhegium and Naxos were razed to the ground. Hipponium and Caulonia were depopulated. Catane was sacked and its original population sold into slavery. Centuries later, the Greeks of Italy would recall 'that worst mischief of all that came to any of the cities was the tyranny of Dionysius.'[1] Nor would he be remembered with affection by the inhabitants of Syracuse. Twenty-five years after his death, when Timoleon had overthrown the tyranny, the people of Syracuse would vote to condemn him and to tear down his statues, along with those of the other tyrants. Only those of Gelon were spared.

A large part of this hatred of Dionysius would have been the toxic political legacy that his thirty-eight years of tyranny had bequeathed. For the first three centuries after their founding, the Greek cities of Sicily had followed a political path common to many Greek cities: an aristocratic government which was overthrown by tyrants, who were then in turn driven out by the people. The only difference would be the importance of military leadership in the roles of the tyrants of Sicily. This was a result of the Greeks' ongoing campaigns to conquer more lands from the other inhabitants of the island. During this period, Gelon, the first tyrant of Syracuse, won an historic victory over the Carthaginians at Himera. This allowed him to portray himself as the saviour of Greek civilization from the threat of barbarian invasion. It also gave tyranny in Sicily a prestige, and a legitimacy, that it had in no other part of the Greek world.

After the immediate threat of the Carthaginians had been removed, the Sicilian people, in a like manner to other Greeks, rid themselves of their tyrants and created more representative forms of government. The democracy in Syracuse would thrive for sixty years. It would, however, suffer a crisis when the Carthaginians returned in 410. The rapid loss of Selinus, Himera and Akragas would cause the people to lose faith in their leaders' military abilities and even their loyalty. Dionysius was able to convince the people to grant him emergency powers in the hope that he would deal effectively with the Carthaginian threat.

Once in power, Dionysius was able to use his position to make himself a new tyrant and rule for the rest of his life. By the time of his death, Dionysius was reputed to have left his son an empire reputedly 'bound fast by adamantine chains.'[2] The easy succession of Dionysius the Younger after the death of his father had demonstrated the truth of this assertion. For the next 155 years of its existence as an independent political entity, Syracuse would be governed by a succession of tyrants for all but twenty of those years.

Continuous tyranny was not, however, the usual form of government of Greek cities outside of Sicily. Other cities would endure tyrannies, but would eventually drive them out, and more representative governments would return. The Syracusan *demos* would continue to attempt to regain its rule over the city but would never succeed. What made the situation in Syracuse so different?

The most obvious answer was the constant threat posed by the Carthaginians, one of the major powers of the age. The invasions of 410 and 406, along with the destruction of Selinus, Himera, Akragas, Gela and Camarina, appear to have left lasting scars in the memories of the Greeks of Sicily; they feared that their civilization would be destroyed by barbarians. Dionysius was able to portray himself as the new saviour of Greek civilization. The continued Carthaginian threat most likely played a role in Dionysius the Younger's succession. The treaty that his father had concluded would have been made in his own name and therefore annulled by his death. His successor was forced to make a new peace, and for a short period war again looked possible.

The Carthaginians would honour this new treaty and would not invade Greek Sicily again for another twenty years. Yet during this period there would be no less than six new tyrants in Syracuse. The Carthaginian invasion of 345 would be the result of conflict between two of these tyrants, one of whom would ally himself with the hated enemy and invite them into Syracuse. Although the Carthaginian threat was a major factor, it is unlikely to have been the sole cause of the continuation of the tyranny.

A brief look forward at these events is useful in understanding the continuation of tyranny in Syracuse. One contributing factor was the enormous wealth of the Greeks of Sicily. Procuring a part of this wealth had allowed Dionysius to build his fortress on Ortygia and employ large numbers of mercenaries. From this stronghold, Dionysius and the later tyrants could rule in safety while using their army of mercenaries and informers to terrorize their opponents. Much of this wealth was in the hands of individuals who were enormously rich by Greek standards. Dion would offer to supply Dionysius the Younger with 'fifty swift triremes for the war, and maintain them at his own cost.' Later, while in exile, his personal wealth meant that 'he was a brilliant figure among the Greeks, to whom the affluence of the exile gave some idea of the power of the tyrant.'[3] This wealth allowed Dion to raise his own private army of mercenaries before he returned to Sicily.

Ten years after Dionysius' death, the *demos* would rise up against the tyranny and, with the assistance of Dion's private army, drive the tyrant out of the city and besiege him within the walls of Ortygia. Almost immediately, the rebels would split along class lines due to the chasm between rich and poor. The radical democrats would pass that most revolutionary of measures: 'a distribution of land, urging that liberty was based on equality, and slavery on the poverty of those who had naught.'[4] Dion, an aristocrat and follower of Plato, would have none of that. He would use his mercenaries to set himself up as tyrant and murder the leading democratic politician. One of his own followers would murder Dion due to ambition, but he, in turn, would be murdered by his own mercenaries when he could no longer pay them. Syracuse would fall into chaos as rival tyrants battled for a personal supremacy that had nothing to do with the Carthaginian threat.

There appears, therefore, to be no single reason for the persistence of tyranny in Syracuse. Rather it was a combination of the constant Carthaginian threat, the legacy of Gelon, the manipulation of class conflict and the extreme wealth of some individuals that allowed later tyrants to successfully emulate Dionysius.

The peace of 367 between Dionysius and the Carthaginians would be, like all those that preceded it, a truce that recognized an existing stalemate. As long as two powerful empires occupied and coveted the same island, further war between the two peoples was inevitable.

Notes and References

Preface

1. Thucydides was an Athenian general during, and wrote a history of, the Peloponnesian War (431–411). He died in 395 before he could complete his work. Later Greek and Roman historians considered him to have established objective history. Like all good historians, however, he was not without his prejudices, which will become apparent during this work. Plutarch (*c* 46–120 AD) is best known for his biographies, which compared the paired lives of famous Greeks and Romans. Although invaluable, this work has its limitations, for as Plutarch readily admits he was a biographer not a historian. Plutarch (*Alexander* 1) confesses that:

   > It is not Histories that I am writing, but Lives; and in the most illustrious deeds there is not always a manifestation of virtue or vice, no, a slight thing like a phrase or a jest often makes a greater revelation of character than battles when thousands fall, or the greatest armaments, or sieges of cities.

   Such a method produces obvious shortcomings for any military history based on Plutarch's writings. Fortunately, his work is a valuable source of material that helps understand the characters of his subjects.

Chapter 1

1. This date is the most widely accepted and is based on the chronology given by Thucydides (6.3). An alternative date of 757 can be calculated by using the chronology given by Diodorus (14.88). All the dates for these early foundations may differ by several years depending on which estimates and sources are used.
2. Strabo 6.2.4.
3. Snodgrass, A, *Archaic Greece* (London, 1980), pp. 123–4.
4. Thucydides 1.2.
5. Strabo 6.2.2.
6. Thucydides 6.2.
7. Strabo 6.2.4.
8. Polyaenus 5.5.1–2. Polyaenus was a Macedonian by birth. He wrote a book on the stratagems of war, which he dedicated to the emperor Marcus Aurelius (161–180 AD).

9. Vellius Paterculus 1.2, translated by FW Shipley,
    http://penelope.uchicago.edu/thayer/e/roman/texts/velleius_paterculus/home.html;
    also Pliny, *Natural History* 16.216, 19.63.
10. Dionysius of Halicarnassus 1.74.
11. Garbini, G, 'The Phoenicians in the Western Mediterranean', in *The Western
    Greeks: Classical Civilization in the Western Mediterranean* (London, 1996), p.
    126.
12. Thucydides 6.2.
13. Herodotus 1.163. Herodotus (c. 484–425) wrote a history of the Greek and
    Persian Wars of the fifth century and their origin. He is alternatively known as
    'the father of history' or, largely unjustly, as the 'father of lies'.
14. Justin 43.4. Justin's claimed his work was an anthology, excerpted from the
    earlier work of the historian Pompeius Trogus, omitting all that was not pleasur-
    able to read or did not supply a moral lesson. The date of composition is hotly
    disputed, with the period *AD* 144–230 being the most likely. Justin appears to
    have been extraordinarily careless in his method of composition and has a poor
    reputation as an historian.
15. Strabo 4.1.5.
16. Strabo 4.1.5.
17. Burn, AR, *Persia and the Greeks* (London, 1984), p. 146.
18. Thucydides 1.13.
19. Garbini, p. 127. See also Strabo 4.1.5.
20. Justin 43.4.

Chapter 2

1. Aristotle, *Oeconomica* 1345b–1346a. Aristotle (384 BC – 322 BC) was a Greek
    philosopher, a student of Plato and teacher of Alexander the Great. He was born
    in Stageira in northern Greece. Aristotle was a prolific writer on a broad array of
    subjects including the political history of Athens. He is generally considered to be
    one of the most important founding figures in Western philosophy.
2. Austin, MM, 'Hellenistic kings, War, and the Economy', in *Classical Quarterly* 36
    ii (1986), pp. 460–1.
3. Forrest, WG, *The Emergence of Greek Democracy* (London, 1972), p. 55.
4. Thucydides 1.15.
5. Herodotus 9.71.
6. Perhaps best argued by van Wees, H, *Greek Warfare: Myths and Realities*
    (London, 2004), especially pp. 153–183.
7. Matthew, C, 'When Push Comes to Shove: What was the *Othismos* of Hoplite
    Combat?', in *Historia* 58:4 (2009), pp. 395–415. Xenophon (*c* 430–354) was an
    Athenian cavalryman, mercenary commander and historian. As such, he is a valu-
    able primary source on ancient military matters.
8. Herodotus 7.9.
9. Hanson, V. *The Wars of the Ancient Greeks* (London, 1999), p. 57.
10. Translated by T Campbell, http://www.poetry-archive.com/t/martial-elegy.html
11. Xenophon, *Hellenica* 4.15.13.
12. Hesiod, *Works and Days* 212ff., translation by HG Evelyn-White.

http://omacl.org/Hesiod/works.Html
13. Translated by J Porter,
    http://homepage.usask.ca/~jrp638/DeptTransls/Theognis.html
14. Forrest, pp. 112, 119.
15. Andrews, A. *The Greek Tyrants* (London, 1969), p. 38.
16. Aristotle, *Politics* 5.7.
17. Diodorus 7.9
18. Aristotle, *Politics* 5.5.
19. Plutarch, *Lycurgus* 2.
20. Pausanias 3.3.1.
21. Aristotle, *Athenian Constitution* 1.5
22. Aristotle, *Athenian Constitution* 2.11.
23. Aristotle, *Athenian Constitution* 2.14.
24. Aristotle, *Athenian Constitution* 3.20.
25. Dionysius of Halicarnassus 7.2–11.
26. Diodorus 7.10
27. Thucydides 8.97.
28. Polybius 2.41 and Pausanias 7.7.1, Achaea; Aristotle *Politics* 5.4, Ambracia;
    Herodotus 4.161, Cyrene; 5.30, Naxos in Ionia; 7.155, Syracuse; 7.164 Cos.
29. Robinson, EW, *The first democracies: early popular government outside Athens*
    (Stuttgart, 1997), pp. 73–78.
30. Translation by EC Marchant, http://www.perseus.tufts.edu/cgi-
    bin/ptext?doc=Perseus%3Atext%3A1999.01.0158;
    query=chapter%3D%233;layout=;loc=2.1
31. Thucydides 3.82.

Chapter 3

1. Dunbabin, TJ, *The Western Greeks: the history of Sicily and south Italy from the
    foundation of the Greek colonies to 480 BC* (Oxford, 1948), p. 406.
2. Aristotle, *Politics* 5.3.
3. Herodotus 1.164.
4. Justin 18.7.
5. The whole episode of Malchus' campaigns is rejected by Picard, GC & C,
    Carthage (London, 1968) pp. 56–7 as a tale invented to justify the Carthaginian
    custom of human sacrifice. This denial does appear, however, to be overly scep-
    tical.
6. Justin 19.1.
7. Polyaenus 5.6.
8. Herodotus 6.23.
9. Thucydides 6.4.
10. Pindar, *Nemean Odes* 9.39–40. Translation at, http://www.perseus.tufts.edu/cgi-
    bin/ptext?doc=Perseus:text:1999.01.0162&query=line%3D%23940
11. Diodorus 10.28.
12. Polyaenus 5.6.
13. Dunbabin, p. 378.

Chapter 4

1. Herodotus 7.158. See also Justin 4.2, 19.1 and Dunbabin pp. 411–2.
2. Herodotus 7.156.
3. For a full discussion of this policy see: Lomas, K, 'Tyrants and the polis: migration, identity and urban development in Sicily', in *Ancient Tyranny* (Edinburgh, 2006), pp. 95–118. Lomas pp. (98–100, 104) identifies thirty such forced displacements carried in Sicily, mostly by Syracuse. Twenty-four are carried out by tyrants and only six by the democracy. All but one of the latter are the expulsion of mercenaries linked to the tyrants or the assisted repopulation of cities by their exiles or refugees.
4. Thucydides 3.57–8.
5. Translated by M Hadas and J McLean, *Euripides Plays* (New York, 1960) pp. 176–7.
6. Herodotus 7.163.
7. Diodorus 11.1.
8. Burn, pp. 306–307, n.30.
9. Diodorus 11.20; also Herodotus 7.165.
10. Polybius 6.52.
11. Green, P, *Diodorus Siculus, books 11–12.37.1: Greek history 480–431 B.C., the alternative version/Diodorus, Siculus; translated, with introduction and commentary* (Austin, 2006), pp. 46–7 and 74.
12. Dunbabin, p. 424.
13. Diodorus 11.21.
14. Diodorus 11.72; Dunbabin, p. 424.
15. Frontinus 1.11.18, see also 1.11.17.
16. Herodotus 7.165.
17. Diodorus 11.22.
18. Herodotus 9.62–63. This translation by GC Macaulay at http://etext.library.adelaide.edu.au/h/herodotus/h4m/chapter9.html
19. Diodorus 11.22.
20. Diodorus 11.23.
21. Dunbabin, 425–6.
22. Diodorus 11.25.
23. Diodorus 11.24.
24. Plutarch, *Timoleon* 23.

Chapter 5

1. Diodorus 11.67
2. Pindar, *Pythian* 1.75, translation at, http://www.perseus.tufts.edu/hopper/text?doc=Perseus%3Atext%3A1999.01.0162%3Abook%3DP.%3Apoem%3D1
3. Diodorous 11.53.
4. Xenophon, *Hiero.*
5. Diodorous 11.67.
6. Diodorus 11.68.

7. Diodorus 11.72.
8. Diodorus 12.26.
9. Thucydides 7.55, also 8.96.
10. See Green (2006), pp. 142–3; Thucydides 6.72–3; Aristotle, *Politics* 5.4.
11. Thucydides 6.17.
12. Diodorus 11.76.
13. Diodorus 11.92.
14. Green (2006), pp.174–5, 188–89, posits that the aristocrats of Syracuse saw Ducetius as a useful tool against the democrats. The treachery of Bolcon may have been a result of these sympathies, as was the later Syracusan inaction when Ducetius returned.
15. The dating of this treaty is much disputed and relies on the evidence of a very fragmentary inscription. The date can be any of a number between 458–417, with 454 being one possibility. This was, however, a period of far-flung Athenian adventurism, including expeditions to Cyprus, Phoenicia and Egypt.
16. Diodorus 12.26.
17. Diodorus 12.29.
18. Diodorus 12.30.

Chapter 6

1. Thucydides 1.95.
2. Thucydides 1.99.
3. Plutarch, *Pericles* 12.
4. Thucydides 1.102
5. Green, P, *Armada from Athens* (London, 1970) pp.16–19.
6. Thucydides 3.36.
7. Aristophanes, *The Knights,* translated at, http://drama.eserver.org/plays/classical/aristophanes/the-knights.txt/document_view
8. Thucydides 2.7.
9. Thucydides 3.86.
10. Green (1970), pp.22–23.
11. Plato, *Gorgias*, translated by B Jowett, http://www.ilt.columbia.edu/publicATIONS/Projects/digitexts/plato/gorgias/gorgias.html
12. Plutarch, *Alcibiades* 17.
13. Aristophanes, *The Knights.*
14. Thucydides 4.1.
15. Thucydides 3.82.
16. Green, p.65.
17. Xenophon, *Hellenica* 5.1.31.
18. Xenophon, *Hellenica* 2.3.21, 2.4.21.
19. Thucydides 6.72.
20. Thucydides 1.22.
21. Thucydides 4.64.
22. Thucydides 4.59–60.

23. Aristophanes, *The Acharnians,* translation at, http://drama.eserver.org/plays/classical/aristophanes/the-acharnians.txt; See also, Plutarch, *Alciabides* 21.
24. Caven, B, *Dionysius I War-lord of Sicily* (New Haven and London, 1990), p.48.

Chapter 7

1. Plutarch, *Nicias* 6.
2. Plutarch, *Nicias* 5.
3. Plutarch, *Nicias* 2.
4. Plutarch, *Nicias* 4.
5. Plutarch, *Alcibiades* 2.
6. Plutarch, *Comparison of Alcibiades and Coriolanus* 5.
7. Aristophanes, *The Frogs,* translation at,
    http://drama.eserver.org/plays/classical/aristophanes/the-frogs.txt/document_view
8. Thucydides 6.15.
9. Plutarch, *Nicias* 12; also *Alciabides* 17.
10. Thucydides 6.8.
11. Diodorus 13.2.
12. Thucydides 6.1.
13. Plutarch, *Pyrrhus* 14
14. Thucydides 6.18.
15. Thucydides 6.33; Diodorus 13.2 gives figures of 140 triremes and 7,000 troops
    from the allies alone, which would give a troop total of 9,200; Plutarch Alcibiades
    20 says 140 triremes but his troop figures agree with Thucydides.

Chapter 8

1. Plutarch, *Alcibiades* 22–3.
2. Plutarch, *Nicias* 15.
3. Plutarch, *Nicias* 16.
4. Thucydides 6.66. Dascon was on the coast, about 1km south of the temple hill.
5. Plutarch, *Nicias* 16.
6. Thucydides 6.67.
7. Thucydides 6.69.
8   Thucydides 6.68.
9. Thucydides 6.69.
10. Xenophon, *Agesilaus* 2.
11. Thucydides 6.69.
12. Thucydides 6.70.
13. Thucydides 6.71. Diodorus 13.7 gives the number of Syracusan dead as 400.
14. Plutarch, *Nicias* 16.
15. Thucydides 7.42.
16. Plutarch, *Nicias* 16.
17. Aristophanes, *The Birds,* translated at,
    http://classics.mit.edu/Aristophanes/birds.html

18. Kagan, D, *The Peace of Nicias and the Sicilian Expedition* (Ithaca and London, 1981) pp. 239–41.
19. Thucydides 6.88.
20. Plutarch, *Nicias* 16.
21. Thucydides 6.72.
22. Green (1970), p.164.
23. Plutarch, *Nicias* 16.

Chapter 9

1. Thucydides 6.90.
2. Kagan, pp. 249–255.
3. Kagan, p. 259.
4. Green (1970) 187.
5. Green (1970), pp. 205–7. He continues this line of argument with a largely invented account of an assembly in Syracuse, pp. 213–4.
6. Kagan, pp. 267–8.
7. Thucydides 7.2.

Chapter 10

1. Plutarch, *Nicias* 19.
2. Demonstrated in Aristophanes, *The Clouds*: 'this fine cavalier, who only knows how to look after his long locks, to show himself off in his chariot and to dream of horses!' translated at http://classics.mit.edu/Aristophanes/clouds.html
3. Thucydides 6.11.
4. Polyaenus1.42.1; Plutarch, *Nicias* 19.
5. Thucydides 7.4.
6. Plutarch, *Nicias* 17.
7. Thucydides 7.5.
8. Thucydides 7.6.
9. Thucydides 7.11–12.
10. Plutarch, *Nicias* 20.
11. Thucydides 7.24.
12. Diodorus 13.9.
13. Thucydides 7.33.
14. Plutarch, *Nicias* 20.
15. Thucydides 7.35.
16. Thucydides 7.37.
17. Plutarch, *Nicias* 20.
18. Thucydides 7.40.
19. Thucydides 7.42.

Chapter 11

1. Green (1970), p 281.
2. Thucydides 7.42.
3. Plutarch, *Nicias* 21.
4. Thucydides 7.44.
5. Thucydides 7.44.
6. Thucydides 7.54–5.
7. Thucydides 7.48.
8. Plutarch, *Nicias* 22.
9. Plutarch, *Nicias* 23.
10. Plutarch, *Nicias* 24.
11. Thucydides 7.56.
12. Plutarch, *Nicias* 25.
13. Thucydides 7.62.
14. Plutarch, *Nicias* 25.
15. Thucydides 7.66–8.
16. Plutarch Nicias 25.
17. Thucydides 7.70.
18. Diodorus 13.14–15.
19. Thucydides 7.71.
20. Plutarch *Nicias* 25.

Chapter 12

1. Thucydides 7.73.
2. Thucydides 7.78. Here ravine could be less spectacularly translated as river valley, and cliff could be rendered as crag.
3. Kagan, pp.341–44; Green (1970), pp. 321–44.
4. Thucydides 7.84.
5. Plutarch, *Nicias* 27.
6. Diodorus 13.19.
7. Plutarch, *Nicias* 27–28.
8. Plutarch, *Nicias* 28.
9. Thucydides 7.87.
10. Plutarch, *Nicias* 30.
11. Thucydides 8.1.
12. Thucydides 7.58.
13. Diodorus 13.112.

Chapter 13

1. A second century Roman Consul who ended every speech to the Senate with the exhortation that: 'Carthage must be destroyed!' Author's translation.
2. Diodorus 13.34–35.

3. Thucydides 8.84.
4. Xenophon, *Hellenica* 1.1.27–31. Here I have preferred Xenophon's version of events to that of Thucydides (8.85) who places these events in 411 but appears to be anticipating future events.
5. Diodorus 13.43.
6. As the French historian Serge Lancel cautions his readers, 'one of our best experts in Semitic studies warned us not so long ago that it is impossible to retrace Carthage's internal history.' Lancel, S, *Carthage: a History* (Oxford, 1995), p. 110.
7. See for instance Herodotus 7.166; Diodorus 13.43, 14.34.
8. Aristotle, *Politics* 2.11. This view of the Carthaginian constitution is largely repeated in Polybius 6.51. 'For there were kings, and the house of Elders was an aristocratical force, and the people were supreme in matters proper to them, the entire frame of the state much resembling that of Rome and Sparta.'
9. Lancel, p 113.
10. Justin 19.2.
11. Dion Chrystostom *Discourse* 25.7, translated by JW Cohoon, http://penelope.uchicago.edu/Thayer/E/Roman/Texts/Dio_Chrysostom/home.html
12. Strabo 17.3.15.
13. Cassius Dio 42.49. Translation by E Cary, http://penelope.uchicago.edu/Thayer/E/Roman/Texts/Cassius_Dio/home.html
14. Diodorus 13.44.

Chapter 14

1. Diodorus 13.55.
2. Diodorus 13.56.
3. Diodorus 13.57.
4. Diodorus 13.57.
5. Diodorus 13.57.
6. Arrian *Anabasis* 1.8; Diodorus 17.13. See also Justin 11.3 and Plutarch, *Alexander* 11.
7. Homer, *The Odyssey* Book 14. Translated by S Butler, http://classics.mit.edu/Homer/odyssey.14.xiv.html
8. Polybius 9.26.
9. Diodorus 13.59.
10. Diodorus 13.62.
11. Diodorus 13.63.
12. Diodorus 13.65
13. Diodorus 13.75.
14. Diodorus 13.79. Cicero, *In Verrem* 2.35, claims that the new city was founded by survivors of the first Himera. The two statements are not incompatible, as under the terms of a treaty signed in 405, the original inhabitants were allowed to return. The Greeks would then appear to be a majority of the population as they sent troops to join Dionysius in 397.
15. Diodorus 13.80.

Chapter 15

1. Diodorus 13.81.
2. Diodorus 13.84.
3. Diodorus 13.85.
4. Polyaenus 5.7.
5. Polyaenus 5.10.4. Also Frontinus 3.10.5.
6. Diodorus 13.87.
7. Caven, p. 48.
8. Diodorus 13.88.
9. Diodorus 13.89.

Chapter 16

1. Polybius 15.35. See also Aelian, *Varia Historia* 12.43; Diodorus 13.96 and Isocrates, *Letter to Philip* 65.
2. For example, Polybius 35.12 describing the secretary of Antiochus III: 'The slaves of one of the royal "friends," Dionysius, the private secretary, marched along carrying articles of silver plate none of them weighing less than a thousand drachmae.'
3. Cicero, *De Divinitus* 1.20. Translated by WA Falconer, http://penelope.uchicago.edu/Thayer/E/Roman/Texts/Cicero/home.html
4. Aristotle, *Politics* 6.5, 6.10.
5. For examples see Xenophon, *Hellenica* 1.7.12–15, 2.2.15.
6. Diodorus 13.91.
7. Diodorus 13.92.
8. Diodorus 13.92.
9. Diodorus 13.94.
10. Diodorus 13.94–95.
11. Herodotus 1.59.
12. Diodorus 13.96. Perhaps using similar words to those of Peisistratus who told the Athenian people that they should 'go home and attend to their private affairs, while he would himself for the future manage all the business of the state.' Aristotle, *Athenian Constitution* 15 http://classics.mit.edu/Aristotle/athenian_const.1.1.html
13. Although drawing historical parallels is always tenuous at best, one is reminded of Hitler's use of the Reichstag fire to pass emergency measures and his employment of the SS as a private army.
14. Caven, p. 158. Caven goes on further to claim that the assembly maintained the right to decide 'on questions relating to war, peace and taxation.' This I believe was not the case.
15. Tod, MN, ed., *A Selection of Greek Historical Inscriptions* vol. ii (Oxford, 1948) no. 123, lines 19–24. Authors' translation.
16. Aristotle, *Politics* 5.10.
17. For a full discussion of the costs of making war, see Champion, J, 'The Causes of the Third Diodoch War 315–311 BC', in *Slingshot*, 213 (2001) pp. 3–6. If this figure appears excessive, it should be noted that the Athenians, with a much

smaller force, spent 2,000 talents on their two-year siege of Potidea. Thucydides 2.70.
18. Herodotus 3.90. Thucydides 1.96, 2.13. The Athenian tribute later rose to 600 talents.
19. Porphyry of Tyre, F42, F43.
20. Caven, p. 163.
21. Aristotle *Oeconomica* 1349a.
22. Polyaenus 5.2.19; Aristotle *Oeconomica* 1349b.
23. Aelian *Varia Historia* 1.20.
24. Aristotle, *Politics* 5.11.
25. Plutarch, *Moralia* 805–813. Translated at, http://penelope.uchicago.edu/Thayer/E/Roman/Texts/Plutarch/Moralia/Praecepta_gerendae_reipublicae*.html
26. Diodorus 14.64, 14.70.
27. Nepos, *Of Kings* 2. Translated by Rev. JS Watson, htp://ancienthistory.about.com/library/bl/bl_text_nepos_livesmisc.htm#Kings
28. Polyaenus 5.2.15. See also 5.2.16 for a similar tale.
29. Nepos, *Of Kings* 2; Plutarch *Moralia* 338b, Justin 21.1.
30. For a full a discussion and extensive list of the citations: see Sanders, LJ, *Dionysius I of Syracuse and Greek Tyranny* (Beckenham, 1987), pp. 8–9 and p. 36 n. 28.
31. Cicero, *De Republica* Book 3. Translated by F Barham, http://oll.libertyfund.org/?option=com_staticxt&staticfile=show.php%3Ftitle=546&chapter=83303&layout=html&Itemid=27

Chapter 17

1. Diodorus 13.111.
2. Diodorus 13.112.
3. Diodorus 13.113.
4. Diodorus 13.114.

Chapter 18

1. Diodorus 14.7.
2. Diodorus 14.8.
3. Diodorus 14.10.
4. Polyaenus 5.2.14; Diodorus 14.10.
5. Diodorus 14.10.
6. Plutarch, *Moralia* 855c. Diodorus 14.14.
7. Polyaenus 5.2.5.
8. Diodorus 14.18.
9. Diodorus 14.18.
10. Diodorus 14.40.

Chapter 19

1. Diodorus 14.41.
2. Diodorus 14.41
3. Diodorus 14.44.
4. Diodorus 14.45.
5. Diodorus 14.45. Oldfather's translation of this chapter renders the Greek verb *parakaleo* as 'urged'. In this context, and others where the tyrants address the assembly, I prefer the more forceful meaning of 'demanded'.
6. Diodorus 14.48.
7. Polyaenus 5.2.6. Caven, p. 102 suggests that the fighting may have occurred at the southern end of the lagoon, near Lilybaeum. I believe the ancient accounts describe the northern end of the bay.
8. Polyaenus 5.2.6.
9. Diodorus 14.50.
10. Diodorus 14.51.
11. Diodorus 14.52.
12. Diodorus 14.52.
13. Polyaenus 5.2.17.
14. Diodorus 14.54.

Chapter 20

1. Polybius 1.42.
2. Diodorus 14.56.
3. Diodorus 14.58.
4. Diodorus 14.60.
5. Diodorus 14.61.
6. Diodorus 14.68.
7. Diodorus 14.65.
8. Diodorus 14.62.
9. Diodorus 14.64.
10. Diodorus 14.65.
11. Diodorus 14.65-6.
12. Caven, p.116, believes that the entire episode is concocted by the tyrant's Athenian detractors: 'I believe that it is much more likely to have come from a collection of rhetorical exercises (under the heading of 'Speeches against Tyrants') – unless that it is a product of Diodorus' own pen.' All ancient authors embellished speeches, and no doubt Diodorus elaborated Theodorus' address. I believe, however, that Diodorus records too much specific detail for this episode to be a later invention and that he records a genuine, historical event.
13. Diodorus 14.71.
14. Diodorus 14.74.
15. Diodorus 14.75.
16. Diodorus 14.74.
17. Polyaenus, 5.10.1.

18. Polyaenus, 5.2.11.
19. Diodorus 14.75; Justin 20.1.

Chapter 21

1. Strabo 6.1.3.
2. Livy 8.27; Justin 23.2.
3. Diodorus 14.100. The army consisted of 14,000 infantry and 1,000 cavalry. Although a large and wealthy city, Thurii is unlikely to have been able to field 14,000 hoplites on its own, so the figure most likely includes light infantry and mercenaries, or perhaps some of the allies had arrived.
4. Livy 9.2.
5. Diodorus 14.103.
6. Diodorus 14.105.
7. Diodorus 14.107.
8. Diodorus 14.111.
9. Thucydides 6.16.
10. Diodorus 16.109.
11. Lysias 33.6. Translated by WRM Jones, http://old.perseus.tufts.edu/cgi-bin/ptext?doc=Perseus%3Atext%3A1999.01.0154;query=toc;layout=;loc=33.6 Plutarch, *Themistocles* 35, tells of a similar denunciation by Themistocles against the earlier tyrant Hieron: 'Themistocles made a speech among the assembled Hellenes, urging them to tear down the booth of the tyrant and prevent his horses from competing.' This passage is usually discredited and believed to have been a fabrication based on Diodorus' account of Dionysius' troubles.
12. Diodorus 15.6.
13. Plato, *Republic* 8. Translated by B Jowett, http://classics.mit.edu/Plato/republic.9.viii.html
14. Plato, *The Seventh Letter*. Translated by J. Harward, http://classics.mit.edu/Plato/seventh_letter.html
15. Plutarch, *Dion* 1.
16. Diogenes Laertius 3.18. *Lives of the Eminent Philosophers* vol.1 (London, 1925). Translated by RD Hicks.
17. Plutarch, *Dion* 5.
18. Diodorus 15.7.
19. Plato, *Republic* 8.
20. Diodorus 15.7.
21. Caven Pp. 169–175.
22. Diodorus 15.13.
23. Diodorus 15.14 claims he captured 1,000 talents, of which he kept over 500. Presumably his men kept the rest. Polyaenus' (5.2.21) account is possibly a garbled version of the same incident.

Chapter 22.

1. Translated by Francis Brooks, *De Natura Deorum (On the Nature of the Gods)* (London, 1896).
2. See Stylianou, PJ, *A Historical Commentary on Diodorus Siculus, Book 15* (Oxford, 1998), pp. 200–201. I have accepted 378 as the most likely date for the end of the war. The following narrative is structured around this belief. Caven, pp. 187–8, argues that Diodorus' original account has been lost and what survives is a later epitome. He dates the end of the war to the winter of 376/5 (p. 200).
3. Cicero, *On the Nature of the Gods* 3.34.
4. Dionysius of Halicarnassus 20.10.
5. Livy 24.3. The other sources for the campaign are: Dionysius 20.7; Justin 20.5 and Aelian, *Varia Historia* 12.61.
6. Justin 20.5.
7. Polyaenus 6.16.1.
8. Diodorus 15.16.
9. Diodorus 15.17.
10. Polyaenus 5.2.10. This campaign seems to be the only logical place for this and the following stratagems recorded by Polyaenus.
11. Polyaenus 5.10.5.
12. Diodorus 15.16.
13. Diodorus 15.17.
14. Diodorus 15.17.
15. Caven 200–201.
16. Dionysius of Halicarnassus 20.7.
17. Strabo 6.2.10. This passage might possibly refer instead to Dionysius the Younger.
18. Diodorus 15.73.
19. Justin 20.5.
20. Justin 20.5.
21. Diodorus 15.73.
22. Justin 20.5.
23. Diodorus 15.73.
24. Diodorus 15.74.
25. Plutarch, *Dion* 8.
26. Plutarch, *Dion* 10.
27. Nepos, *Dion* 2; Plutarch, *Dion* 6.
28. Diodorus 15.74.

Chapter 23

1. Dionysius of Halicarnassus 20.7.
2. Diodorus 16.5. The phrase was popular in antiquity being repeated by Aelian, *Varia Historia* 6.12 and Plutarch, *Dion* 7, 10.
3. Plutarch, *Dion* 6, 15.
4. Plutarch, *Dion* 37.

Bibliography

Andrews, A, *The Greek Tyrants* (London, 1956).

Austin, MM, 'Hellenistic kings, War, and the Economy', in *Classical Quarterly* 36 ii (1986) pp. 450–466.

Berger, S, *Revolution and Society in Greek Sicily and Southern Italy* (Stuttgart, 1997).

Burn, AR, *Persia and the Greeks* (London, 1984).

Caven, B, *Dionysius I War-lord of Sicily* (New Haven and London, 1990).

Champion, J, 'The Causes of the Third Diodoch War 315–311 BC', in *Slingshot*, 213 (2001) pp. 3–7.

Dunbabin, TJ, *The Western Greeks: the history of Sicily and south Italy from the foundation of the Greek colonies to 480 BC* (Oxford, 1948).

Finley, MI, *Ancient Sicily* (London, 1979).

Fischer-Hansen, T, (ed.), *Acta Hyperborea 6: Ancient Sicily* (Copenhagen, 1996).

Forrest, WG, *The Emergence of Greek Democracy* (London, 1972).

Green, P, *Armada from Athens* (London, 1970).

Green, P, *Diodorus Siculus, books 11–12.37.1: Greek history 480–431 BC, the alternative version/Diodorus, Siculus; translated, with introduction and commentary* (Austin, 2006).

Hanson, VD, *The Western Way of War: Infantry Battle in Classical Greece* (Oxford, 1988).

Hanson, VD, *The Wars of the Ancient Greeks* (London, 1999).

Kagan, D, *The Peace of Nicias and the Sicilian Expedition* (Ithaca and London, 1981).

Lewis, S, (ed.), *Ancient Tyranny* (Edinburgh, 2006).

Lancel, S, *Carthage: a History* (Oxford, 1995), translated by A Nevill.

Leighton, R. Sicily, *Before History: An Archaeological Survey from the Paeolithic to the Iron Age* (New York, 1999).

Matthew, C, 'When Push Comes to Shove: What was the *Othismos* of Hoplite Combat?', in *Historia* 58:4 (2009) pp. 395–415.

Picard, GC & C, *Carthage* (London, 1968), translated by D Collon.

Pugliese Carratelli, G, (ed.), *The Western Greeks: classical civilization in the Western Mediterranean* (London, 1996).

Robinson, EW, *The first democracies: early popular government outside Athens* (Stuttgart, 1997).

Sanders, LJ, *Dionysius I of Syracuse and Greek Tyranny* (Beckenham, 1987).

Scott, M, *From democrats to Kings* (London, 2009)

Tod, MN, (ed.), *A Selection of Greek Historical Inscriptions* vol. ii (Oxford, 1948).

Snodgrass, A, *Archaic Greece* (Berkeley, 1980).

van Wees, H, *Greek Warfare: Myths and Realities* (London, 2004)

The following translations of the ancient sources were used:

Aelian, *Varia Historia*, translated by G P Goold (London and Cambridge, Massachusetts, 1997).

Aristotle, *Oeconomica,* translated by G C Armstrong, http://old.perseus.tufts.edu/cgi-bin/ptext?doc=Perseus:text:1999.01.0048&query=section%3D%2314

Aristotle, *Politics,* translated by B Jowett, http://www.constitution.org/ari/polit_00.htm

Aristotle, *Athenian Constitution,* translated by Sir FG Kenyon, http://www.constitution.org/ari/athen_00.htm

Arrian, *The Campaigns of Alexander,* translated by A de Selincourt (Harmondsworth, 1958).

Diodorus Siculus, *The Library of History* Books 5–7, translated by G Booth, http://books.google.com.au/books?id=NCsUAAAAYAAJ&printsec=frontcover&dq=diodorus+siculus+booth&cd=1#

Diodorus, *The Library of History IV,* translated by C H Oldfather (London and Cambridge, Massachusetts, 1946).

Diodorus, *The Library of History V,* translated by CH Oldfather (London and Cambridge, Massachusetts, 1950).

Diodorus, *The Library of History VI,* translated by CH Oldfather (London and Cambridge, Massachusetts, 1954).

Diodorus, *The Library of History IV,* translated by CL Sherman (London and Cambridge, Massachusetts, 1952).

Dionysius of Halicarnassus, *Roman Antiquities,* translated by E Cary, http://penelope.uchicago.edu/Thayer/E/Roman/Texts/Dionysius_of_Halicarnassus/home/html

Frontinus, *Stratagemata*, translated by CE Bennet, http://penelope.uchicago.edu/Thayer/E/Roman/Texts/Frontinus/Strategemata/home.html

Herodotus, *The Histories,* translated by A de Selincourt (Harmondsworth, 1954).

Justin, *Epitome of the Philippic History of Pompeius Trogus,* translated by J S Watson, http://www.forumromanum.org/literature/justin/english/index.html

Livy, *The History of Rome,* translated by Rev. C Roberts, http://www.forumromanum.org/literature/liviusx.html

Pausanias, *Guide to Greece, volume 2: Southern Greece,* translated by P Levi (Harmondsworth, 1971).

Plutarch, *Parallel Lives,* translated by B Perrin, http://penelope.uchicago.edu/Thayer/E/Roman/Texts/

Polyaenus, *Stratagems,* translated by R Shepherd, http://www.attalus.org/translate/polyaenus.html

Polybius, *The Histories,* translated by W R Paton, http://penelope.uchicago.edu/Thayer/E/Roman/Texts/Polybius/home.html

Strabo, *The Geography of Strabo,* translated by H L Jones (London, 1917).

Thucydides, *The Landmark Thucydides,* translated by R Crawley (New York, 1998).

Xenophon, *Agesilaus*, translated by H G Dakyns,
    http://ancienthistory.About.com/library/bl/bl_text_xenophon_agesilaus.htm
Xenophon, *Hiero*, translated by H G Dakyns,
    http://www.gutenberg.org/dirs/1/1/7/1175/1175.txt
Xenophon, *A History of My Times (Hellenica)*, translated by R Warner
    (Harmondsworth, 1966).

Index